Audrey Hepburn

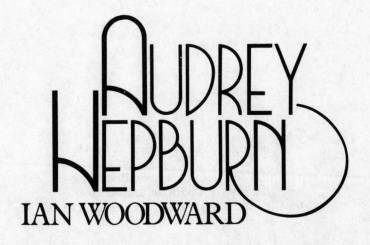

AUDREY HEPBURN

IAN WOODWARD

W.H. ALLEN · LONDON
A Howard & Wyndham Company
1984

Copyright © Ian Woodward 1984

Printed and bound in Great Britain by
Mackays of Chatham Ltd, Kent
for the Publishers, W.H. Allen & Co. Ltd
44 Hill Street, London W1X 8LB

ISBN 0 491 03480 6

CONTENTS

HEPBURN ON HEPBURN

'My life isn't theories and formulae. It's part instinct, part common sense. Logic is as good a word as any, and I've absorbed what logic I have from everything and everyone . . . from my mother, from training as a ballet dancer, from *Vogue* magazine, from the laws of life and health and nature.'

'I tried always to do better: saw always a little further. I tried to stretch myself.'

'I went through a period of first success. Then there was the inevitable change: the bad newspaper articles. Some people don't care about that, but I do. I'm hurt. I feel it. I don't think I've done anything dreadful. Sometimes you do things for reasons the press doesn't know. But I'm happy to go on as I have.'

'I never read articles about me because it makes me nervous to know what others think of me. I used to suffer so from gossip columns. There's never been a helluva lot to say about me. . . .'

PREFACE

*'There must be something wrong with those
people who think Audrey Hepburn doesn't
perspire, hiccup or sneeze, because they
know that's not true. In fact, I hiccup more
than most.'*

IN THE ENTIRE star-studded history of Holly-
wood, no other screen goddess has held herself so aloof from
the standard public trivialities of superstardom as Audrey Hepburn. She has never flaunted her sex or her glamour trappings.
Although she owns no yachts or castles, she is a multi-
millionairess and lives like a work-a-day princess: almost from
the beginning, Frank Sinatra dubbed her 'the Princess'. Yet she
travels all over the world with less fanfare than a junior starlet.
She has probably taken more luxury flights than any member
of the jet-set. She has never been known to lend herself to
stunts which could conceivably further her career. She has, in
short, broken all the rules of how to succeed in Hollywood.

By any standards, her journey from the back row of a
London chorus to the front rank of Hollywood stars and Broad-
way leading ladies was a phenomenal one, and it could only
have happened to Audrey. Her leading men have included
Gregory Peck, William Holden, Humphrey Bogart, Henry
Fonda, Fred Astaire, Gary Cooper, Anthony Perkins, Peter
Finch, Burt Lancaster, George Peppard, James Garner, Cary
Grant, Rex Harrison, Peter O'Toole, Albert Finney, Ben Gaz-
zara, and Sean Connery. None but the best for this Anglo-
Dutch waif.

Audrey has managed to portray in most of her screen characters women of spectacular elegance, groomed, rich and lovely;
yet very much more than cardboard cut-outs. She has long
been dressed by Givenchy. But, for Audrey, the *haute couture*,

vii

the polish and the squeaky clean qualities with which most of her characterisations have been endowed have simply been accessories to an acting talent of stained-glass brilliance. Along the way, with those huge eyes, long neck and barest covering of flesh over her splendid bones, she was always a fashion photographer's dream: Audrey Hepburn and Richard Avedon were a natural.

In a movie epoch when stars were launched with all the regularity of a new ice-cream flavour, Audrey possessed one platinum-plated quality that set her apart in the firmament. It was called *class*. Hollywood loved her, because breeding was the one commodity money couldn't buy. For years she remained the princess she portrayed on the screen in *Roman Holiday* – which brought her that Oscar – enshrined irrevocably on a pedestal like the goddess-myth she had become.

Throughout a movie career spanning more than three decades, Audrey has made relatively few films – just twenty-five. Yet she has decorated more covers of *Life* magazine than any other personality: seven times, equal number one with Marilyn Monroe. Her enduring popularity is unique. She remains firmly entrenched in the box office Top Ten in Japan, the world's second largest movie outlet. 'It's curious,' she muses. 'Maybe I look Japanese.'

A poll conducted recently by a marketing affiliate of the American Film Institute found that among moviegoers and movie buffs, Audrey is (*a*) the second most popular female performer (living or deceased) of the 1950s, after Marilyn Monroe; (*b*) the second most admired actress under seventy (still living), after Jane Fonda (sixth most admired, overall, after Katharine Hepburn, Bette Davis, Garbo, Fonda and Dietrich); and (*c*) that more movie buffs would rather see an Audrey Hepburn film than the films of any other actress under seventy. This is the former ballet girl's achievement.

The Audrey Hepburn story is a story of personality acclaimed, beauty praised and talent rewarded. It is something else besides. With a First Act that reads like a good mystery by her childhood favourite, E. Phillips Oppenheim, a Second Act that embraces the glamour and magic of one of the Broadway fantasy plays in which she herself appeared, and a climactic Third Act in which the beautiful heroine lives happily ever after, this is a modern fairy-tale with a difference. It really happened.

PART ONE

War and peace:
early years in Nazi-occupied Holland

1

'It is too much to hope that I shall keep up
my success. I don't ask for that. All I shall do
is my best – and hope.'

HOLLYWOOD AND BROADWAY surveyed the
horizon and took a deep breath.

Excitement was mounting for the imminent Academy
Award presentations, and tonight – 25 March 1954 – was the
night. Deborah Kerr, toast of Los Angeles and New York, had
been heavily tipped for a special award. No other actress had
accomplished more for British prestige in films and plays during the preceding twelve months.

The ceremony, which was televised live, went off with scar-
cely a hitch. Quick switches were made from Hollywood to
New York and Philadelphia. Four searchlights pierced the clear
California sky as the long limousines pulled up in front of the
theatre and a veritable constellation stepped out to the cheers
of the thousands of enthusiastic fans who jostled to see their
idols.

In New York, meanwhile, the twenty-four-year-old British
star of Broadway's new smash-hit play, *Ondine* – she played a
water-sprite – was making her nightly quota of curtain-calls.
After the last bow had been taken with customary ritual, she
raced from the stage and slipped quickly into a fabulous
sequinned evening gown, a present from her co-star, Mel Ferrer. Within minutes they were both installed in a white
Rolls-Royce and being whisked away by a siren-blowing,
light-flashing motorcycle police escort through the neon-lit
streets of New York to the old Centre Theatre, the Broadway
focal-point of the Oscar awards.

3

Curious heads turned, and knowing, delighted faces smiled well-meaningly as the couple made their way to their aisle seats, where the actress's mother, the Baroness Ella van Heemstra, was already installed. Television monitor sets around the auditorium indicated that the annual Academy Award sweepstakes in Hollywood were about to end with the giving of one of filmdom's highest honours.

'And the best film actress of 1953 is . . .' (an agonising pause ensued while the secret ballot envelope was opened) '. . . Audrey Hepburn for her performance in *Roman Holiday*.'

Audrey Hepburn!

Deborah Kerr applauded wildly, Ava Gardner less wildly. But that was show business. Audrey gasped, opened her mouth to exhale a mute cry of joy and pain, and then buried her face in her hands – a face that was still covered in stage make-up for her role in *Ondine*.

Mel kissed the water-sprite's pale cheek: 'There you are! Didn't I say everybody was rooting for you!'

As Audrey left her seat to acknowledge the honour bestowed upon her by the motion-picture industry, she was visibly trembling. Her willowy, delicate frame seemed likely to snap at any moment. The occasion had clearly got the better of her. When she walked up on to the stage to accept her Oscar, she turned in a dazed manner in the *wrong* direction: in other words, left towards the wings instead of right towards the presentation. The audience roared.

'It was very effective and greatly appreciated,' her old friend, David Niven, would say many years later. 'But I've always meant to ask her: "Were you *really* that dazed?"'

Clutching the Oscar to her modest bosom, she faced the assembled multitude and (it seemed) thanked everybody in the Los Angeles telephone directory 'for making it all possible'. 'I mustn't allow this award to turn my head or persuade me to forget my life's ambition – to become a truly great actress,' she avowed. 'It's the second big film which will prove if I was really worthy of the first.'

But an irrefutable fact remained. A star had been born.

Within a few months she would win five other major awards, for her roles in both *Roman Holiday* and *Ondine*, but it was her Oscar trophy which, when the heat of the night had died down, conspired to generate the most fervent debate. Some sound judgments were made about her talents and,

4

inevitably, some jealousies prevailed. Some pundits felt she had been given an Oscar too soon. For while, it is true, Audrey shared with Helen Hayes and Shirley Booth the distinction of getting him the first time they bid for him, Joan Crawford, they reasoned, went through fifty-eight films before he deigned to notice her, while Loretta Young and Ronald Colman both stood in line more than twenty years for him.

Small wonder that so many people were sceptical about the significance, for better or worse, of the English girl's Oscar. Even Don Hartman, Paramount's powerful chief of production in Hollywood and one of those responsible for giving Audrey her momentous break in *Roman Holiday*, found himself treading the path of caution. 'There is no evidence that Audrey is a full star yet,' Hartman said firmly a couple of days after the award ceremony. 'The question which has to be answered is: "Can she hold up a picture on her own?" Audrey has been called a star after *Roman Holiday*, and she has certainly had a lot of publicity. But we haven't tested yet whether the Hepburn name *by itself*, above a film title, will fill cinemas.'

Even the director William Wyler, who had contributed in no small way to her Oscar success, and who would work with her again on two further films, felt compelled to admit: 'Audrey Hepburn may be the Princess, but Deborah Kerr is the Queen!' Loyalties, and the not-unreasonable assertions that success must be earned, ran high in Tinsel Town.

Yet it wasn't as if Audrey nursed any self-inflated notions about her particular dramatic gifts. 'It's like when somebody gives you something to wear that's too big, and you have to grow into it,' she confided to Mel Ferrer as he accompanied her home after the Oscar liturgy. 'I'm truly happy. My one ambition now is to be an actress.'

The film capital's doubts were based entirely on such physiognomical considerations as feet that were a trifle big for her size and a bustline that did not compensate. Nevertheless, in the words of an enthusiastic woman critic, those feet had the 'sure, golden-slippered tread of a star', and director Billy Wilder even predicted that 'she will make bosoms a thing of the past,' which wasn't good news for Misses Monroe, Ekberg, Dors, Loren, Mansfield and Lollobrigida. Few dared to forecast how a public with Monroe and boobs on its mind was going to react.

Those who wished to keep a sense of proportion observed, not entirely accurately, that she had done almost embarrassingly little: a sad but charming princess in the film *Roman Holiday*, and, on the Broadway stage, a gauche young thing in *Gigi* and a water-sprite in *Ondine*. 'She was praised for a mischievous, ethereal charm which sends critics scampering for phrases they last used when writing about *A Midsummer Night's Dream*,' said critic Milton Shulman. 'Except for this ability to exude an impish, waif-like quality, there is no evidence that Audrey Hepburn can do anything else. Yet this has not hampered the word-tinsellers from lifting her into the exalted company of such proven actresses as Greta Garbo, Katharine Hepburn, and Ingrid Bergman.'

Up to a point, he was right. Audrey had been in Hollywood barely two years and yet, in that relatively short period, the volume of publicity she had received had surpassed even that accorded to many a top-flight actress during her entire career. But Audrey was not the recipient of an Oscar because she possessed a face and a figure. It was because she was a Broadway actress, and those who expected good acting from her on the screen were not hoping for the impossible.

'Of course,' added Shulman, as a final acid drop, 'this surfeit of praise for minor achievements is one of the occupational hazards facing all actors. How quickly these comets turn to ash!'

Certainly in Hollywood, the day after the Oscar ceremony, her disappointed rivals could only have relieved their pangs of envy by watching her roasting at the stake. 'But what would be the use?' snarled an Oscar also-ran who clearly had given the prospect some wishful thought. 'The way this girl's got them moon-eyed, the critics would all be raving it was the most terrific stake scene since Joan of Arc.'

There could be no doubt that the ladies of Hollywood were in possession of ample evidence to support their grievances. The girl from London, with just one Hollywood film and two Broadway stage shows to her name, was being hailed not only as the best film actress in the world, but quite likely the most brilliant in twenty-seven years. Furthermore, said the ladies, when critics wrote about her they abandoned ordinary, earthly words. At worst, they got poetic; at the very worst, mystic. They resorted to 'magical', 'enchanting', 'moon-kissed', 'elfin', 'miracle' and 'witchery'.

What Audrey's actress colleagues disliked more than anything else, and what really brought out the vitriol, was the way in which male critics wrote her love letters instead of reviews.

One of the sharp-tongued ladies of Broadway quoted a passage from the review of *Ondine*, which appeared in the *New York Herald-Tribune* just four weeks before the Oscar ceremony: 'She slips across the stage without touching the floor, and when she is in repose she is lovelier still. A shivering prisoner pinned to a rock, she is every man's dream of the nymph he once planned to meet.'

So, Audrey Hepburn, despite all the awards – and *the* award – was not yet Deborah Kerr. She was not, within her profession, the unadulterated toast of Los Angeles and New York. She was still very much the 'Princess', and there were a lot of right royal duties to perform – and a lot of back-stabbing to endure – before she would become the 'Queen'.

What saved her, at this crucial moment in her career, from unbearable perfection, was that basically she was a very young, naïve, ordinary girl. There seemed to be little chance that she would be spoiled by all the publicity nonsense. In fact she even called some newspapermen 'Sir'.

When Mel read to her some of the adjectives that were flying around in the reviews for *Ondine*, descriptions like 'coltish', 'gazelle-like' and 'other-worldly', Audrey was the first to laugh.

'What they mean,' she said, 'is tall and skinny.'

'Did you know,' Mel then asked, scanning a newspaper interview about her, 'that you have eyes that are "lake-haunted"?'

'Maybe,' she yawned, 'I need some sleep.'

'The beauty experts,' added Mel, 'predict a "dramatic new make-up fashion" to follow your "bat-wing eyebrows". . . .'

'I wish I had the courage to tell them,' she said, 'that I just don't pluck them.'

As far as her private life was concerned, she was something – and somewhere – else. The nightclub gossip-columnists never saw her. When the curtain came down she disappeared to study acting and ballet. An indefatigable pursuit of an unattainable perfection was what alone gave a meaning to her life. She would step off the stage after a scene that still had the audience rocking and would worry to the director: 'I didn't get a laugh with that line. What did I do wrong?'

Audrey, twenty-four-year-old Audrey, was building a career. Yet while most critics contended seriously that she was the most brilliant actress to arrive in Hollywood since Garbo, in the silents of 1927, that was no guarantee that she could last the course. She yet had to prove herself by length of service. The Tinsel Palace awaited the coronation of its princess. . . .

2

'In Holland and Belgium, and afterwards in England, my happiest moments were in the country. I've always had a passion for the outdoors, for trees, for birds and flowers.'

A STEADY DRIZZLE WAS just one more cross for Edda to bear that day as she bolted for cover. It was not the first time her life had been thrown in peril, and it certainly would not be the last. Edda Hepburn van Heemstra, a tall, fragile, dark-haired bundle of nerves, who had celebrated her fifteenth birthday the previous month, had been exposed to the same danger many times before, far too many times before.

The dreadful whip-cracking sound of Nazi gunfire continued sporadically as she made her way home. She turned a corner – and stopped dead in her tracks. A small group of German soldiers, the cause of the commotion, were training their guns on the doors and windows of some old warehouses at the far end of the street. Edda was reminded, yet again, to be extra vigilant.

The streets of Arnhem, once one of the most perfect medieval towns of the Netherlands, were now, in 1944, a dangerous adventure-playground for young Dutch girls to be caught up in. And the wartime drama she would shortly see enacted – the mammoth airborne attack by the British and American paratroops on the occupying Germans, and the Allies' subsequent tragic defeat – would be portrayed, three decades later, in the epic film *A Bridge Too Far*.

Edda would then be known to the world as Audrey Hepburn.

But basic thoughts of survival now occupied Edda's terror-torn mind and, almost instinctively, she found herself escaping down a wet cobbled street which ran parallel to the rapid, blood-polluted waters of the Rhine. In an instant she found refuge beneath one of the ancient, shadowy arches of the County Council building, its lavishly ornate façade pock-marked by bullets. Groups of German soldiers, holding submachine-guns, hurried by within a few feet of her. Then came the rumble of vehicles: motorbikes, trucks and one or two tanks.

That particular day, Edda's private tutor had delivered word that, because of a slight, recurring illness, she would be unable to visit her pupil's home. So Edda journeyed across town to take her lessons at her teacher's house. But what neither teacher nor pupil knew, in that late afternoon as Edda made her way home, was that an emergency curfew had been imposed by the German authorities while a cell of saboteurs was being penetrated and, ultimately, destroyed. The Dutch girl, therefore, had no right to be on the streets.

Still clinging like a limpet to the shadow-shrouded brickwork, Edda became momentarily lost within the crowded confusion of her thoughts. How long she remained in that bizarre condition, no one will ever know. All she would remember was the sudden, sickening realisation that a submachine-gun was pointing at her ribs.

'What are you doing here?' enquired the soldier brandishing his gun. His voice was impatient, businesslike.

Edda showed her leather satchel containing her school books and, as best she could with her limited command of German, explained her predicament. The soldier, a blond young subaltern, seemed to be satisfied that the trembling bag of bones before him was telling the truth. After rummaging quickly through her satchel, and ordering her to remove her shoes to ascertain whether she was carrying messages for the underground movement, he became unexpectedly compassionate. He told her to remain hidden until the end of the curfew, which, in view of the culprits having now been apprehended, would probably be in about half an hour. And he departed as expeditiously as he had arrived.

Edda let out a sigh of relief. Just the previous day, as on many other occasions, she had indeed been conveying messages in her shoes for the underground forces; and several other members of her family had suffered gravely at the hands of the invading Nazis as a result of their own contributions to the Dutch resistance movement.

10

Within a few months of the incident the County Council building would be completely destroyed during the fighting for the Rhine bridges. Only the north gate would survive.

Many years later, Edda, now Audrey Hepburn, the glamorous, immensely rich, world-famous Hollywood star who had mesmerised cinema audiences in *The Nun's Story*, *Breakfast at Tiffany's* and *My Fair Lady*, stood wistfully opposite the site of the old County Council building, recently rebuilt in ultra-modern style and linked to the old gate by a glass tunnel high above the traffic. And beneath a phoenix on the walls of the entrance gate she read the inscription:

DEVASTATA MCMXLIV Brought down by earthly forces.
RENOVATA MCMLIV What God restores has greater strength.

As she stood there, her melancholy eyes scanning the ground floor, her mind drifted back to the wartime drama and to the shadowy arched wall that had become her solace and refuge. And suddenly the film star's head was filled with the memories of a past life which, when somebody decided to write her biography, would probably read like the figment of an author's crazy imagination.

This is her story.

The announcement in the London *Times*, dated 24 December 1927, read as follows:

'Dr A. A. L. Rutgers, Director of Agriculture, Industry and Commerce in the Netherlands East Indies, has been appointed Governor of Surinam (Dutch Guiana) in succession to Baron van Heemstra, whose resignation will take effect on January 4. – *Reuter*.'

The dignified Baron Aarnoud Jan Anne Aleid van Heemstra (Edda's maternal grandfather), Knight of the Dutch Lion Order, Commander of the Order of Orange-Nassau, Grand Officer of the House of Orange, Knight of the Order of the Knights of St John, and now ex-Governor of Surinam but still a familiar and popular figure at the Court of Queen Wilhelmina, was immensely proud of his aristocratic lineage and would defend it to the last. Like his father and paternal grandfather and his uncles and cousins, he was trained as a lawyer; his ancestors' names, in common with his own, were preceded by 'Mr', meaning 'Meester', a title used by Dutch lawyers (equivalent to the British Doctor of Laws degree, LL.D.); in the Netherlands, therefore, he would have been properly referred to as Mr A. J. A. A. Baron van Heemstra. He was born at Huis Slotzicht, Vreeland, on 22 July 1871, and, prior to his appointment as Governor of Dutch Guiana, was first burgomaster of Arnhem and then solicitor-general and deputy justice at the Arnhem Court of Justice. At the slightest opportunity he would remind his daughter Ella, Edda's mother, that their ancestors had occupied positions of honour as statesmen and soldiers since the twelfth century.

On 26 March 1896, in The Hague, the Baron married the Baroness Elbrig Willemine Henriette van Asbeck, the daughter of Baron Gerrit Ferdinand and the Honourable Miss Caroline van Hogendorp, a young lady two years his junior. (His bride would die at Oosterbeek in 1939, some considerable years before his own death in 1957.) From this union there was one son and five daughters. Ella, who was born at Velp, Guelderland, on 12 June 1900, was the Baron's third child. Before her was Wilhelmina Cornela in 1897 and Geraldine Caroline in 1898, and after her came Marianne Jacqueline in 1903, Willem Henrik in 1907, and Arnoudina Johanna in 1911; the title Baroness or Baron was automatically conferred on each of them. During the late 1920s and 1930s, Marianne became lady-in-waiting to Queen Wilhelmina's daughter, Princess (later Queen) Juliana of the Netherlands.

As with many European aristocratic families of long tradition, where one powerful, wealthy house had been strengthened by the bond of marriage with that of another pedigree of comparable stature and prosperity, Ella came of mixed Dutch-Hungarian-French stock. She was also partly Jewish. Although her aristocratic ancestry can be traced back to the twelfth century, the paternal genealogy for the van Heemstra family starts in 1528 with Taecke Obbema, an affluent owner of estates at Oostdongeradeel, Dantumadeel, Tietjerksteradeel, and elsewhere. Following the death of his first wife, Otzen Clant, he remarried in 1528. His bride's name was Auck Heemstra and, according to the so-called *Burmania-boek*, he subsequently adopted for himself, and all his heirs, his second wife's family name of Heemstra. From Taecke Heemstra there is an unbroken line of descendants all the way down to Edda/Audrey.

Taecke Heemstra's son, Feije Heemstra (who later married Ebel Hemmema), was the owner – at fourteen – of vast estates at Wijns; *his* son, Feije van Heemstra (born 1572; married Aelcke Tjarda van Starckenborch), was the landlord of Oenkerke; *his* son, Feije van Heemstra (born 1605; married Maria Bannier), was a lieutenant under Captain Douwe van Andringa; *his* son, Feije van Heemstra (born 1630; married Tjits van Aysma), was a major in the regiment of the Stadthouder's Guards, sergeant-major in the Burmanian regiment, and variously commander of the town and country of Ravenstein, commander of Breda, and colonel and commander of Emden; *his* son, Schelte van Heemstra (born 1665; married second time, as widower of Lutske van Burmania, to Catharina van Scheltinga), was variously governor of Prince Johan Willem Friso, sergeant-major, alderman and member of the Admiralty Council of Amsterdam; *his* son, Willem Hendrik van Heemstra (born 1696; married Wya Catharina van Glinstra), was variously administrator of Kollumerland and Nieuw-Kruisland, dike-reeve of Kollumerland, administrator of the polder districts of Kollumerzijlen and Munnikezijlen, and postmaster-general; *his* son, Schelto van Heemstra (born 1738; married Wiskje van Scheltinga), was attorney at the Amsterdam District Council and the Admiralty Council of Amsterdam, burgomaster of Bolsward, and owner of vast areas of forests; *his* son, Baron Willem Hendrik van Heemstra (born 1779), married Johanna Balthazarina van Idsinga in 1803, and was Edda's great-great-great-grandfather; *his* son, Mr Frans Julius Johan, Baron van Heemstra (born 1811), married Baroness Henriëtta Philippina Jacoba van Pallandt in 1837, and was Edda's great-great-grandfather; *his* son, Mr Willem Hendrik Johan, Baron van Heemstra, Knight of the Order of Orange-Nassau (born 1841; married Wilhelmina Cornelia de Beaufort, 1866), was a member of the Provincial States of Utrecht and burgomaster of Driebergen, and was Edda's great-grandfather; *his* son, the dignified Baron Aarnoud van Heemstra, who married the Baroness Elbrig van Asbeck, was, of course, Edda's grandfather and Ella's father. He died in The Hague on 30 December 1957, aged eighty-six.

Whatever else Edda may have eventually suffered from, it would not be an identity crisis; she would know exactly who she was and where she came from; portraits of her ancestors hung in museums, galleries and private houses throughout the Netherlands. How could she forget?

Edda's mother, Ella, was raised according to the strict social conduct of the Dutch nobility: groomed thoroughly to exhibit those traits of confidence, strength, bearing and leadership which were deemed to be such highly prized qualities. In the Netherlands, as in every European country except England, high state office or duty was an almost exclusive prerogative of the nobility. For the Dutch gentleman and lady, public activity was a matter of personal sense of duty, and Ella would have come into the world with her future duties to the Royal household already planned and sealed – although, in the event, *the* Royal duty, that of lady-in-waiting to Holland's future queen, Juliana, went to Ella's younger sister, Marianne.

A substantial part of Ella's childhood was spent on the family's magnificent estate at Doorn, in Utrecht, the central and smallest province of the Netherlands. Many fine old castles existed in the province, and Ella and her family resided in one of them, Het Kasteel de Doorn. (Today, under its new name of Huis-Doorn, it is run as a stately-home-cum-museum, being open to the public each year between 15 March and 31 October.) Surrounded by an exceptionally wide, deep moat, and set in hundreds of leafy acres, the fortress's halls and rooms were resplendent with large, gilt-framed portraits of the household's noble ancestors.

One spring morning, when daffodils covered the estate in great carpets of yellow, the Baron summoned his daughter to the library to administer some stern parental advice. He reminded Ella of the family's long, illustrious heritage, and implored her not to indulge in any activity that would deviate from the honour of the Heemstra dynasty.

'Whatever you do,' he began, as he attempted to light his traditional Dutch pipe, with its china bowl, cherry-wood stem and horn mouthpiece, 'whatever you do, don't associate with the stage or with actors and actresses. You'd bring disgrace on the family.'

Ella frowned. Many years later she would explain: 'I tried to obey my father. But I grew up wanting more than anything else to be . . .' (she paused) '. . . well, English, slim, and an actress.'

While she was growing up, ambitious political events were being enacted across the border in Germany which would have catastrophic repercussions not merely on the Baron's family but on the families of the entire world. On 9 November 1918, when Germany, facing defeat in the First World War, had risen

14

against Wilhelm II, the Kaiser abdicated, and the following day – urged by Hindenburg – fled to the Netherlands, along with the Empress Augusta and their son, the Crown Prince. Eighteen months later, with the ex-empress seriously ill, the exiles felt themselves to be a burden to their amiable host, Count Bentinck, who had provided shelter to the imperial family at his castle at Amerongen; and, indeed, soon after, Wilhelm managed to buy from the Baroness Elbrig van Heemstra – Ella's mother – the old castle-home at Doorn, where the exiled emperor proceeded to absolve administrators and officers of their oath of loyalty to him, though he did not formally renounce his rights.

At the end of the war, the Treaty of Versailles declared that he was a 'war criminal' and that he should be handed over to the victorious Allies for trial; but the Dutch refused to give him up, and the matter was not pressed further by London. For the remainder of his life he nursed vague hopes for the restoration of the monarchy in Germany; and when, in 1941, he died at the van Heemstras' castle at Doorn, Hitler granted him a military funeral. Thus, at the castle residence Ella knew so well as a girl, the long line of German emperors and Prussian kings had come to an end.

Just prior to the exiled Kaiser's arrival at Doorn, Ella's family had already taken up residence at their fine old ancestral estate near Arnhem; and it was at Arnhem, on 11 March 1920, that Ella – three months short of her twentieth birthday – was married to the Honourable Jan Hendrik Gustaaf Adolf Quarles van Ufford, Knight of the Order of Orange-Nassau. Five years her senior, and born and raised at Noordwijk-Binnen, he was the son of the Honourable Mr Jan Hendrik Jacob and the Baroness Adriana Collot d'Escury and, in his time, was First Lieutenant of the Horse Artillery and ADC to Queen Wilhelmina. But it was a stormy marriage, they argued about almost everything, and they were divorced in the Netherlands East Indies five years later. There were two sons, Ian (or Jan) and Alexander.

By this time Ella's father, the Baron, had been appointed by Queen Wilhelmina to be the new Governor of Dutch Guiana, or Surinam. Here, in that little-known part of South America between the river Orinoco, the river Amazon and its tributary the Rio Negro, and the Atlantic Ocean, Ella and her sons enjoyed a brief sojourn. Orchids, sometimes with stems twelve feet high, grew all around the Governor's house, and gigantic vines festooned the trees of the residential grounds. The land over which her father ruled as Governor was originally British, but in 1667 was given to the Dutch in exchange for New York. The Baron presided over a colony of some 63,000 square miles, whose products consisted largely of cacao, coffee, sugar, rice, maize, bananas, rum, bauxite, and gold. Yet, as blissful as her stop-over might have seemed in the capital, Paramaribo, with its glittering diversions of parties and state banquets, Ella – now more customarily addressed as the Baroness van Heemstra – was drawn back irresistibly to her European homeland. During her earlier stay in the Dutch East Indies, following the dissolution of her marriage to Jan Hendrik, she had met an influential Anglo-Irish banker named John Victor Anthony Hepburn-Ruston and, although there had been an instant mutual attraction, the relationship was little more than platonic. She had only recently gone through with her divorce, and John, too, had just been divorced in San Francisco from his first wife, Cornelia Wilhelmina Bisschop. And so, having returned to Arnhem, Ella boarded the next boat for the Indonesian capital of Batavia (now Jakarta), and, on 7 September 1926, she and John were married. They eventually left for Belgium, where John now managed the Brussels branch of the Bank of England, which handled the finances and properties of the Baron's family.

John, the son of Victor John Hepburn-Ruston and Anna Catharine Wells, was born in London on 21 November 1889, and was therefore nearly twelve years older than his new bride. He was of above-average height, dark-haired, with thick, bushy eyebrows. His jaw was square, his brown eyes all-perceiving, and he was reasonably (though not exceptionally) good-looking; and yet he had a manner about him which people found immediately compelling: a man of charisma. Women adored him. Ella, certainly, was drawn instantly to this striking man who was such a virtuoso in matters where economics and accounting were the black and white notes of the pecuniary keyboard.

Their first and only child was born on 4 May 1929, on John's fine old estate near Brussels. Edda Kathleen Hepburn van Heemstra, a long baby with the prettiest, 'laughing' eyes, came into the world at a time of grave economic and political unrest. The impending slump of 1929, with the crash of the New York Stock Exchange, would shake the financial structure of the whole world to its foundations. No continent would escape the catastrophe, but in Europe its consequences would be tragic. The slump would sweep through Belgium, the Netherlands and Germany like a hurricane, leaving wreckage and despair in its wake.

In Britain the elections of May 1929 resulted in the defeat of Stanley Baldwin and the formation of a Labour Government under Ramsay MacDonald; but in time the economic crisis grew so grave that MacDonald was obliged to form a coalition, the National Government, which included Conservatives, Liberals and a splinter group of the Labour Party. In the Soviet Union, Stalin resumed an orthodox line in respect of the collectivisation of farms, and large numbers of peasant proprietors – the *kulaks* – were liquidated, just as other capitalist elements had been disposed of ten years earlier. In Belgium, three weeks after Edda saw her first light of day, the Catholic Party won the elections; and Herbert Hoover was into his second month as the thirty-first president of the United States.

In Hollywood, Mary Pickford and Douglas Fairbanks began work on their first 'talkie' together, *The Taming of the Shrew*; but, in London, theatre managers were fearing that the talkies would take business away from West End theatres. Certainly the popularity of talking and singing pictures had reached such a pitch in Britain that, reported the *Daily Express*, more than three hundred new cinemas were being built or were about to be built. The golden age of the movies was born.

If, politically and financially, the world was in a catastrophic mess, at least the artistic and cultural climate in which Edda was raised would be seen one day to be especially apt for one of the twentieth-century's most original and sensitive children. Her perceptiveness was apparent from the beginning. Although she was raised with two boisterous older half-brothers, Ian and Alexander, either on the estate near Brussels or at her mother's castle-like house on the van Heemstra's manor near Arnhem, it would eventually become obvious to the Baroness – as Ella would continue to call herself – that little Edda much preferred her own company and was consequently becoming more and more withdrawn. And yet she could also be a creature of contradictions, mentally introspective yet revealing great bursts of physical tempestuousness.

She was three years old when she made her first acquaintance with the England whose filmgoers she would later conquer. Each winter thereafer she attended school here. It was on her first visit to England that Edda displayed the first early indication that she was destined to become a performer. The Baroness had taken her, and the boys, to an afternoon band concert when they were visiting Folkestone, on the south coast, and at some point she managed to disappear from her mother's side. When the Baroness was just beginning to think the worst and in the process of asking passers-by to help in a search for the lost child, someone pointed out a little girl on the far side of the bandstand, dancing up and down in time to the music. A small audience had collected around her.

'E-d-d-a!' the Baroness cried out with relief.

The enthralled dancing girl proffered a quick wave in recognition, and continued to entertain the crowd. The Baroness watched in amazement, a proud little smile stealing across her face. Years later she would explain: 'Edda did that kind of thing without any prompting from me or other adults. It was spontaneous and natural, so she didn't appear to be one of those awful little prodigies.'

Although a quiet, reflective child, given to day-dreaming and dressing-up in her mother's clothes, Edda was not the 'sweet little girl' type. She was thin, and frequently sickly, but tomboyish in spirit and would race Ian and Alexander to scale the trees and jump the fences on the estate. And, unlike most other little girls, she bore no regard for dolls. When, from time to time, the Baroness tried to interest her daughter in such playthings, Edda would leave them in a pile in the nursery, complaining 'They're so *silly*', and years later she would confess 'They just never seemed real to me.' For the remainder of her life she would be a realist.

Throughout these early years, Edda continued to maintain a mostly cloistered, protected life, living alternately between the family's estates in Holland and Belgium and winter schooling in England, a life of nannies and private tutors. She never wanted for anything, and yet she was seldom the happiest of children.

Parental tensions, barely discernible to begin with, later explosive in nature, gradually made their impact. The Baroness had already endured one painful divorce, and her marriage to John now seemed to be heading for the rocks as well. They were constantly quarrelling over the Baroness's money matters; and the more stormy the marriage became, the more tense was the atmosphere of Edda's home life. She inevitably suffered, as little children everywhere suffer when life at home isn't secure. Her personality, always frail in character, changed dramatically. She became over-sensitive, developed an acutely introverted nature, and sought refuge by hiding in the green fields around her family's estates – and eating compulsively. Hiding and eating became the two most important impulses in her small world.

'It was either chocolates, bread or my nails,' she would later explain as she looked back on those unhappy days.

Although she developed a strong attachment to both of her older half-brothers, she seldom made friends with children of her own age. More and more she began to find solace in the dogs, cats, rabbits, horses and other livestock that were part of the estates, as well as in the animals, birds and plants of the surrounding countryside, whose company she would share and treasure for many hours of every day. And, like many children who are not inclined towards gregariousness, she was an ardent reader. A favourite volume of fiction would accompany her on every out-of-the way rural ramble, when, at some point, she would squat beneath an old willow and lose herself in another world. 'I was brought up,' she reminisced later, 'with an enormous love of Rudyard Kipling.'

Although she dearly loved the elder of her two half-brothers, Ian, she grew up more closely with the younger one, Alexander, a lad just four years older than herself.

'Alexander's the original bookworm,' she recalled, 'and when we were children he was devoted to Kipling. I admired him so much that I read all Kipling's books because I wanted to be like him. And I followed everything else he read, too. The result was that before I was thirteen I had read nearly every book by Edgar Wallace and Edward Phillips Oppenheim, who wrote a long series of romantic mysteries about secret international documents, shifty diplomats and seductive adventuresses. Those were real adventure books, and to me as a girl they had far more appeal than books like *Topsy Goes to School.*'

John's work for the bank in the meantime continued to take him abroad a great deal, and it was while he was away on these prolonged business excursions that his daughter found her only real moments of peace and inner contentment. Without the sound of incessant quarrelling ringing in her ears, and spared the vivid images of two parents bickering and feuding,

Edda's introverted nature would find itself momentarily reprieved. A bright, sunny child took over the shell of the earlier down-in-the-mouth little girl.

She got on very well with her mother, and her mother in turn worshipped the daughter whom, she was well aware, was far too sensitive to remain unaffected by the interminable war of words on which she and John were engaged. The quarrelling, ironically, brought mother and daughter ever closer, and between them there existed an awesome rapport, an extraordinary bond of love and respect which would be with them forever. If the Baroness ever worried about anything, it was that, in trying to compensate for the emotional turmoil that sometimes ripped through the house like a tornado, she was often inclined to shower Edda with too much love. She felt guilty of over-indulgence.

While away on his excursions, Edda's father fell in with a pro-Nazi political group, with whose sympathies he became increasingly involved and infatuated. How much the Baroness herself was involved in her husband's political fanaticism cannot be accurately gauged. It is almost certain that, taking into account that Nazism and genteel European aristocracy did not always make the most compatible bed-fellows, her involvement would have been peripheral, casual and executed purely from a sense of wifely accord. At any rate, it has been difficult to find any evidence connecting her with the movement, except for a solitary, fleeting reference in David Pryce-Jones's exhaustive monograph on Unity Mitford, who was Hitler's English girlfriend and the sister-in-law of the guiding force of the British Union of Fascists, Sir Oswald Mosley.

The author reflects on 'how eerie the Nazi insistence was on photographing their moods of power', and goes on to explain that 'the photographs of Unity and her group friends . . . have about them something hectic, a factitious comradeship, all straight lines of faces, smiles, and arms linked for the statement to the camera. Here is the jollity on the steps of the Brown House, with Unity and Sister Pam and Mary, Coleridge Hills and his wife (J. C. Hills) and Baroness Ella van Heemstra, who was a Mosleyite with her first husband Ruston (*sic*.). . . .'

Unity subsequently shot herself in Munich on the outbreak of the Second World War, during which John would eventually find himself blacklisted for being pro-Nazi and for having joined Mosley's black-shirted Fascists. Pryce-Jones supplies no precise date for the 'eerie' photographs in question, although they are mentioned in a section of his book dealing with May of 1935: a significant date.

It was at about this time, and certainly in 1935 itself, that John and the Baroness separated under strange circumstances, the aberration being directly attributable to the erring husband. (It would be another three years, however, before they became legally divorced.) One day, offering neither rhyme nor reason, John simply walked out on his family, never to be heard from again. As one who knew the family later recalled, 'He left no recollections to which Edda or her mother wished to cling.' In later years, certainly, Edda would claim to remember little about him, 'except that he was fond of horses'. To this day, nobody knows where John is, whether or not he became aware of his daughter's fame – or, indeed, whether he is still alive. Edda told a magazine interviewer in 1954 that her father was living in Ireland. The shadowy figure became an enigma to the last.

The Baroness subsequently took Edda and the boys back to Arnhem, and life went on much as before: private tutorage, winter schooling in England, an enclosed, exclusive existence that seemed to be designed, ironically, to cultivate Edda's brooding introspection. At long last her divorce was declared absolute, an annulment widely believed to have been the result of disagreements over the management of the van Heemstra money. It was an old story: the husband who misappropriated his rich wife's family fortune. History was littered with such men, and John was merely following in a long tradition.

The divorce brought with it some inevitable inter-family repercussions, most notably the crucial question of Edda's custody. John's attorney noted that at the time when he left his family, Edda was so retiring and shy that her behaviour alarmed him. The Baroness, too, realising that her unhappy marriage was the cause of her daughter's personality problem, was now resolved more than ever to take drastic steps to change things. The divorce decree, as it happened, solved everything. It stipulated that Edda should attend an exclusive English girls' school near London so that John could exercise his visitation privileges. The Baroness was at first concerned about the possible adverse influence such an arrangement might have on the development of Edda's delicate personality, but in time she became reconciled to it.

21

Edda, meanwhile, was filled with terror. To be separated yet again from her mother, this time in the company of complete strangers, was the last thing in the world she would have sought. She longed for the security of a stable family background, for the company of her dear half-brothers and of the animals on the estate. But now the nine-year-old girl, who spoke English and French fluently, was bound for England and all that that implied in terms of untold loneliness.

At the end of the first term, the Baroness joined Edda in England. When she arrived at the school to greet her daughter, the child was blossoming with good health and gushing with exciting reports on the progress of her first ballet lessons. A teacher confirmed that Edda was showing a natural aptitude for dancing. She would go far.

But all was not auspicious, even if on the surface it appeared so. It was during her period at the English boarding-school that Edda began to suffer the migraine attacks which would afflict her for the rest of her life. The change was too revolutionary for a youngster of Edda's sensitive temperament. Dancing lessons apart, the small girl simply could not cope; it is debatable whether any young girl could have coped with such a revolution.

None the less, the Baroness returned to her rented accommodation in central London, situated not far from Regent's Park, confident that Edda was thriving on the strict regime of the English preparatory-school system. The well-ordered, often harsh, Victorian discipline of the school, plus the close contact with other girls of her own age and (sometimes) class, transpired to be exactly the 'magic formula' which Edda needed at that time in order to be drawn out of herself.

She was still making steady progress in that direction when, in the summer of 1939, she was holidaying with her mother and her two half-brothers at her grandmother's house in Arnhem. While the prospect of returning to her English school after the summer break did not exactly fill her with unbridled joy, neither was she smarting from the soul-destroying fears which had consumed her the previous year. She was blissfully happy, possibly for the first time in her life.

But war in Europe was fermenting. At any moment, the course of history would be changed.

3

'We went underground after Hitler marched in. . . .'

W HEN ENGLAND FINALLY declared war on
Germany in September 1939, the Baroness reasoned that Holland would be by far the safest place for Edda, and so she completely ignored John's pleas to return their daughter to her English school. She chose, instead, to install the three children in the van Heemstra estate just outside Arnhem. Later she enrolled Edda, Ian and Alexander at a small school in Arnhem itself, and allowed Edda to continue her ballet training at the Arnhem Conservatory of Music. Although, at this time, she spoke two languages with precocious fluency, Edda had never uttered more than two or three words of Dutch. The prospect of having to attend a school where a 'foreign' language was spoken filled her with great anxiety.

'That first morning in school,' she would say in retrospect, 'I sat at my little bench, completely baffled. I went home at the end of the day, weeping. For several days I went home weeping. But I knew I couldn't just give up. I was forced to learn the language quickly. And I did. Considering what was to happen to me later, it was a useful basic experience.'

One evening, some months later, during a period of high political tension – when a major confrontation with Germany seemed imminent – the Sadler's Wells Ballet (today's Royal Ballet), spearheaded by its brightest jewels, Margot Fonteyn and Robert Helpmann, were appearing at Arnhem: a town, incidentally, just twelve miles by road from the German border. During the performance, which included Frederick Ashton's

Horoscope, a ballet about young lovers ruled by the signs of the zodiac, Hitler's tanks started to roll into Holland. Fonteyn and the company were told to finish the show, board their buses and leave as quickly as possible. But, at the final curtain, the Baroness – who had been instrumental in arranging the visit – decided to make a thank-you speech to the company. It went on and on and on, in Flemish; then she repeated it in English. Finally, she insisted that her daughter Edda should present a bouquet of fresh tulips to Margot Fonteyn. At last the company, leaving behind the lavish costumes, sets and orchestral scores for *Horoscope*, piled into their buses and made their bid for freedom.

That night, sitting up in bed with the printed programme of the dance company from Britain in front of her, Edda decided that one day she too would be a ballerina like Margot Fonteyn. She could think of little else. She felt intoxicated. *She wanted to become a ballet dancer.*

And yet there were other, more pressing matters to occupy people's minds. The Nazis had invaded the Netherlands. Arnhem was occupied. Life for the child would become something far removed from her dreams of rich music and decorous dancing.

As Edda recalled later, 'We heard the news over the radio. All civilians were ordered to remain indoors and to close their shutters, and we were warned not to look out of the windows. Naturally, we all peeped out. I know I did. And it was uncannily strange. In an invasion, one expects fighting; but there was no fighting. We saw the grey uniforms of the German soldiers on foot. They all held machine-guns and they marched in looking spick and span and well disciplined; then came the rumble of trucks and tanks – and the next thing we knew was that the Germans had taken complete charge of the town.'

On 10 May, less than a week after Edda's eleventh birthday, Queen Wilhelmina issued a 'flaming protest' at the German invasion of her country – during the First World War she had declared her government's firm intention to maintain the integrity and neutrality of the Netherlands – and then decided to leave for England with her family, which included Princess Juliana. All this came as a profound shock for most of the Dutch people, who had been completely unaware of what was going on in the rest of the world. Wilhelmina and her family arrived in London three days later, followed by her Cabinet.

24

From her new vantage point, she later became the symbol of the resistance movement in the Netherlands, keeping the loyalty of the great bulk of her people and exhorting them in broadcasts over Radio Orange to hold on until liberation should come. The Baroness and her family, who rarely missed the broadcasts, would soon be numbered among Queen Wilhelmina's staunchest supporters.

'On the surface, life remained normal,' the Baroness told a family friend, *en route* to a town some miles away. 'The Germans tried to be civil and to win our hearts. They were always excessively polite, and would step out of the way of women walking on the pavement. But this didn't last for long.'

In fact, tension mounted.

'We heard stories of sabotage and whispers of an underground movement,' she continued. 'Some hostages were taken and shot as an example to others. The soldiers were no longer polite to us. We were pushed off the pavements as a reminder that they were the conquerors.'

The wealthy people of Holland were among the first to feel the full impact of the invasion. All Dutch gold in private possession was requisitioned, and Dutch silver coinage was replaced with zinc. In retrospect, the Baroness's decision to remain in Arnhem was all the more odd, taking into account her Jewish ancestry. The van Heemstra estates and property holdings, and most of the family fortune, were immediately seized by the Germans. In the course of time, one of Edda's uncles – one of the foremost lawyers in the country and one of her best-loved relatives – was arrested by the Gestapo during a retaliation action designed to halt underground sabotage activities (a German troop train had been blown up). When the resistance movement continued, he was placed before a firing squad with five other hostages and shot; and when the underground still continued to operate, the attorney's son, one of Edda's closest cousins and a member of the royal court, was arrested and, later, he too was executed. Edda then watched, with horror in her dark eyes, as Ian, the older of her half-brothers, was dragged away by force to a concentration camp. They were all regarded as enemies of the Third Reich. The occupation was a complete reign of terror and for many young Dutch girls it was even worse. The Baroness's daughter learned a great deal at too early an age.

'At times like this,' she would say, 'you learn about death, privation, danger, which makes you appreciate safety and how quickly it can change. You learn to be serious about what counts.'

Edda's knowledge of French and English proved to be a liability under wartime occupation, and her name was as good as a time-bomb; for the remainder of the war she lived under an assumed name, which to this day she has never revealed. In public, the pigtailed schoolgirl never uttered a word of English: the enemy's eyes and ears were everywhere. There was no such thing as being *too* careful. She lived a shadowy life, and started to learn to speak Flemish, which she set about with application and tenacity, though she still travelled into town for her schooling, in itself a severe hardship. Eventually she gave up school and was given a tutor, but she maintained her ballet studies at the Arnhem Conservatory. Some time later she herself provided dancing lessons at a local academy but, after a while, was compelled to abandon these as well, though she continued to offer lessons at home, where the Baroness had installed a dance barre in an empty room. At an age when most girls were tripping over the polished floor at a school concert, Edda was giving ballet tuition to youngsters not much younger than herself.

'I had decided to become a dancer and I was very serious about it,' she would explain in subsequent years. 'And I wanted to dance solo roles. Pavlova was my ideal. I had any amount of books and magazines on dancing. I loved music and I was fanatically dedicated and I desperately wanted to do these roles because they would allow me to express myself. I couldn't express myself while conforming to a line of twelve girls. I didn't want to conform. I was going to hit my mark and I was working very hard.'

Quite soon, however, civilian food was severely rationed and the strain on Edda began to tell. She became thin and, subsequently, extremely ill. The Baroness decided that perhaps it would be to the whole family's advantage, and not least to Edda's, if they moved. With the help of some local friends they eventually found a house on the outskirts of the town. It hardly offered the opulent comforts of the old mansion, but it was perfectly adequate to the emergency needs of Edda and Alexander. There were three bedrooms and a serviceable kitchen, with a round, cast-iron stove in one corner, from the rusty flue of which more fumes tended to escape into the room than into the outside world. She can still describe in vivid detail the feeling of the family huddled around the stove, for the experience imbued her forever with an uneasy sense of 'how delicate it all is. Human relationships. Family. Any minute a bomb can blow it all away.'

The over-sensitive young girl was confronted daily with brutal reality – a reality which she, and millions like her, had to live with or go under. Arnhem was a grim and fantastic place for a child to be. The acute food shortage would leave her with a permanently delicate stomach and with asthma, which would keep her awake at night, intermittently, for the rest of her life. And there would be the nightmares, when the horrors of war-torn reality mingled insanely with the fevered imagination of nocturnal slumbers.

'I saw families with little children, with babies, herded into meat wagons – trains of big wooden vans with just a little slat open at the top and all those faces peering out at you,' she would tell Curtis Bill Pepper – but this was actuality, not the remembrances of some horrid hallucination or dream. 'And on the platform,' she went on, 'were soldiers herding more Jewish families with their poor little bundles and small children. There would be families together and they would separate them, say-ing, "The men go there and the women go there". Then they would take the babies and put them in another van. I tell you, all the nightmares I've ever had are mingled with that.

'People all have fears, but mostly they are distant and unknown to them. They are afraid of death which they haven't gone through, they are afraid of getting cancer which they don't have, they are afraid of getting run over which hasn't happened. But I've known the cold clutch of human terror. I've seen it, I've felt it, I've heard it.'

All those who, like Edda, saw, felt and heard it, became increasingly determined to voice their disgust. The first open act of rebellion was a strike in February 1941 in protest against the rounding-up of Jewish youths in Amsterdam and, later, elsewhere. As a result of the strike, many municipal councils were dissolved a month later and their powers transferred to the provincial burgomasters and commissioners, who by now were either Nazis or fellow-travellers.

The Nazi measures against the Dutch Jews, or rather the Jew-ish Netherlanders, led progressively to the introduction of the Star of David, which they were forced to wear prominently.

27

However, a large part of the Dutch population, Arnhem included, took the fate of their Jewish fellow-countrymen to heart; of the 130,000 Jews living in the Netherlands at the time, some 30,000 went into hiding. The resistance movement furnished them with fake identity cards, ration books and *Ausweise*, cleverly forged on underground presses.

Edda, dutifully, played her part. German soldiers who passed her in the streets, on her way to and from the Conservatory, never dreamed that in the shoes of this long-legged girl were coded messages for the underground forces. Neither did they nurse any suspicion that she was giving dancing recitals in the private houses of the town – secret recitals at which funds were collected for that same resistance work. Those secret gatherings behind locked doors and curtained windows – attended in real peril since there were Nazi edicts about the number of people who could meet at one place – were Edda's first audiences.

The Baroness, inspired by Queen Wilhelmina's exhortations, became increasingly involved in underground activities, and it was but a matter of time before Edda and Alexander would be recruited and asked to contribute their services to the cause of the Dutch freedom-fighters. Edda was a natural contact, because the Arnhem Conservatory was used as a centre for raising funds and recruiting saboteurs, their subversive activities conducted under the cover of musical concerts, ballet performances and other entertainments. At these 'black' concerts, where the audiences were placed in as much danger as the artists, the pianist would be compelled to play so softly that the music could barely be heard. Edda not only danced: she was frequently also the pianist. Often she performed with one of her classmates, Joyce Vanderveer, a friendship which would survive the war and be rekindled many years later across the Atlantic.

It was impossible to buy ballet shoes unless a permit had been obtained from the Chamber of Commerce, so Edda was forced to dance in old slippers. Her mother and friends helped her to make dresses out of curtains and old sheets. Invitations to a 'tea party' were sent to reliable underground movement sympathizers, and there was usually an audience of about 100 people, all paying as much as they could afford. Edda danced her versions of the classical ballets – *Coppélia*, *Swan Lake* and *The Nutcracker*. And always, as she whirled and pirouetted, she strained to hear, above the music, the knock of the secret police at the door.

Although her first dream was to be a ballet dancer, 'like Margot Fonteyn', her appearances at the 'black' concerts were not in the customary role of a snowflake or sprite. Certain physical limitations ruled against such an eventuality. 'I never was a raindrop, though I was dying to be,' she told a friend. 'I was a "boy". I had to lift up the little girls because I was so tall.'

But in time her strength waned and she could no longer be the 'boy'. Long periods of living without milk, butter, eggs, sugar and meat began to take its toll. The near-starvation diet brought with it severe anaemia; later, in her adult years, she would find it impossible to put on weight: she would be the eternal 'hungry waif'. But the schoolgirl Edda, with her huge eyes and tiny face, was indeed hungry.

'When you have had the strength to survive starvation,' she would say many years later, 'you never again send back a steak simply because it's under-done.'

As money grew tight the family jewel box was emptied to buy food; but most of the time Edda simply had to scrounge for it. A meal often consisted of little more than endive (a species of chicory with curled leaves) and a little bread. (Just the thought of endive, after the war, would turn her stomach. 'I never want to see any again,' she would wail.) During the winter and spring months she survived for long periods on tulip bulbs. So weeks and months of starvation whittled away the emerging womanly shape; the girl who, by her own description, was already plain and bony thin, became a shadow of her former self.

Edda's frail condition came to a head one day while she was having her usual ballet tuition at the Conservatory. Even in a class of dancing girls where thinness was the norm rather than the exception, Edda's sickly, puny frame stood out. Her stomach that day was gripped by sharp pangs of hunger as she tried desperately to listen to what the teacher was saying. With hands that visibly trembled Edda gripped the practice barre and struggled to perform a series of bends with the other girls in the class. As her knees bent for the fifth time, the blood drained from her pale cheeks and she was enveloped in the whirling, sickening blackness of a deep faint. Moments later she opened her eyes and looked up from the floor to see a ring of faces around her.

'Don't try to move,' the old man said tenderly. 'Just lie there for a while. You've been trying too hard. These exercises are too difficult for you; you're not strong enough.'

Edda managed a weak smile as some of her strength returned. 'I feel better now,' she said unconvincingly. 'Let's go on with the lesson.'

'Don't talk nonsense,' replied the white-haired dancing master. 'You're in no condition to go on. You must have some rest. When did you eat last?'

Edda, still slightly dazed, thought for a second. Then she answered: 'I had some bread yesterday morning, but I'm not hungry.'

'Not hungry?' moaned the old man in sympathy. 'No food since yesterday and you want me to believe you're not hungry? You're a very good dancer, but a very poor liar.'

When the dancing master had ended the lesson and sent the other girls home, he helped the dazed Edda into his office and sat her down on a creaky wooden chair. From the bottom drawer of a battered filing cabinet, he brought out a familiar-looking red ball of Edam cheese.

'I've been hoarding this for an emergency,' he explained, 'and this is an emergency if I've ever seen one.' He sliced off a generous chunk and held it out to Edda. 'Here,' he said, 'eat this piece. It will give you a little strength.'

After eating the cheese, Edda was surging with new energy. Soon she was chattering away about how she dreamed of becoming a ballet star – 'just like Margot Fonteyn'.

'You keep dreaming, young lady,' the old man said, 'and one day your dreams are bound to come true.'

One day, indeed, her dreams would come true beyond her wildest expectations. And yet if dancing was not to be the source of that fame, it would be the springboard. But become a movie star? Thin, ugly Edda become a *movie* star? Had the Baroness, or Joyce or her half-brothers suggested such a thing, Edda would have laughed, and then asked why she was being teased.

Many years later she told her writer friend, Henry Gris: 'Like so many other teenagers, I had tremendous complexes. I would have no sooner thought of my face on the screen as I would that anyone would want me for anything at all in the movie line. I didn't think much of my looks. In fact, I thought I was such an ugly thing that no one would ever want me for a wife.

'Oddly enough, when I was a child I didn't even comprehend

30

the meaning of the word film star the way children the same age do today. I was growing up in a world where such things were totally foreign matter. Holland of my childhood was a million miles away from the world of movie make-believe. The truth of it is, I didn't even know Hollywood existed. I had never read about old Hollywood and its fabulous personages. Nor did I get an opportunity to read about a contemporary Hollywood. All this passed me by without my even once stretching out a teenager's hand to grab for it. I didn't know, and I wasn't curious.

'I saw very few movies because they were German. I refused to go to see Nazi movies. One of my brothers [Ian] had some old records but he was taken off to Germany before I could get interested in them. I was growing up with people much older than myself. I was going to dancing school every day with my little satchel. In it were my sandwiches and my music. I was studying and dreaming of Pavlova and Diaghilev. To all intents and purposes I had been cut off from the world of youngsters my age because the war had made me a prisoner not just physically but mentally, never allowing me to peep out to see what was really outside. In the oppression of occupation I for one had been left to my own devices. And these devices drew me into the enchanted world of music, where one didn't have to talk, just listen. Eventually, music became everything as I could not go on dancing. It was the war, and the war diet, and the anxiety and the terror.'

Her dancing, during those bleak years when death constantly lurked round the corner, had been her exclusive comfort and balm; and now, through the agency of malnutrition, even that pitiful solace had been denied her. Anxiety and terror now dominated her life. During the course of the occupation some four hundred thousand non-Jewish Dutch workers were forced to work in Germany's war industry as slave labourers. The growing resistance around Arnhem led to sharper Nazi reprisals and correspondingly stronger counter-measures from the underground movement. More than once Edda had endured nerve-racking near-misses while engaged in ferrying coded messages for the resistance. A recent encounter with a young Nazi officer, when she had been searched, her shoes included, now precipitated a cold sweat whenever she thought of it. Better not think about such things. . . .

4

'I'm a very interior person.'

TWO MONTHS BEFORE liberation, with the smell of freedom in the air, the German police initiated steps to round up women to work in their military kitchens, hospitals and camps. Girls were literally picked up at random off the streets of Arnhem, herded into trucks and despatched to their destinations. One day on her way home from a message-conveying mission, Edda rounded a corner . . . and all at once her heart seemed to fill her throat. She was consumed by an instant nausea.

'Fräulein! Kommen Sie hier . . . schnell, *schnell!'*

Not more than thirty feet away a German army sergeant, his submachine-gun directed menacingly at Edda's body, suddenly commanded the girl's undivided attention. Her feet were momentarily glued to the pavement; she could not have moved, even if she had so desired. Behind the grim-faced soldier, huddled in a tight, nervous knot in the middle of the road, a small group of Dutch women hostages were being herded by several more German men-at-arms. Edda possessed sufficient presence of mind not to beat a hasty retreat while the German's gun beckoned her to join the assembled womenfolk. Still clutching her leather satchel, containing some sheet-music, a few stale crusts of bread and a small flask of apple juice, Edda moved swiftly in a daze towards her large, thick-set antagonist. She was pushed without ceremony, face-first, against the wall of a house and searched.

As the group of women, some of them sobbing, were

marched to German headquarters, Dutch traders and office workers watched the doleful procession with expressionless masks; but a numbed hate coloured their eyes as they surveyed the captors. 'We won't forget this' – the sentiment was inscribed enduringly on their souls. The herd filed past the little general stores where Edda and Alexander had often succeeded in scrounging cut-price endive and potatoes. She hoped against hope that Alexander might, just might, be on his way to the shop at that very moment and therefore be in a position to inform the Baroness of his sister's plight; but that sort of thing only happened in books, she thought. Presently, they came to a halt on the perimeter of the town, a mostly residential area which had seen better days. All but one of the German soldiers had gone off to corral more women. The solitary guard, his rifle propped against a lamp-post, proceeded to remove a tobacco pouch from a breast-pocket and roll a cigarette.

Edda could hardly believe it. Was this her one and only opportunity? Her eyes were everywhere, and her mind was made up in a flash. Although suffering from malnutrition for almost a year, and so frail that even dance exercises were no longer possible, she would risk life and limb and attempt an escape. In an instant she had made a dash for it and was round a corner and down an alley before the guard even had a chance to grab his rifle, let alone fire a shot.

By chance, satchel-in-hand, she had stumbled into a damp, dark cellar. There was a tiny arrow-slit window at ceiling height, some empty wooden boxes and some old newspapers on the floor, and, for company, a family of hungry rats. Edda shivered; it was August, and outside the sky was blue and the sun warm and bright, but down in her hell-hole the fifteen-year-old girl shivered – and wept.

Always brave and indomitable in spirit – at those times, at least, when called upon to be brave and indomitable – Edda now succumbed to feelings of utter dejection and hopelessness. What would become of her now? What would the Baroness be thinking? Oh, how worried she would be when her beloved daughter failed to return home.

Despair and fatigue gradually subsided into impenetrable sleep. When she awoke, curled up in the foetal position on the forbiddingly cold, dusty floor, a thin shaft of light filtering through the cobwebbed arrow-slit, she seemed to be no longer

33

confused. True, she did not know what day it was or how long she had slept, but involuntary, short-term hibernation had purged her mind of its former melancholy.

She rose to her feet, stretched her aching limbs, and fumbled in the gloom for her satchel. From it she extracted a piece of crisp-hard bread and the flask. How long circumstances would compel her to remain in the rat-hole she could not accurately predict, but, she felt absolutely certain, it would be many days. Her 'food supply' must therefore be strictly rationed.

And so, as day receded into night, and blackness into greyness, Edda's life-cycle became meaningless and without sense of duration. From time to time her body trembled and her heart froze as the rumble of Nazi tanks and trucks shook the cellar's foundations; on one occasion a squad of German soldiers disgorged themselves on to the street immediately in front of the cellar's arrow-slit and she was convinced that, unknown to her, she had been spotted running into the building and that now they had come to flush her out. She watched, slumped in one corner, as booted feet shuffled past the tiny window. And then they were gone.

Some days she experienced terrible internal pains and, even in the poor light available, she noticed that her faeces were no longer brown but chalky grey. She grew progressively weaker; she could not remember when she last ate or drank, because her wretched 'supplies' had disappeared . . . how many days ago? The time had arrived when she must abandon her hide-out. Her pains were now so severe that, she reasoned, to be caught by the Nazis and despatched to a camp could not possibly be as harrowing as the agonies that were tormenting her body at that moment.

One other consideration occupied her attention. Arnhem, and the surrounding villages, were suddenly caught in the crossfire of Montgomery's parachutists and the Wehrmacht. Fears that the building would be shelled finally gave her the resolve to move. That evening Edda crept from her cell and disappeared into the night. Here and there German armoured vehicles stood guard, but otherwise the streets were suspiciously deserted – a blessing and a curse. She would need to be zealously sharp-eyed and seek her homecoming by way of stealth, dark alleyways and dimly lit passages.

At last, daughter and mother were reunited. When Edda was stronger, the Baroness would admit that she had thought the worst, that her daughter was dead or that she had been abducted and was languishing in some distant German slave-labour camp. For the moment, though, Edda required immediate medical attention. The family doctor brooded silently, and then announced: 'Jaundice. She's developed a serious jaundice infection, probably due to a vitamin-K deficiency, by which I mean a lack of green, leafy vegetables –'

'Such as endive,' Edda interrupted, and grimaced.

'How long,' asked the doctor, 'was she in hiding?'

'Nearly a month.'

Edda looked shocked.

'Nearly a *month?*'

'Three weeks and four days, to be exact,' the Baroness explained.

Edda's condition would slowly pick up, though for the rest of her life she would always appear to be in need of a good square meal. Quite simply, her metabolism had suffered a severe setback. It was in a state of deep shock. If Edda had never needed to watch her weight in the past, now, more than ever, in the future, she would certainly never need to concern herself about it – except to try to put weight *on*. It would be a futile battle.

But now another quite different battle raged. Earlier that summer, American and British forces had made their way from the Seine and liberated much of Belgium and France. By the middle of September they were ready for a further push forward and, inevitably, this meant crossing the Rhine. The Allies had conceived a plan which, if successful, might have ended the war by Christmas 1944. This was to drop large bodies of airborne troops behind the enemy's lines at several places in the Netherlands. They were to capture the towns of Eindhoven, Grave, Nijmegen, and Arnhem, the roads between them, and the road bridges over the Maas, the Waal, and the Rhine at the last three. Such an operation would enable the British 2nd Army to advance rapidly to the very frontier of Germany.

Of all this activity Edda was ignorant, although underground reports had warned her family to be ready for 'something' – and that 'something' came on 17 September, when the first British party landed just west of Arnhem; it subsequently reached the north end of the bridge and held it.

'There was a sudden terrible noise.,' Edda would recall of that first landing. 'Everything seemed to become a burning

35

mass. No one knew quite what was going on. Then we saw the German and British wounded being taken past. Everything was chaotic. We all had to stay indoors.

'We took in friends who had come from other parts of the town, and there were thirty-seven sleeping in our house. Evacuees from the north streamed into Arnhem . . . ninety thousand of them. And, after that, conditions were worse than they had ever been. It was almost impossible to feed all the people staying with us, and we had to buy black-market flour from Mr Riemens, which we made into a sort of porridge.'

The second British group landed next day, but, because the weather was cloudy and foggy over the British airfields from which they started, they arrived many hours later than had been planned. It was a delay that would have grave repercussions, for it gave the retreating German troops sufficient time to be diverted and to attack the much more lightly armed airborne troops.

'Because of the shortage of food in the town,' continued Edda, 'the Nazi commander in charge ordered all surplus civilians to leave. I still feel sick when I remember the scenes. It was human misery at its starkest – masses of refugees on the move, some carrying their dead, babies born on the roadside, hundreds collapsing from starvation.'

The heroes in Arnhem held on for ten long days. But on the nights of 26/27 and 27/28 September those who remained unwounded were withdrawn across the Rhine in assault boats and found their way back to their comrades of the 2nd Army. Out of 10,000 men who went into the fight, more than 7,500 were lost – killed, wounded, or missing.

On one occasion, the Baroness hid six British airmen in her wardrobe while the Gestapo searched her home. Later, one of the airmen, slightly injured, remained behind at the Baroness's house while the other five joined their comrades. For thirteen days and nights he was concealed in another cupboard, which was little bigger than a coffin. Eventually, fit enough to leave, he bid adieu – with a parting gift of the Baroness's last bottle of champagne secreted in his jacket.

Nine years later, while reading an English Sunday newspaper, the Baroness discovered for the first time that the airman had reached England safely. He was Lieut.-Colonel Anthony Deane-Drummond. 'I was really keeping the champagne to celebrate Queen Wilhelmina's return,' she said. 'But I'm glad I gave it to him. He was such a brave man.'

What the brave man did not know, and perhaps could never know, was that he escaped the house not a moment too soon. For, not long after, Edda and her family suffered the terrible experience of having their home bombed to the ground. Edda, Alexander and the Baroness escaped with nothing but the clothes they wore. The devastation was so dreadful that nothing survived the impact; even the old cast-iron stove had exploded into a dozen jagged pieces. Everywhere was havoc and ruins; after the battle of Arnhem only 282 houses were habitable.

The Baroness promptly found temporary accommodation at the home of friends. It was a large house, with several floors, and for twenty-four hours, despite the noisy chaos of hostilities all round them, the van Heemstras seemed reasonably comfortable. Unfortunately, a German squad had set up a radio transmitter on the upper floor of the house and, accordingly, the British suspected Edda's family of being collaborators. There was a sudden terrifying confusion as a group of British soldiers burst through the front door and brandished their submachine-guns at the frightened fifteen-year-old girl who stared at them with big eyes out of hollow cheeks. Edda flung out her arms in a desperate, life-saving bid to stop them shooting. 'Please don't! It's not how it seems –' and she stuttered out an explanation just in time to save her life.

The medieval heart of Arnhem, and the great road bridge over the Rhine, were destroyed in the fighting. Gone, too, under so much rubble, was the beautiful old County Council building. When the battle was over, a great proportion of the Dutch people of the town, who had given the British so much, were driven from their homes by the Germans, who stole silver, linen and anything else they could carry away. The occupying forces knew it would only be a short while before the Allies came in strength.

Such heroism as the Allies displayed was not to go unrewarded, and Field-Marshal Montgomery was later to write in a letter to General Urquhart: 'There can be few episodes more glorious than the epic of Arnhem, and those that follow after will find it hard to live up to the high standard that you have set. In years to come it will be a great thing for a man to be able to say, "I fought at Arnhem."'

In years to come, Edda would also be able to tell her children, 'I was there', though she would say it rather differently: 'I wouldn't have missed it for the world – anything that happens to you is invaluable. Just the same, mingled in all the nightmares I've ever had are the war, and the cold clutch of human terror. I've experienced both.'

Liberation finally came with the German surrender on 5 May 1945, a day after Edda's sixteenth birthday. A new future opened up for Edda and for the Dutch people. When the British troops returned to Arnhem to clear it of mines and booby-traps, Edda ran out into the street to welcome them. She danced and smiled and jumped with joy and longed to kiss every single one of the conquering soldiers.

'I stood there watching them,' she would recount. 'The joy of hearing English spoken, the incredible relief of being *free* – it's something you can't fathom.'

She tried to verbalise what freedom meant. Freedom was something you could smell. 'Freedom,' she said, 'smelt like English cigarettes.'

5

*'On the one hand maybe I've remained
infantile, while on the other I matured
quickly, because at a young age I was
very aware of suffering and fear.'*

FOLLOWING LIBERATION, EDDA volunteered for
work as a nurse in a rest home for Dutch soldiers. She derived
enormous satisfaction from the job. She felt she was repaying
in some small measure the prodigious sacrifices the men in her
care had made for all those who had lived under the pernicious
dominion of Nazism. It was an epoch that would haunt her forever.

'The war,' she said once, 'left me with a deep knowledge of
human suffering which I expect many other young people
never know about. The things I saw during the occupation
made me very realistic about life, and I've been that way ever
since. Don't,' she added, 'discount anything awful you hear or
read about the Nazis. It's worse than you could ever imagine. I
came out of the war thankful to be alive, aware that human
relationships are the most important thing of all, far more than
wealth, food, luxury, careers, or anything you can mention.'

While working at the rest home, Edda accepted gifts of food
and chocolates from her grateful patients. It was like make-
believe. She had never seen so many bars of chocolate, and,
because she had been deprived of food for so long, she became
a compulsive eater. On one occasion she ate seven bars of chocolate all at once, quickly, and became violently ill. She still had
tremendous re-adjustments to make.

There were also the disappointments, those lingering ulcers
of peace-after-war. Through the aegis of a close family friend in
London, Edda learned that she had been awarded a scholar-

39

ship to the famous Rambert School of Ballet, the offshoot of an equally renowned company. Marie Rambert, a Polish dancer who had coached the great Nijinsky in the difficult rhythms of Stravinsky's *The Rite of Spring*, founded in 1930 what is today England's oldest dance company – the Ballet Rambert. The choreographer Frederick Ashton, whose *Horoscope* had been performed in Arnhem on the eve of the Nazi invasion, was its prize discovery, and, for several years, Alicia Markova its ballerina. Robert Helpmann was a frequent guest star, as was Edda's idol, Margot Fonteyn. Alas, for financial reasons, and because of some uncertainty regarding her national status, Edda would have to forgo the offer for the moment.

During the occupation the Nazis had destroyed many of the van Heemstra property holdings, and the family estate outside Arnhem had been demolished in the crossfire. Although the Baroness still owned property in Belgium and Holland, it was impossible to sell it. The only possessions which could be used to raise money were a few jewels. Rather than remain in Arnhem and try to rebuild, the Baroness decided it was more important to move to pastures new. Ian had returned from his German concentration camp and so the family, now reunited, moved to Amsterdam.

Edda, meanwhile, began to think about her future. Her determination to become a dancer remained as resolute as ever. The Baroness, too, had always possessed great ambitions for Edda: she would be a dancer, or perhaps even a musician or an actress. For she recalled how, in her own youth, she had dreamt, daydreamed, that one day she might become an actress – despite the Baron's admonishments. It was now her fondest wish that Edda should fulfil those dreams.

Though ruined financially, the Baroness was undaunted and secured a job as a cook-housekeeper in the service of a wealthy Dutch family, in the basement apartment of whose house the van Heemstras found cheap but comfortable lodgings. With the little money that was left over each week, Edda was able to resume her ballet training in Amsterdam. There, over the next three years, she assumed a 'European style', a distinctive look and an approach to work, that stemmed directly from her Russian ballet teacher, a disciplinarian named Olga Tarassova.

'I would train for two or three hours at a time,' the pupil would relate years later, 'and even if I were purple in the face and covered with sweat, she would shout: "Stand up, van Heemstra – don't slouch!" That gave me strength.'

'With Edda,' Madame Tarassova would then privately confess to the Baroness, 'with Edda, ballet is as natural as drinking water.'

Although Edda thrived under the dictatorial, iron-fisted rule of her Russian teacher, she had become a young woman, with all the attendant emotions and thoughts. Something was missing in her life. Romance. She had no time, though, for boyfriends. 'Somehow,' she would later complain, 'my world remained close shut.'

But then almost as quickly the sunshine would appear from behind the clouds. 'To me,' she would enthuse, 'the sublime joy spelled out a chance to go to a concert. Alone, of course. It is strange how certain things remain imprinted in your memory. Thus I can clearly see myself trudging to the Concertgebouw in Amsterdam, proudly clutching a season ticket to a concert series.'

One day at her dancing academy, while engaged on the perfection of some *grands battements* with Madame Tarassova, the class was visited by the Dutch film director Charles Huguenot van der Linden. He was about to start work on a movie called *Nederland in 7 Lessen* ('Dutch in 7 Lessons'), and he was on a last-minute mission to find a pretty young lady to play the small role of an air stewardess. The part demanded, primarily, dignity and sophistication of its player. The director was joined in due course by the film's associate producer, H. M. Josephson, and the two men sat quietly in one corner of the mirrored studio. Once or twice they discussed this or that girl with Madame Tarassova, but mostly they chatted privately among themselves.

At the conclusion of the class, the two men from the film studio seemed to be in mutual agreement. 'So it's that tall, thin girl with the *eyes*,' van der Linden told Josephson. 'Let's have a word with her.'

That afternoon Edda could not return home fast enough to inform the Baroness of her fabulous luck in securing a small role in a new film. She would be required for three days' work, starting the following Tuesday.

'They want me to *act*,' Edda said proudly. 'Can you imagine – I'm a stewardess on an aeroplane! Isn't that just the most marvellous thing?'

The Baroness smiled. 'It is indeed.'

Edda was eighteen and a half when she made her film début.

Van der Linden has always claimed, rightly, that it was *he* who discovered the young lady who was to become the toast of Hollywood – not all those who would later profess that distinction.

The following year, with the lifting of the currency restrictions on European travel, and with Ian and Alexander having left home for a life of adventure in the Dutch East Indies, Edda prevailed upon the Baroness to allow her to go to England and accept her scholarship with the Rambert School of Ballet. She was in complete accord with her daughter's wishes. But first there was 'an awful fuss' with the Dutch and British embassies over the question of Edda's Belgian-Irish-Dutch background. Finally, the required visas came through. Although the Baroness had still not managed to sell her properties in Holland and Belgium, she had nevertheless saved and planned prudently. Sufficient funds had been raised, in fact, to enable them to pay their fares and to leave the country with £35 in cash.

The ballet student would also leave with a new name. Henceforth she would be known as –

Audrey Hepburn.

PART TWO

English rhapsody:
the dancer finds her voice

6

*'I am not beautiful. My mother once called
me an ugly duckling. But, listed separately,
I have a few good features.'*

CROSSING THE NORTH SEA from the Hook of
Holland, which was more than usually choppy, the nineteen-
year-old ballet student began to wonder if it was worth it. The
girl whose stomach had endured the atrocities of Nazism, now
felt like death warmed up as the passenger steamer went into yet
another Big Dipper routine. Why, she thought, with her head in
the lavatory bowl, why did she nurse such mad notions about
studying in England?

All that preoccupied Audrey and the Baroness on disembar-
king, however, was their appointment in London with Marie
Rambert. It was a two-hour train journey away, and time was
limited because they possessed only enough money for food
and lodgings in a cheap hotel, near King's Cross, for three days.
They took an Underground train from Liverpool Street Station
to Notting Hill Gate, where, at an old church hall built in 1850
and now renamed the Mercury Theatre, Madame Rambert's
famous ballet studio was situated.

Madame Rambert, then aged sixty – she would remain active
for another thirty-odd years – received Audrey and the Baroness
cordially in a tiny, dark office, the walls of which were covered in
framed lithographs of the immortals of the Romantic ballet
movement: Carlotta Grisi, Lucile Grahn, Fanny Elssler and
Marie Taglioni. As the Baroness and the ballet director engaged
in an all-embracing conversation that took in the Sadler's Wells
Ballet's precarious visit to Arnhem, the student stared uninhi-
bitedly at the great legend about whom she had read so much.

45

Witty, wiry and emotional, small and agile, with chin high, eyes visionary, Audrey noticed that everything about her was alive and alert. She would also discover, later, that the future Dame of the British Empire – Mim to her friends, Madame to her company and students – was a teacher renowned for whacking her pupils' knuckles with a stick when they were caught with folded arms or slouched shoulders. To think, she mused, that she had once thought Madame Tarassova a determined taskmaster!

The scholarship took care of tuition costs only; food, clothes and lodgings had to be paid for by Audrey and the Baroness – and in two days their money would run out. At that time, in post-war Britain, food-rationing was still in operation, and 1s 4d (7p) worth of meat was the ration per person a week; since Audrey and the Baroness were unable to get at their money in Holland and Belgium, they almost starved. Never had they felt so destitute, even in wartime Arnhem. But Providence, as always in the Audrey Hepburn story, shone over her in all her wanderings. Marie Rambert, recognising her talent, took the poor ballet student into her terraced home in Camden Hill Gardens (where she and her husband, Ashley Dukes, had lived since 1919) and housed, fed and schooled her for six months. It was a lifesaver.

'I was always short of money,' Audrey would recall, 'although I did all sorts of little odd jobs outside of school hours. My first class was at 10 a.m. and my last was at 6 p.m., so it was work, work all day and into the night.'

In 1983, some thirty-five years later, and now a film star whose name was a legend, Audrey would fly to London to attend a gala held at Sadler's Wells as a tribute to the enduring, adventurous spirit of Marie Rambert. (She died in 1982.) And, in a moving, self-reflective speech from the stage, Audrey would state publicly her gratitude to the lady who, fondly, always referred to her as 'my pupil'.

'I owe her a great deal,' Audrey would tell the gala audience, which included the Princess of Wales. 'She was a great inspiration and a wonderful friend to me.' She would describe herself as a 'failed ballerina', and explain that, because she was too tall, she could never find a partner who was big enough for her. At the end, above all, she would say an eloquent 'Thank you, dear Mim.'

The Baroness, for the time being, found temporary employment in a florist's shop, then worked briefly as an interior decorator until she was appointed manager of a block of Mayfair flats, just off Park Lane. It was here, at No 65 South Audley Street, having now vacated the dingy King's Cross hotel, that she managed to scrape together just enough money to rent a single room; after a while she could afford another room, and, as manager, with a cheap-rent concession, she finally enjoyed sufficient means for a whole apartment. Audrey later moved in, and the Baroness's nameplate was duly affixed to the door, a little below her daughter's. Over the letter-box was a knocker in the form of a big gold key, which belonged to the family's castle at Doorn.

On the other side of the road, almost directly opposite the front entrance to the red-brick Victorian flats, Bill Allen has been selling roses, daffodils and carnations since 1933, first with his mother, then in his own right. His stall, painted dark green, stands at the corner of a house, almost boxed-in by black wrought-iron railings. He is now in his early sixties, grey-haired, rosy-cheeked and untroubled – a 'real Londoner' and proud of it – but he still talks about the Baroness and 'her girl' as if it was yesterday.

'The Baroness was a good customer,' said Bill, his eyes clouding slightly. 'Sometimes she'd give me a little present, like a box of chocolates. She lived up there, mate – two floors up. . . .' He gestured to two large adjoining windows. ''Course, the place has changed a bit since then. I mean, there wasn't a Chinese restaurant on the ground floor in them days. Very polite, the Baroness, very gracious; always had time for a chat. You could tell she had class . . . a real *lady*. Her girl wasn't anything exceptional to look at, mind you. Very plain, really, as I recall; but she laughed a lot, always giggling, like teenagers do. Reckon they must have had a bit of money to live in one of those flats; this is one of the most expensive streets in London to bed-down in. Only the toffs could afford to live here, governor.'

Well, even Bill didn't know *everything* about the Baroness and Audrey. But the 'anglicisation' of Audrey Hepburn, six months after her inauspicious arrival in London, had begun.

Like the Baroness, Audrey had been making herself busy. The moment her classes with Rambert were over each day, she would make the rounds of West End auditions for musical stage shows, but with no luck. She would also visit theatrical agents. It had become a matter of some considerable concern to Audrey that she should supplement the Baroness's meagre household budget. During holidays, therefore, she found such diverse jobs as dental assistant and filing clerk, and in the evenings she gave the occasional French lessons. But mostly she worked part-time as a £7-a-week model for fashion and beauty photographers, in which pursuit she made her first big public impact in London.

Even then her offbeat beauty, combined with a pixie-like naïveté and natural dignity, beguiled everybody who met her. In fact, with her innate breeding, and long-legged good looks, the photographers had found a subject on whom they could really go to town. Her ability to wear high-fashion costumes, furthermore, would one day contribute not a little to her success in films. Her modelling experience, certainly, was the genesis of a lifelong desire – some might call it compulsion – to be meticulously dressed. From that time on she would become an avid reader of fashion magazines.

It was during her involvement in high fashion that she came to realise two important factors about herself. First of all, that her colouring lacked definition. She therefore started to wear black, white or muted colours such as beige or soft pinks or greens. 'These colours,' she concluded, 'tend to make my eyes and hair seem darker whereas bright colours overpower me and wash me out.' Secondly, because of her height and angular build, she could not wear padded or squared shoulders, and so she often cheated on her armholes and collars to give an illusion of narrow rather than wide shoulders. And she wore low-heeled shoes to give the impression that she was smaller than her 5ft 7in. All her career she would be obsessed by her tallness and would rarely be seen wearing high-heeled shoes.

One day a touring ballet company's representative visited the Mercury Theatre to recruit young dancers for an extended tour. Audrey was among the girls offered a permanent spot. Only a week earlier she had affirmed to the Baroness: 'To be a ballerina really is the only dream of my life.' Here was The Great Opportunity. Yet she was undecided about what to do.

Just the previous day, Audrey had been one of ten girls chosen from 3,000 applicants for one of the coveted spots in the front-line chorus of the London production of the Broadway hit musical, *High Button Shoes*. She was certain she had been disastrous at the audition, yet she came out a winner. She told a writer friend a few years later: 'The trouble was I knew nothing about modern dance steps, and my ear wasn't attuned to the rhythms. I don't know how I had the nerve to try for it in the first place.'

At the audition itself the show's producer, Jack Hylton, stopped the thin, dark girl in the middle of her dance number. She was standing in the centre of the bare stage at the London Hippodrome. 'All right, miss,' he said matter-of-factly. 'Leave your name.'

The girl had stepped from a crowd of one hundred hopefuls. She gave her name, rushed off into the wings, and burst into tears.

'Audrey Hepburn, age nineteen,' wrote the stage manager. He made a mental note that the Hepburn girl was worth £8 10s a week and not a penny more.

'I feel suddenly rich and secure,' she told the Baroness that night. 'Even though I've trained as a classical ballet dancer, with the full classical, pulled-back hair and my feet turned out even when I go for a stroll down the street, I've actually landed a part in the chorus of a *musical comedy*,' she observed with a note of outrageous incredulity in her voice. 'Who would have imagined?'

But the very next day, with the offer of a full-time job in a ballet company, she found herself even more perplexed. Did she want to follow in the footsteps of Margot Fonteyn or Ruby Keeler? That evening, after some deliberation, she chose the musical. Explaining that decision, Audrey said: 'I'm finding that my height is a handicap in ballet and that I might have to slave for years to achieve only limited success. I can't wait years; I need money badly.'

Sharing the chorus line with Audrey was a vivacious girl named Kay Kendall, later to get her big break in the hit comedy film *Genevieve*. She would also marry Rex Harrison. At one time the two girls were dancing as many as twenty-eight performances a week in *High Button Shoes*, while Audrey went on with her studies at Marie Rambert's school; sometimes she'd be joined by Kay, and, once a week, at a London gymnasium, they would indulge in strenuous physical training lessons. Gradually, to her complete surprise, she suddenly discovered that she was actually *enjoying* musical comedy. Lew Parker, one of the American stars of the show, mused to a colleague one evening: 'She isn't an outstanding dancer, is she? But she has a personality that attracts you immediately. You know what I mean – *there is "something" about her.*'

Make a note of that phrase, for it will crop up again and again in the Hepburn story. It remains nebulous. The 'something' cannot be defined because it is applied to an indefinable quality – the magic which makes a star of a chorus girl. But whatever the 'something' was that she possessed, no one was interested just then. Audrey was happy beyond belief, though, because she was earning her first-ever regular salary. She was contributing at last to the family budget – and she was paying back small sums of money to Marie Rambert for her kindness during Audrey's first six months in London.

Many years later, talking to a friend who had noted how youthful-looking she always seemed to be, Audrey commented: 'Other than being thin, I look younger because I've always looked after my skin. I use moisturisers, I sleep at least eight hours – and early, too – and I walk an awful lot.'

For decades to come, Audrey would be the classic Peter Pan. People would invariably get her age wrong – to her advantage. She would be years younger than she seemed. It would be a recurring theme in her life. Even Marie Rambert got it wrong. Talking to a reporter less than six years after Audrey's arrival at the Mercury Theatre, Rambert explained: 'I think she may have been sixteen.' But what was three years among friends? 'She had lovely long limbs,' she then added more accurately, 'and her eyes were beautiful. Although I did not groom her as a ballerina, I always knew she would get on. She was such a good worker, a wonderful learner. If she had wanted to persevere in ballet, she might have become an outstanding ballerina.'

Lack of perseverance was not ordinarily one of Audrey's weaknesses, but then she had an awful feeling that time was running out. She was a girl in a hurry. The search for a career had begun in earnest.

'She was always saying that she had big feet,' Rambert recalled. 'I never noticed it. I always thought them charming. It was because of her height that I couldn't consider her for my company. Audrey, however, had to do something. She made no bones about the fact that, her family having lost everything in the war, she had to work. So she went out and got that work – in some revues.'

It didn't happen quite like that. Unknown to Audrey, one of

50

London's leading impresarios, Cecil Landeau, went to the London Hippodrome to see *High Button Shoes*. It was early in the new year, and, when the producer caught sight of the high-kicking, long-legged girl with the ear-to-ear smile, he liked what he saw. 'The first impression,' he told Logan Gourlay, 'was made by a pair of big dark eyes and a fringe flitting across the stage.' Landeau made some enquiries after the show and was informed that the young woman who had bewitched his eye was named Audrey Hepburn. 'Never heard of her,' he mumbled under his breath, and disappeared into the night, having made a note of the name. A month later, he offered Audrey a part in a lavish new revue he was just about to put into rehearsal. It was called *Sauce Tartare*.

In common with Sir C. B. Cochran, Britain's leading theatrical impresario of the 1920s and 1930s, famous for revues featuring 'Mr Cochran's young ladies', Landeau had a flair for choosing girl dancers with personalities which reached across the footlights in dazzling shows like *Cockles and Champagne*. His ventures as a theatrical impresario frequently landed him in the London bankruptcy courts; he aimed high and paid the price. Revues of such lavishness and epic proportions had not been mounted in the West End since Cochran's day. As a human being he may have left much to be desired – many singers, dancers, comedians and actors who worked with him have described him as a 'nasty man' – but his ability as a talent-spotter could not be faulted.

Landeau devoted the best part of a year to the preparation of *Sauce Tartare*. He travelled some fourteen thousand miles in his search for the best possible cast and, indeed, once rehearsals got under way, Audrey found herself involved in a truly international show. It included South African Zoë Gail and South Americam singer Jan Mazurus, with featured dancers from Russia, Norway and Spain. Two other leading artists were from Holland and Belgium, comedienne Renée Houston hailed from Scotland, and the music was by a calypso band from Trinidad led by a Portuguese pin-up girl named Miguelita. Star of the show was the black American singer Muriel Smith. She sprang to fame on Broadway six years earlier in *Carmen Jones* and was described by the American press as 'a swivel-hipped, passionate wench with a gorgeous voice'.

Rehearsals proceeded apace – until the first dress rehearsal. Landeau threw up his arms in despair. The show, he felt, lacked cohesion and panache. From a stalls seat some twelve rows from the front, Landeau brought the show to a halt by clapping his hands loudly and uttering some ill-considered profanities. 'It's just not good enough,' the forty-four-year-old showman told the assembled cast. 'You're simply not yet ready for the public. We're going to have to postpone the opening night.'

But the company insisted on going through with the production even if it meant working at it all night. And 'work at it' was exactly what Audrey and her colleagues did . . . from midnight until an hour before the official curtain-up. Produced and directed by Landeau, compèred by Patricia Dare, with lyrics and music by Geoffrey Parsons and Berkeley Fase, and comedy sketches by Ronald Frankau and Claude Hulbert, the £25,000 revue – true to show-business tradition – *did* go on. It opened on 18 May 1949, at the Cambridge Theatre, to rave notices. 'Gay, topical and tuneful,' enthused the *Daily Telegraph*. The London *Evening Standard* went one better, noting that Honoria Plesch's colourful costumes and décor could 'bear comparison with the old Cochran Pavilion revues', and adding that Landeau's first revue production since the war was 'inventive, tasteful and witty for far more of the time than we have come to expect in such shows'.

A much-relieved Cecil Landeau slept peacefully that night. 'If it had failed,' he announced next morning after reading the reviews, 'I would have gone back to films.' Instead, he stayed on to help shape Audrey's future career.

7

*'I've been lucky. Opportunities don't often
come along. So, when they do, you have to
grab them.'*

THROUGHOUT THE RUN of *Sauce Tartare*, Audrey
continued her ballet classes with Marie Rambert and, periodically, undertook photographic modelling assignments to supplement her income. In addition, every Saturday morning, she
attended movement classes arranged for the acting profession
by Betty and Philip Buchell at their studios in the West End of
London. The Buchells, as teachers and choreographers, had
won great renown for their work on various films with Anna
Neagle.

Robert Flemyng, who would appear with Audrey some
years later, recalled: 'One Saturday I went in for my movement
class as usual and there, exercising at the barre, was one of the
most enchanting little creatures I had ever seen. A whispered
enquiry elicited from Betty that her name was Audrey Hepburn
and that she was in the chorus of *Sauce Tartare*. She was very
shy, but over the weeks we all got to know her, and love her.
We all realised that beneath that shy little elfin exterior lay a
strong will and determination, and we felt that she would *do*
something.'

Audrey herself would later reflect, 'When I think of myself at
twenty, I was very much at sea. I wasn't at all sure what life
was all about.'

None the less, it was a happy, carefree period for the young
dancer. She was free of responsibilities for the first and only
time in her life. She led, in fact, a regulated, uncomplicated
existence, unenslaved by romantic attachments or the kind of

high-pressure career-making that, within two years, would dominate her days.

Meanwhile, Audrey and Alma Cogan, a singer who was also in the cast of *Sauce Tartare*, deepened their offstage friendship. They would drink coffee together in a little café behind the theatre and reflect on their future. 'One day,' Alma would say dreamily, 'I'll be a famous singer.' And, no less dreamily, Audrey would reply: 'One day I'll be a famous actress.'

The prospective famous actress told David Lewin: 'I have always reached for something just above my head. If I have been able to hold on, it is because I seized every opportunity and worked extra hard. Nothing came easily. In musicals I was the tense, rigid girl trained for ballet who had to watch everyone else to find out what to do.'

Even so, her efforts did not go unnoticed. The young society photographer Antony Beauchamp, who had achieved some measure of fame for his startling cover-picture of wife-to-be Sarah Churchill for *Life* magazine, and whose photographic studies of such movie immortals as Greta Garbo and Vivien Leigh were universally admired, went to see *Sauce Tartare* one evening and was immediately mesmerised by Audrey.

'I kept looking again and again at the startling eyes which were never still,' he later recalled. At that time he was engaged on preparing a series of pictures for a leading London fashion house, and he was looking for a new personality. 'There, on the stage, at the right-hand side of the chorus,' continued Beauchamp, 'I believed I had found her.' So, after the show, he went backstage and asked to see 'the chorus girl with the eyes', and was introduced to Audrey.

'How would you feel,' he asked, 'if I said I'd very much like to photograph you?'

'Flattered,' she said, 'but I couldn't possibly afford your fees.'

'I'll photograph you for nothing,' he assured her. 'You can pay me later.'

At once Audrey's face became well-known in all the up-market glossy magazines. But Beauchamp was convinced she had a much brighter future as an actress. One day, therefore, he sent her to a friend who was a theatrical agent. That evening, in her dressing-room at the Cambridge Theatre, she wrote a letter to the society photographer: 'It may seem strange for a girl to send a man a box of chocolates, but these are the

54

hand-made ones you said you liked. I am sure that not many people thank you for what you have done for them. . . . I am going to the agent today. . . .'

The agent, incredibly, turned Audrey down. He was not the first to do so, and he would not be the last.

Towards the end of the year, box office receipts for *Sauce Tartare* – in common with other West End shows – had dwindled to a financial danger-point. To attract more customers, Landeau initiated an experimental period of cut-price tickets for the stalls and dress-circle 'at the pre-war figures of half-a-guinea, seven shillings, and six shillings'.

But none the less, *Sauce Tartare* folded soon after, in the new year, and Audrey, who had been on a £10-a-week salary, found herself out of a job. But not for long. Within a week of the demise of the old revue, Landeau was already at an advanced stage in the planning of its successor. *Sauce Piquante* went into immediate rehearsal and opened on 27 April 1950, again at the Cambridge Theatre.

Audrey, who was still little more than a featured dancer, was this time involved in several sketches – all of them with the show's funny men and women. Among them was ex-cabin boy Norman Wisdom, impersonator Douglas Byng, quick-fire David Hurst, burlesque-happy Joan Heal (who had appeared in Audrey's previous two shows), and radio's Bob Monkhouse. Muriel Smith was again the dusky, exotic principal singer; actress Moira Lister, in her first revue, struck a nice balance between glamour and fun as Vivien Leigh in a parody of *A Streetcar Named Desire;* while crooner Marcel le Bon provided sufficient Latin glamour to send all female hearts a-flutter.

In one sketch, 'Non Compos Mentis', featuring Norman Wisdom as a lunatic in a railway carriage, Douglas Byng as a military general and Bob Monkhouse as a porter, Audrey would first walk on in a saucy 'French waitress' costume to announce the hilarity to come. Her contribution was invariably more appreciated than the sketch that followed.

One of the dancers, a statuesque Scandinavian named Aud Johanssen, whose magnificent bust would have induced a combined inferiority complex among Jayne Mansfield, Bette Midler and Dolly Parton, would come off stage cursing: 'I can't stand it! I know I've got the best tits on stage, and yet they're all staring at a girl who hasn't got any.'

Even Diana Monks, the show's principal dancer, would

make her stage exit crying – and continue to weep in the wings. 'They're looking at bloody Audrey,' she would sob to the rest of the girls. 'We don't stand a chance. We might just as well stay in our dressing-rooms.'

As Bob Monkhouse recalled: 'The standard of dancing in *Sauce Piquante* was of a superior quality, but Audrey's was the poorest dancing in the show. If she'd been a good dancer, the other girls would not have minded so much, but everyone knew that she was the least talented among them. They all loved her offstage, but hated her on, because they knew that even if she just jumped up and down, the audience would still be attracted to her. What Audrey had in *Sauce Piquante*, and what has sustained her through a fantastically successful and well-managed career, was an enormous, exaggerated feeling of "I need you". Anthony Newley had this at one stage; the message was urgent: "I'm helpless – I need you." When people sense this, they respond to it immediately, perhaps not realising why they're doing so. And Audrey had it in abundance, that same air of defencelessness, helplessness. I think everybody in the audience thought, "I want to look after little Audrey." She seemed to be too pretty, too unaware of the dangers.'

Landeau, always quick to appreciate what should be exploited, realised at once that Audrey had something quite exceptional to offer. After initiating her services in a couple of chorus numbers, he promoted her into several set pieces – and raised her salary to £15 a week. In one number, in which she was exquisitely dressed as a Dresden shepherdess, she would nightly draw loud, prolonged applause the moment the curtain went up.

And she did so without even raising her little finger. 'It was quite extraordinary,' observed Monkhouse. 'She simply signalled that infectious, impish grin, which seemed to go from one earhole to the other. She looked incredibly radiant because, at that time, it was uncontrolled. The lips actually turned inside-out and the eyes went sort of potty, like a Walt Disney character. It was so lovely, one stepped back a pace. She later learned to tone it down a bit.'

Audrey became the embodiment of the show's title. Theatre critic Milton Shulman, never the easiest of men to please, reflected a few years later: 'She had no lines to say, no part to play. But with her infectious grin and her bouncing enthusiasm

Audrey Hepburn's direct maternal ancestry:

Feije van Heemstra
(1572-1618)

Feije van Heemstra
(1605-36)

Schelte van Heemstra (1665-1733) and his wife
Catharina *née* van Scheltinga (1666-1724)

Willem Hendrik van Heemstra
(1696-1775)

Wiskje van Scheltinga
(1746-95)
(wife of Schelto van Heemstra)

Baron Willem Hendrik van Heemstra (1779-1826) and his wife
Johanna Balthazarina *née* van Idsinga (1783-1850)

Audrey's great-great-grandparents, Baron Frans Julius Johan van
Heemstra (1811-78) and Henrietta Philippina Jacoba *née*
Baroness van Pallandt (1810-81)

Audrey's great-grandparents, Baron Willem Hendrik Johan van
Heemstra (1841-1909) and Wilhelmina Cornelia *née* de Beaufort
(1843-1927)

Audrey's grandfather, Baron Aarnoud Jan Anne Aleid van Heemstra (1871-1957)
(This photograph, and the twelve previous pictures, reproduced by courtesy of Iconographisch Bureau, The Hague)

Audrey with her mother, Baroness Ella van Heemstra (born 1900), daughter of the Baron above
(Associated Press)

Arnhem, about 1930
(Gemeentearchief Arnhem)

Arnhem, 1945, after the German occupation
(Gemeentearchief Arnhem)

The Rhine bridge, Arnhem (about 1938), as Audrey knew it
(Gemeentearchief Arnhem)

Baron Aarnoud van Heemstra's Doorn Castle (Het Kasteel
de Doorn), Utrecht, where Audrey's mother was raised and where
Germany's exiled Kaiser Wilhelm II spent his last years
(Huis-Doorn)

Official residence in Arnhem of the Queen's Commissioner,
a post held between 1926 and 1944 by Audrey's uncle,
Dr Schelte Baron van Heemstra *(Gemeentearchief Arnhem)*

Audrey's aunt, the Baroness Marianne van Heemstra (far right),
lady-in-waiting to Princess Juliana of the Netherlands (second from
left), in the company of Queen Wilhelmina (left) and her
lady-in-waiting, the Baroness van Heekeren
(Associated Press)

Audrey, aged fourteen, in her first stage appearance, singing and dancing in an operetta produced in Arnhem *(Rex Features)*

Audrey, aged seventeen, participating in an end-of-term concert arranged by her ballet school in Amsterdam *(Rex Features)*

The Mercury Theatre in north London, former home of the Ballet Rambert company and its associate school, where, from 1948, Audrey studied classical ballet under the eye of the company's founder, Marie Rambert
(Zenka Woodward Picture Library)

With dancer Babs Johnston at the audition for Jack Hylton's West End production of the Broadway hit musical, *High Button Shoes*, London Hippodrome, 1948
(Popperfoto)

Number 65, South Audley Street, the London home from 1948 (and for many years thereafter) of Audrey and the Baroness. Their flat is situated on the second floor, immediately above the restaurant
(Zenka Woodward Picture Library)

High jinks on the roof of London's Cambridge Theatre, where Audrey and fellow dancers Aud Johanssen and Enid Smeeden were appearing in Cecil Landeau's revue, *Sauce Tartare* (1949)
(Keystone)

she actually looked as if she was enjoying herself. Perhaps it was this marked contrast with what the rest of us were feeling that made her as conspicuous as a fresh carnation on a shabby suit.'

The actress Diana Coupland, at that time a band singer with Geraldo, can still vividly remember being mesmerised by Audrey in *Sauce Piquante*. She talks of 'this incredible charisma'. 'It had nothing to do with Audrey's dancing,' insists Miss Coupland. 'She really wasn't as good as the other girls. In fact, she wasn't anything special as a dancer, period. But she *glowed*. And it was strange, because she wasn't pretty in the sense that we regard "pretty" today. It was a very unusual look, just as Leslie Caron or Bette Davis were considered unusual. Yet she beamed: the smile was wide and full of life, and she had the most beautiful eyes. The whole audience was drawn towards "that girl with the eyes".'

Van Johnson, in London for a Royal Command performance, went to Claridges one day for a cocktail meeting with his agents, Robin Fox and Laurie Evans. Audrey was with them. 'I can still see her now, this cute little girl sitting in the corner,' says the red-haired freckle-faced star of *State of the Union* and *The Music Man*. 'She had these big, beautiful eyes, and bones – I just remember bones. She was wearing white gloves and a sort of sailor's hat with streamers hanging down, and I was just smitten by her innate manners and breeding and her quiet, inner confidence. The only other person I ever met with similar qualities was Grace Kelly.'

The publicist assigned to promote *Sauce Piquante*, John Newnham, was told by Landeau: 'Keep an eye on that girl. She's worth watching.'

Newnham went out with her on a photographic session to the South coast. At Rottingdean, the photographer stared wistfully at a concrete 'rock' several feet from the water's edge.

'If we could only get you on to that, it would make a lovely setting,' suggested the man with the camera.

'I think I could make it with a long enough run,' said Audrey. 'If I do fall in – well, I've got a change of clothes with me!'

The jump, fortunately, was safely negotiated, but it probably wouldn't have worried her unduly if she had missed and got a soaking. It would just have been something to laugh about.

Later, the photographer noticed a high wall with a picturesque house behind it. 'I think,' he suggested tentatively, 'I could get another lovely shot if you could pose on that wall.' But then he quickly changed his mind: 'It's a bit *too* risky. . . .'

'Stand below it and catch me if I fall, and I'll try it,' the young dancer volunteered.

With helping hands from publicist and photographer, Audrey scrambled up on to the wall. Everyone was happy: more sensational pictures. 'Let me tell you,' Newnham quipped to Audrey on the way back to London, 'even my sergeant-major would have hesitated before instructing us to do that when battle-training!'

One of Britain's most influential press agents at that time was Frederic Mullally, whose public-relations firm handled some of the biggest show-business names around. He spotted Audrey in *Sauce Piquante*. 'Immediately,' he said, 'I recognised her star potential. By comparison, every other girl in the chorus-line seemed dull, lifeless and rather artificial.'

With a well-planned publicity boost, mused the publicist, Audrey could shoot to the top. So he arranged for one of his staff photographers to take some glamour pictures of her at his Mayfair offices. He would then circulate the prints to all the picture editors in Fleet Street. He explained to Audrey that these would be 'pin-up' pictures and that she should therefore come along with a suitable choice of low-cut sweaters and briefs. His partner, Suzanne Warner, a young American publicist, would take charge of the session.

Soon after Audrey arrived Suzanne called her boss into the studio. She was worried. And one look at Audrey told Mullally why. 'She was wearing a brief enough pair of shorts,' explained Mullally, 'but above that was a high-necked sweater. And the trouble was that the sweater was certainly doing nothing for Audrey – and Audrey was doing as near as nothing to the sweater!' It was not the first time a press agent had come against this problem of anatomical insufficiency. Mullally turned to his American assistant.

'There's an easy way out,' he suggested enigmatically.

'I'm all ears.'

'Well, it's summed up in the edict: *"What God's forgotten, we stuff with cotton."* It never fails.'

Suzanne set to work. Diplomacy was called for . . . yet be too subtle and Audrey might miss the point. She drew the chorus girl aside and gently explained the problem – and the solution. Audrey could not believe what she was hearing. She blushed, set her mouth and shook her head.

Suzanne pleaded with her. The photographer pleaded with her. Mullally pleaded with her. Finally, wilting under so much verbal pressure, Audrey agreed to 'just a slight' extension of her normal endowment. Suzanne led her away, still infusing brilliant scarlet, for the necessary adjustments.

The resulting picture, published in a big-selling Sunday newspaper, was the first and only photograph ever taken of Audrey wearing (to use a phrase of the time) 'gay deceivers'. A copy of the picture went into Mullally's office files, with the caption: 'Audrey Hepburn – and friends.'

Many years later, when asked what she would alter if she could miraculously change something about herself, she promptly answered, 'Oh, I'd like to be not so flat-chested, I'd like not to have such angular shoulders, such big feet, such a big nose.' But with the same humorous tone she added, 'Actually, I'm very grateful for what God's given me. I've done pretty well.'

What God had given her was a face which lotion manufacturers in Britain discovered long before the hawk-eyed film scouts – a nameless face which was helping to sell Lacto-Calamine, a popular beauty preparation. For years she gazed from magazine and newspaper advertisements with those wide, limpid eyes, a soft fringe curling across her forehead, and an elusive suggestion of mischief.

One critic, reaching for a phrase, referred to her 'splendid emaciation'. To a writer she confessed: 'I never thought of myself as a beauty. I'm the sort of person who has done the best with what I've had. I was too thin and I had no bosom to speak of. Add them up, and a girl can feel terribly self-conscious.'

It was towards the end of the run that her lifelong love affair with animals manifested itself. One miserable night Muriel Smith arrived at the stage door clutching a bedraggled, mud-splattered kitten which she had just saved from the wheels of a lorry outside the theatre. It was in a dreadful state. Bob Monkhouse subsequently decided to look after the animal, because otherwise it would certainly have died. But it was too young to feed itself – it just looked dimly at the saucer of milk – and Monkhouse had little idea what else to do to encourage it to feed. And then Audrey appeared from the chorus girls' com-

munal dressing-room, came to the rescue, and started to organise things. She asked Peter Glover, one of the dancers, to
empty a threepenny sachet of cigarette-lighter fuel. Audrey
then snipped off the end with a pair of nail scissors, washed it
under the tap, filled it with milk, made a pin-hole in the other
end – and the kitten lapped it up.

'After about a week,' reported Bob Monkhouse, 'I took the
kitten home and he stayed with me and my then wife for about
six years before, unfortunately, he was run over by a car. We
called the cat Tomorrow, at Audrey's suggestion. It was rather
a rude joke, stemming from the fact that we had a male cat that
had been castrated, and you know what they say about tomorrow never coming. Audrey was rather good with jokes.'

He quoted his first conversation with her during rehearsals
for the show. She told him: 'I'm half-Irish, half-Dutch, and I
was born in Belgium. If I was a dog, I'd be in a hell of a mess!'

After *Sauce Piquante*, Landeau was fully convinced that
Audrey would reach stardom not as a dancer but as an actress.
At first she laughed at him, because she was acutely aware that
not only was her theatrical experience limited in the West End
to just one musical and two revues, but that in all her years on
earth she had seen only half a dozen plays. Then her large dark
eyes widened as he explained how he proposed to prepare her
for the future. First she would have to do something about her
voice, which was then too high and squeaky. He sent her for
coaching in dramatic art to Charles Laughton's old teacher,
Felix Aylmer, one of Britain's finest character actors who, in
films, played mainly schoolmasters, bankers and bishops and
who, additionally, had just been elected president of Equity,
the actors' trade union. He would be knighted in 1965.

'He taught me to concentrate intelligently on what I was
doing,' she said later, 'and made me aware that all actors need
a "method" of sorts to be even vaguely professional.'

While Aylmer worked on her vocal squeak in the afternoons,
Landeau taught her how to project the new voice by sitting in
the empty auditorium after the show while she declaimed
Shakespeare from the stage. The resulting voice would become,
when movies beckoned, one of her most distinguishing charac-
teristics.

Her life now consisted of kissing the Baroness goodbye each
morning and embarking on a pyrexic day of dancing classes,
drama tuition, modelling assignments, auditions, visiting

agents, rehearsals, appearing in the show, and returning wearily at night to the Baroness at their South Audley Street apartment. It permitted, perhaps by design, no time in her schedule for serious boyfriends. There is no recorded romance in Audrey's life until her twenty-first birthday. That evening she arrived at the theatre's stage door to find a nosegay of red roses and an affectionately composed card awaiting her. It was signed 'Fondly – Marcel.'

Marcel le Bon, the handsome young Frenchman who was one of the star singers of *Sauce Piquante*, courted the long-legged dancer with the same unfaltering devotion that his goddess courted her career. They saw a great deal of each other and their colleagues awaited 'an important announcement'.

Landeau, conscious that the burgeoning romance might jeopardise an already-ailing show, decided to take it upon himself to make the announcement himself. He told the two love-birds that he had just entered a 'no-marriage' clause in Audrey's contract, as well as in the contracts of the show's three other junior principals, Patricia Dare, Enid Smeeden and Diana Monks. He explained that he had also taken out an insurance against any of them marrying; none of the girls were even engaged.

Audrey accepted Landeau's unique gesture, regarding it as something of a joke. The 'no-marriage' clause, however, went much deeper than mere pique. As always with Landeau when one of his shows was sinking, he began to grasp at straws and take outlandish measures if the financial and mental turmoil became too much for him.

The revue finally closed in June after only six and a half weeks – 'killed by the heat-wave', said an aide – causing Landeau to lose about £20,000 and most of the cast their jobs. The following year the impresario would once again find himself in the bankruptcy court. But Landeau was the archetypal phoenix; until he could gather momentum (and more money) for a new revue, he arranged with one of London's top night-clubs to present a potted version of the old revue as a glittering floor-show, entitled *Summer Nights*.

The cabaret opened early in July at Ciro's, the famed night-spot where, one historic evening, Gladys Cooper got a glass of champagne poured over her head by Tallulah Bankhead. Audrey was kept on as part of a four-girl line-up, but Marcel was given the boot.

If the demise of *Sauce Piquante* appeared to be Marcel's swan-song, the ensuing floor-show proved to be very much a watershed in the career of his loved one. More people 'discovered', or claimed to 'discover', Audrey during her season at Ciro's than at any other period. From this point in the story, a multitude of well-meaning 'talent-scouts' will occasionally appear to tell of the time they first caught a glimpse of the high-kicking girl in the line-up: *their* discovery. Stanley Holloway, in fact, in his autobiography, comments perceptively on the large number of people 'who have genuinely kidded themselves into believing that they were the first to recognise Audrey's potential radiant talent.'

On one occasion the Australian leading man John McCallum and his actress wife, Googie Withers, visited Ciro's with former American teenage film star Bonita Granville and her Texan oil millionaire husband. 'We had a table near the cabaret,' McCallum recalled, 'and I found that I couldn't take my eyes off one of the dancing girls. Nothing unusual in that, but this girl – Audrey Hepburn – was different. She had large, doe-like eyes, and an elfin look. But what set her apart from the others was a certain indescribable kind of élan, which generated magnetism. Googie noticed my preoccupation, and agreed immediately, as did the others, that the girl "had something". The next day I phoned my agent, John Findlay, of Linnit and Dunfee, and told him about her . . . and the agency signed her up.'

At this time, Audrey's usually well-ordered routine was turned on its head. After finishing at Ciro's around two in the morning, she and one or two other girls would walk home through Piccadilly ('It was so lovely: so safe. Now all that seems a different world,' she observed in later years), and would get to bed at around 3 a.m. She would usually sleep until midday, have a quick bite to eat, and then arrange to meet Marcel and a few other members of the old cast of *Sauce Piquante*, who were still out of work. Audrey had agreed to help them work up a proposed new cabaret act, with which they hoped to tour the country. It was a busy, crazy time.

8

*'It really was the only dream of my life, to be
a ballerina. The acting was a surprise to me.
It still is.'*

Located in Golden Square, Soho, just a short
distance from Ciro's, was the headquarters of Associated
British Pictures (now controlled by EMI). And it was here, in a
small third-floor office, that there worked a man generally con-
sidered to be the shrewdest casting director anywhere. Robert
Lennard's international influence was prodigious. Directors
John Huston and Fred Zinnemann would not make a film in
Europe without Lennard casting for them.

This great starmaker, who had entered the film industry in
1930 as an assistant director to Alfred Hitchcock, and who, in
the course of time, put Laurence Harvey, Kenneth More,
Richard Todd, Terence Stamp, Richard Harris, Olivia Hussey
and many others in front of the film cameras, was a small,
sprightly man with patient, light-blue eyes. 'What I look for
first is talent, never conventional good looks,' he once
explained. 'I can't define it even after all these years in the business, but I can sometimes recognise it after only a fifteen-
minute interview in the office.'

One night at Ciro's he found the indefinable. When the
floor-show was over, he asked Audrey to call round at his
office the next day. But when some of his colleagues looked her
over, they were far from impressed.

'What can you do with her?' one of them asked. 'She's flat-
chested, and she's got pop eyes.'

'That's as may be,' Lennard retorted, 'but she has star quality.'

A few days later Lennard bumped into Mario Zampi, an Italian film-maker working in Britain who was acquiring a growing reputation as the director of semi-crazy film comedies. Zampi informed the casting director that he was currently preparing a new comedy, called *Laughter in Paradise*.

'I'm still on the look-out,' Zampi disclosed, 'for a pretty young actress for one of the leading roles. Any ideas?'

Lennard told him about Audrey, and about another young dancer.

'They're appearing in Cabaret at Ciro's,' he said. 'Go and have a look and see what you think. If nothing else, you'll have a damned good evening. Landeau, as usual, has put together a marvellous show.'

Zampi and the film's scriptwriter, Michael Pertwee, wasted no time and, after the pubs had closed, went to the nightspot to assess the two chorus girls.

'They were both very pretty,' Pertwee later recalled, 'but Audrey was more than that. She took our breath away.'

'She made you feel so *warm*,' added Zampi, who was so enthusiastic about Audrey that he later went to see the show time and time again just to look at her.

A meeting was arranged at the film's production office for the following afternoon.

'Talking with her,' Pertwee added, 'only served to convince us both that she had to play the leading part of Lucille Grayson, even though she had absolutely no acting experience. So she was offered the role. To our chagrin, after a few days, she turned it down – "for personal reasons".'

She had written the following letter to them: 'I'm sorry. I've just signed to do a short tour in a show. I can't break the contract. It wouldn't be fair.'

The role was subsequently given to Beatrice Campbell, an actress six years Audrey's senior and a 'veteran' of several films; two weeks earlier she had just finished shooting *The Mudlark* with Alec Guinness. Nobody was more disappointed than the Baroness, because she knew the *real* reason behind her daughter's seemingly foolish decision. It could be described in three little words: Marcel le Bon.

Audrey, Marcel and 'the gang' were all set to take their new cabaret show on the road when, inexplicably, the promised bookings fell through. Marcel, more dejected than ever, felt he had failed not only himself but everyone else. His dark moods finally became too much for Audrey, and they went their separate ways. Impulsive by nature, he packed his few belongings and boarded the next ship for the United States. Audrey's 'personal reasons' for declining the glossy film offer had disappeared overnight and, a few days after Beatrice Campbell had been officially signed, the dancer went rushing back to the film company.

'If the part's still available, and you're not too mad with me, I'd be thrilled to do it,' she told Zampi.

Zampi wasn't in the least mad with her and felt wretched for not having waited a few more days before casting the role. He gave her the bad news, and her sad doe-eyes screwed him up even more inside.

'Look, Audrey, I very much want to use you in my picture,' Zampi then said. 'But the only role not yet cast is a bit-part of a girl who sells cigarettes. Do you want to do it?'

'Yes,' Audrey said without hesitation. 'When do I start?'

'You start and finish on the same day,' the director informed her. 'The role requires just a day's work.'

A magnificent cast, headed by Alastair Sim, Fay Compton, Joyce Grenfell, Guy Middleton, George Cole, Hugh Griffith, Ernest Thesiger, A. E. Matthews, Eleanor Summerfield, John Laurie and Anthony Steel, had been assembled for the film – a witty study of human nature, concerning an eccentric prankster who leaves his heirs a fortune if they discharge amiably embarrassing or criminal tasks. Audrey had been allocated just one line of dialogue: 'Who wants a ciggy?' But on the strength of that one line, and that one day's work, she was offered a seven-year contract by Associated British (ABC). 'Think it over,' they said. 'No need to rush.' Her film career was launched. Starmaker Lennard had done it again. 'We were all aware that Mario Zampi had found someone rather special,' George Cole would remember many years later. 'A buzz of excitement ran through Pinewood,' added Eleanor Summerfield. 'Everyone who had seen the rushes of Audrey's one little scene were quite convinced that a new star had arrived.'

For the moment, however, the 'new star' would have to content herself with being a bit-part actress – while maintaining her nocturnal employment at Ciro's. The routine suited her admirably. Producers and directors, hearing through the grapevine that an exciting new girl had entered their world quietly through a back door, were sufficiently intrigued to try her out.

65

Before the year was through she would take on another four films.

She went almost immediately into *One Wild Oat*, a modest bedroom farce based on a popular West End comedy by Vernon Sylvaine and directed by Charles Saunders. In the film, starring Robertson Hare and Stanley Holloway, Audrey played an hotel reception clerk. It was little more than an 'extra' role. But the picture, about an old flame who sets out to blackmail a highly respectable solicitor, ran into censorship problems and, in the course of cutting, most of Audrey's bits ended up on the floor. The problem was, Audrey was the 'wild oat', and the censor objected to some of the visual and sexually verbal insinuations. Fortunately, she was still (barely) visible in two quick scenes.

Associated British next cast her with Joan Greenwood, Derek Farr, Helen Cherry, Nigel Patrick and Guy Middleton in *Young Wives' Tale*, a mild but palatable comedy based on Ronald Jeans' stage play about England's postwar housing shortage and set mainly in the Victorian home of the Bannings, 'not far from Kensington Gardens'. Director Henry Cass, having watched Audrey at work in her previous film, felt so confident in her ability to do justice to a scene, no matter how brief, that he offered her the minor featured role of Eve. The film today looks a very *English* comedy, and very dated, with lots of 'by joves' and 'crikeys' in the dialogue. Yet there could be little doubt that Audrey gained immeasurably from the experience – and from the director's confidence in her.

But not everyone on the set shared Cass's considerable optimism. One member of the production team was overheard talking to a colleague one day. 'She ought to go back to dancing,' he jeered. 'She'll never make it as an actress.'

'I probably hold the distinction,' Audrey would admit some time later, 'of being one movie star who, by all laws of logic, should never have made it. At each stage of my career I lacked the experience. But at least I never pretended to be able to do the thing that was being offered.'

Anthony Mendleson, a costume designer at Ealing Studios who rented an apartment in the same South Audley Street building as Audrey and the Baroness, and who became a close friend of the bit-part actress in her early film days, would later explain of this period in her life: 'She was absolutely natural; no "act" at all. She was no different in front of the cameras than she was talking to you in the room.'

All the same: 'No one on the picture knew her terribly well,' said Derek Farr. 'She kept herself very much to herself.' But Farr, at that time one of the big names in the British cinema and soon to star with Michael Redgrave and Richard Todd in *The Dam Busters*, got to know Audrey better than most. He used to drive her back to South Audley Street each evening after the day's work at ABPC's Elstree studios in Hertfordshire. One evening Audrey was unusually quiet.

'What's worrying you?' enquired Farr.

'ABC have offered me a long-term contract – and now I've got to make my mind up,' said Audrey anxiously.

'Do you want it?'

'I don't know.'

'For God's sake, don't,' insisted the actor. 'You're much too good for them.'

'But,' she said, 'I haven't any money.'

'Don't worry – one day you will.'

While waiting around on the set for her turn in front of the camera, Audrey would pass the time constructing attractive little models out of coloured clay. More than one cast member commented on the fact that, should all else fail, she might seriously consider becoming a sculptress. 'The models were quite beautiful,' Helen Cherry would later explain. 'One that particularly sticks in my mind was of Father Christmas on his sleigh, with his red cloak flying behind him. It showed exquisite attention to detail . . . as did Audrey in her acting.'

The allure of true love, meanwhile, beamed in like a comet on her professionally fulfilling but romantically empty life. 'I think love and fear are the most important things,' Audrey would proclaim many years later. 'Whatever you love most, you fear you might lose, you know it can change. Why do you look from left to right when you cross the street? Because you don't want to get run over. But,' she concluded, 'you still cross the street.'

When it came to love and marriage, Audrey's fears were (and always would be) pronounced. From the very beginning, from her first recorded romance with Marcel le Bon, Audrey would try more determinedly than most to make a relationship of the heart 'work'. The traumatic memories of her parents' broken marriage would remain locked in her consciousness forever, and it would become almost a life's mission not to experience the same mistakes herself.

She once explained what she looked for in male companionship: 'The kind of man I'm attracted to can be tall or short, fair or dark, handsome or homely. Physical good looks don't necessarily appeal to me just by themselves. If a man has that indefinable quality that I can only call "warmth" or "charm", then I'll feel at ease with him.'

The man who most satisfactorily fulfilled these criteria, following her break-up with Marcel, was the tall, handsome, charming and eligible James Hanson. He was then the twenty-eight-year-old son and heir of a wealthy Huddersfield businessman who had been compensated handsomely for the loss of his road-haulage company under nationalisation. They met at the party of a mutual friend just after Audrey had completed work on *Young Wives' Tale*, and there had been an immediate chemistry between them. Although, just a few months earlier, Jimmy had been a regular escort of the self-possessed and beautiful Jean Simmons, he was now telling everybody who cared to listen that this latest liaison was the real thing.

At this time the beanpole six-foot-four Jimmy Hanson was fast acquiring a reputation as a wealthy playboy who frequented the most glittering nightspots on both sides of the Atlantic. He was noted for his sartorial elegance and a love of big cars – which, in years to come, as boss of Hanson Air, would be supplemented by an even greater love of snazzy aeroplanes, including a Hawker Siddeley 125 executive jet, and helicopters (a fleet of Bell LongRangers).

On the face of it, the fledgeling multi-millionaire playboy of the Western world was not an obvious candidate for Audrey's affections. For the first half of her childhood she had known wealth and opulence, so riches alone would not necessarily turn her head. She had always avoided men who displayed even a suggestion of unconcealed flamboyance, and yet here was a man who concealed very little when it came to partaking of the better things in life. So what lay beneath Jimmy's debonair charm? By all accounts, very little. For his 'debonair charm' – what Audrey called 'that indefinable quality' – was precisely what attracted the starlet to him. The qualities he possessed, in fact, would be duplicated almost exactly in successive admirers, lovers and husbands. All of them, in varying degrees, would display something of the playboy in their character. What they represented was in obverse proportion to her own quiet, modest, solitary nature: a classic attraction of like with unlike, a potentially lethal meeting of nitric and sulphuric acids with glycerine. She would be fated to living out, and compensating for, a series of incompatible marital relationships that seemed doomed from their conception. She would be fated, too, to enacting the role of the model partner. Yet her role would not be an 'act'. With each relationship and each marriage she would endeavour against all the blatantly obvious odds to make it work; and even when, in private, it was patently *not* working, she would give every indication to the outside world that here was the most blissfully happy *affaire d'amour* since Héloïse and Abélard. So often, alas, her friends would know a different story.

But now, at least, Audrey's blissful heart knew no bounds. She and Jimmy were, to all intents and purposes, inseparable – except that his business interests conspired to separate them on far too many occasions. His trips between England and Canada grew more and more frequent, though when the couple were together their relationship was propelled by a renewed buoyancy. They went to the theatre and the cinema. They were seen at all the best parties and nightspots, and next day their pictures would appear in the gossip columns. In years to come, both Jimmy and Audrey would become irritated by, but grow to accept, such intrusions on their privacy. But now they were both young things trying to make their mark in the world, and life was fun, and who cared about popping flashbulbs? Life was to be lived. They talked of marriage.

9

'Making movies is very hard, unglamorous work.'

WHEN THE ENGAGEMENT of Landeau's *Summer Nights* floor-show came to an end at Ciro's, Audrey relied more than ever on photographic modelling assignments and bit-part work in films to keep her solvent. Modelling, especially, would occupy her time for several months.

Later, explaining this dark period to Henry Gris, she said: 'I was very happy when I was given an opportunity to earn a little extra money by doing bit-parts in movies. This is how I got into movies: not because I thought it was so wonderful to be in one, and, gosh, here's my dream coming true, but because I needed money to live. And so, when another opportunity was offered me, I took it. Gratefully.'

But the mighty Associated British, despite witnessing a quietly impressive performance from Audrey in *Young Wives' Tale*, were still reluctant to push a role her way worthy of her obvious potential. After she finished work on her last film, in fact, they loaned her out – for another bit-part – to Sir Michael Balcon's Ealing Studios. These studios, under Balcon's leadership, enjoyed a well-deserved reputation for their impressive cluster of sophisticated satirical films, productions which were typically British in their irreverent, self-deprecating, understated humour. Among the most successful of the genre were *Passport to Pimlico*, *Kind Hearts and Coronets* and *Whisky Galore*.

In the autumn of 1950, Balcon and his team, headed by associate producer Michael Truman, screenwriter T. E. B. Clarke and director Charles Crichton, were ready to go into production with a film later described by one cinema historian as a 'superbly characterized and inventively detailed comedy, one of the best ever made at Ealing or in Britain.' *The Lavender Hill Mob* starred Alec Guinness as the timid bank clerk who brilliantly conceives and executes a bullion robbery; he is aided and abetted by Stanley Holloway, his fellow lodger and maker of gimcrack souvenirs.

Audrey's part came in the opening sequence, set in a South American airport lounge, in which she was required to approach Guinness, offer him a packet of cigarettes and, after being paid for them, give him a friendly hug. She seems very friendly. She could be his mistress. In fact, she is a hat-and-cloak girl named Chiquita.

Not everyone fell in love with her. Balcon confessed, 'We all have our blind spots. In the prologue and epilogue of *The Lavender Hill Mob* we had a very pretty girl – Audrey Hepburn – selling cigarettes to Alec Guinness. I paid no particular attention to her.' Even Tibby Clarke, who won an Oscar for his screenplay, admitted that Audrey, who spoke just one line, 'struck nobody as star material'.

Nobody, perhaps, except Alec Guinness. During rehearsals for the Rio de Janeiro airport scene, Guinness was immediately impressed by the vision before him. He could not, for the most innocent of reasons, tear his eyes away from her. 'She only had half a line to say,' Guinness would later explain, 'and I don't think she even said the line in any particular or interesting way. But her faun-like beauty and presence were remarkable.' He excused himself from the rehearsal for a few minutes and telephoned his agent. 'I don't know if she can act,' he said, 'but a real film star has just been wafted on to the set. Someone should get her under contract before we lose her to the Americans.' But only a few weeks earlier, and obviously quite unknown to Guinness, Audrey had signed with Associated British – the movie monster that merely 'played' with her. Guinness, however, remaining faithful to a gut feeling which insisted that the vision in *Lavender Hill* was 'a real film star', introduced her to the Hollywood director Mervyn LeRoy, who was then casting his spectacular but ultimately stagy and physically brutal *Quo Vadis*. Guinness hoped that his American friend would cast Audrey in the female lead of Lygia; but the part went to a 'name' – Deborah Kerr.

The British studio's lack of foresight and sense of adventure, meantime, would eventually lose them a world star; after *Young Wives' Tale*, five years would elapse before Associated British decided ever again to employ Audrey in one of their own films. It may have been their intention to do so, at some imminent date, if and when the right vehicle came along, but, in 1951, they much preferred to loan her out to other studios. Which is why, for her next project, she worked once again for Michael Balcon. Among the films being planned for Ealing's twenty-first anniversary programme was *Where No Vultures Fly*, set on location in East Africa with Anthony Steele and Dinah Sheridan, and *The Secret People*, a downbeat political melodrama about European refugees in pre-Second World War London.

It was in this second film, the boldest and least typical of Ealing productions, that Audrey was given her best role to date. The international cast, led by Italy's Valentina Cortesa – who had been a success in *The Glass Mountain* the year before – and the French-Italian Serge Reggiani, was directed by one of the country's best film-makers, Thorold Dickinson. The film's scenario was overwhelmingly 'serious' and quite unlike any other screen project with which Audrey would ever again be associated. Following the murder of their Italian father, a victim of political tyranny in France, Maria (Valentina Cortesa) and her young sister Nora (Audrey) are sent for safety to London. Here, Maria (and inevitably Nora) becomes involved in some assassination business contrived by her lover (Serge Reggiani), from whom she had been separated by political intrigue in Italy.

For the first time in any of her films, Audrey's ballet training proved to be of immediate benefit, for Nora was a ballet student who, by the end of the story, becomes a celebrated ballerina. Although her dancing in the classroom scenes was performed on full point, in the actual ballet sequences Audrey chose to dance on only half-point (on the balls of the feet), a positive vindication of her self-confessed technical weakness in classical ballet; the less-demanding period of cabaret and revue dancing had merely accentuated this weakness. Dancing with John Field, a star of what is now the Royal Ballet and a frequent partner of Beryl Grey, seemed to be a hindrance rather than a help.

'The ballet scenes were a great strain for her – far greater a challenge, in a way, than the scenes calling for acting and spoken dialogue,' recalled Sidney Cole, producer of *The Secret People*. 'She was a little fraught.' Michael Mendleson, Ealing costume designer and friend who worked with her on *Secret People*, would also later note, 'She was very critical of the fact that she wasn't the greatest dancer in the world. She'd been trained as a classical dancer, she knew the ropes, but we all knew it was a great effort for her to do it.'

Both Cole and Dickinson had originally spotted Audrey in *Sauce Piquante*. They were therefore familiar with the dancer with the endless legs who, along with several other actresses, turned up one day at Ealing Studios to screen-test for Nora. Studio executives were subsequently worried that she might be too tall to be credible as Valentina Cortesa's *younger* sister. Unknown to producer or director, however, Valentina, who developed an instant rapport with Audrey, had already worked out a strategy to help the aspiring actress. She had learnt that, following the initial interview, Audrey had not been offered a screen-test.

'I get the impression,' Audrey said, 'that they think I'm too tall.'

'I'll make sure you get a test,' Valentina assured her. 'This is what we'll do. . . .'

The test was called for that afternoon. The camera rolled and Audrey was a success. She was offered the part.

'Didn't I say you'd be in the picture!' laughed Valentina. 'You've just learnt one of the first tricks of the trade – how to engineer Fate.'

Their secret plot? Audrey removed her shoes and Valentina played on her tip-toes; it was an age in movies, after all, where short actors like Alan Ladd stood on boxes and tall actresses like Ingrid Bergman stood in holes in order to compensate for incompatible heights. As ploys, they would not be unknown to Audrey in the years ahead.

'Once we'd seen Audrey's test,' explained Sidney Cole later, 'there was no contest. None of the other actresses looked as *interesting* as Audrey.'

Despite her relative inexperience in films, Thorold Dickinson was convinced that Audrey was the stuff of which stars were made. For several weeks, consequently, he tried to persuade Balcon to buy her ABC contract and sign her up with Ealing. He persevered in vain. 'Balcon was far too conventional to even consider the proposition,' Dickinson would lament. 'And, anyway, Audrey's behaviour was always too modest to attract the attention of strangers.'

But Cole was more realistic where Audrey's potential talents were concerned. 'I think,' he would explain later, 'that it would be going too far to suggest that, at the time, one said "Ah, here's a potential star!" It very rarely works like that. She had enormous charm, was a beautiful young woman, and was very graceful as a dancer, and she had a great deal of quality – but that doesn't necessarily lead anywhere. If you look at *Secret People* now, you can see with hindsight a certain amount of inexperience coming through – but her charm of manner worked very well.'

Valentina, Dickinson, and Serge Reggiani were unusually supportive to the young ex-dancer with the burning enthusiasm, while Irene Worth (that *superb* actress) would have liked to help, but felt too inhibited – and too modest – to do so. Irene Worth was then appearing at London's New Theatre in T. S. Eliot's *The Cocktail Party* and had been asked by Dickinson to take a small role in *The Secret People* in order to help Serge Reggiani with his English.

'We had a night's location,' Miss Worth remembered, 'and Audrey and I sat in the back of someone's car to get away from the cold and damp and the dreadful lassitude which sets in with waiting to be called for the next scene. Audrey was naturally very worried about it since she was so inexperienced in acting. The work didn't go very well and I remember how I thought to try to help her but felt it would be presumptuous for me to say anything and I recall, with admiration, how Serge stepped in and helped her, so specifically and strongly.

'We all adored him, especially for his magnificent performance with Simone Signoret in *Casque d'Or*. Audrey turned to him like water in the sand and took his help with concentration and openness. She seemed to have qualities of endurance and patience and a powerful will to 'get it right', to learn. One got the feeling that she had been through privations in the war, but I never asked her personal questions.'

Irene Worth then stressed, importantly, that Audrey was a novice – 'and one is very "closed" at the beginning'. But, she added, 'What was already fully apparent was her natural, unselfconscious sweetness, which has never been corroded.'

One other important factor which contributed greatly to Audrey's baptismal period in films was, ironically, her very lack of experience. Although she had appeared on stage, she had never played a straight acting role, so she did not have to endure the painful process of an experienced stage actor – of having to adapt to a different medium, of having to go right against a theatre training, of *underplaying*.

'The film itself was rather like a fairy-tale for her,' said Sidney Cole. 'To be given the second female lead in *Secret People* completely overwhelmed her, as if she knew in her heart that she wasn't really ready for so great a burden of responsibility. At the same time, though, she didn't give you the feeling of being helpless: she needed guidance as an actress, yes, but not as a person.'

The 'serious' nature of the film's scenario was much relieved for Audrey when an old friend from her *Sauce Piquante* days arrived on the set. She and Bob Monkhouse laughed a lot together. Monkhouse had become the BBC's first contract comedian, and, with schoolfriend Denis Goodwin, had formed a highly successful script-writing team, concocting thousands of radio and television shows for Arthur Askey, Jack Buchanan, Bob Hope, Jack Benny and themselves. While engaged on *Secret People*, in which he played a Cockney hairdresser, Monkhouse and Goodwin had three radio shows running at the same time, and most days Monkhouse would be busy on the set, wearing his white hairdresser's coat, typing his comedy scripts.

Audrey took a great interest in the scripts, especially the contents of one particular routine intended for *Workers' Playtime*.

'You look lost for words!' Audrey said one day, glancing over Monkhouse's shoulder. 'That's not like you.'

'I need a gag to finish the routine, which is all about how poor my childhood was,' said the funny man.

'Why don't you say that you were so poor as a family that you didn't even have any cheese to put in a mouse-trap, and so you had to draw a picture of a piece of cheese to put in the mouse-trap?'

'Well, that's quite funny,' said Monkhouse, 'but it's not really a complete joke.'

'All right,' added Audrey, 'you could then say that you caught a picture of a mouse.'

Monkhouse would laugh when recalling that joke three decades later. 'Do you know,' he said, 'I did that gag for years. I'd be doing all my usual patter about my so-called "poverty-stricken" childhood, how we wore knives and forks for jewellery, and I'd say "We were so poor, we couldn't afford a piece of cheese for a mousetrap, so I drew a piece of cheese. And what do you think I caught? A picture of a mouse!" And whenever I did it, I could see Audrey's serious little face, how she stood there like a schoolgirl, how she slowly worked out this sensational joke.'

Although Audrey's part in *The Secret People* was relatively small, she was given an above-the-title credit, immediately below the names of Valentina Cortesa and Serge Reggiani – 'a fact which reflected how pleased we were with her performance,' producer Cole disclosed later.

But this film, unfortunately, would do little to further Audrey's career. 'We never disguised the fact,' Dickinson confessed, 'that *Secret People* was what you would call an "art house" subject, not for the general public so much as for a smaller audience. It wasn't supposed to be a film that would get all its money back here. But when the film failed in England they didn't, in fact, try to sell it in Europe at all.'

After the press show, Ealing scriptwriter Tibby Clarke encountered Audrey outside the cinema. 'Please don't abandon us for Hollywood,' he implored her.

'I'm sorry,' she answered without hesitation, 'but I'll not give you any such promise!'

And, certainly, Audrey would never again work in Britain for a British film company, though it would not be for any lack of trying on the part of the latter.

Working as a personal assistant to Thorold Dickinson on *Secret People* was a high-placed young man named Alfred Shaughnessy, whose stepfather was equerry first to King Edward VIII, then to George VI, and who, in the 1970s, would become script editor and principal writer of television's *Upstairs, Downstairs* series. In partnership with John Eldridge, a talented young documentary director, Shaughnessy decided to secure a property and persuade Balcon to let them make it under the auspices of a new production company called Group Three, whose brief was to make low-budget films of quality and originality.

They came up with *Brandy for the Parson*, based on Geoffrey Household's hilarious novel about a young couple on a yachting holiday who become unwittingly involved in smuggling brandy into Britain. Shaughnessy's screenplay impressed Balcon sufficiently for the Ealing boss to give the film the go-ahead. The two film-makers were now confronted with the problem of casting the three star parts, comprising (in Shaughnessy's words) 'Bill Harper, the orthodox young man on holiday; Petronilla, his girlfriend; and Tony Rackham, the debonair young adventurer who gets them involved in the smuggling operation.'

'John and I had been chatting up Audrey Hepburn, who was just becoming much talked about, and urging her to play Petronilla,' Shaughnessy explained. 'She was in *Secret People* so we were seeing her at the studio most days. She had followed the progress of our script with interest, and said she would be delighted to do our picture next.'

As soon as the first draft of the script was ready, Shaughnessy gave Audrey a copy to read. The following day she handed it back. 'Lovely,' she said with a sweet but mischievous smile, 'but I couldn't play Scene 42. The censor wouldn't allow it.'

Shaughnessy grabbed his 'harmless, innocent and thoroughly wholesome' script from her hands and flicked through the pages. Scene 42? It read as follows:

Scene 42. INT. CABIN OF YACHT. DAY (STUDIO)
Petronilla is awake, dressed in Bill's pyjamas. *She is peeing out of the porthole.*

'The ladies in the script-typing pool had omitted the letter "r", either by accident or design,' the writer later chuckled.

Weeks went by, meanwhile, because of some internal disagreements about the film's budget. Until Shaughnessy was accorded the final 'OK' from Group Three, he was unable to make legally binding contracts.

'Audrey's agent, Kenneth Harper, kept on ringing me for news but I couldn't commit myself,' Shaughnessy related. 'One day Harper rang to say that he'd had an offer for Audrey to go down to Monte Carlo and play in a film with a bandleader called Ray Ventura [who also produced the film]. It was a nothing part but she was to have a Dior dress, the money was good, and it would mean a month in the sun. Nevertheless, she'd still rather do *Brandy for the Parson*.

'I pointed this little pistol at Group Three's head, but they still couldn't give me a start date or a commitment. So Audrey had to go. John and I were shattered. Later, when we'd started the picture, I had a postcard from her from Monte Carlo saying how sad she was not to be with us, "especially as I hear you've got the lovely James Donald" or words to that effect.'

In addition to James Donald, a Scottish actor then a big name in the cinema, the film's principal triumvirate was completed by Kenneth More, and, in 'Audrey's part', Jean Lodge (Shaughnessy's wife). 'I often reflect,' Shaughnessy later recorded, 'that had Audrey come down with us to Devon and played the not very rewarding part of Petronilla, her break [in Hollywood] might have been longer coming. But come it would have, in the end, for she had dazzling, devastating star quality.'

Yet would that be enough?

10

'I'm sorry. I can't act.'

THE NIGHT BEFORE leaving for Monte Carlo, Audrey met America's famed show-business columnist Radie Harris for the first time at a dinner-party given in the scribe's honour at Mayfair's most popular private club, Les Ambassadeurs; and Radie, unknown to the starlet, would soon become Audrey's close friend and confidante. Also at the party was the American socialite leading lady of 1940s films, Faye Emerson – who had flown over to spend a few days with Radie – plus Humphrey Bogart, John Huston, Sam Spiegel and Lauren Bacall. The newspaper lady's hosts were James and John Woolf of Romulus Films.

Audrey, whose contact in films until now had been with purely home-produced British actors, was speechless, literally, over meeting Humphrey Bogart, whom she had always admired. She had never met a legend – not, at least, a Hollywood Legend – and if anybody had told her that one day she would be Bogie's co-star, she would have retorted: 'Nonsense! I'll never be in the same class as him.'

The aspiring film actress, none the less, was being seen in the right places by the right people; she would never forget Valentina Cortesa's advice about 'engineering Fate'. Radie, in the process, quickly discovered Audrey's great charm, and drew her out by asking a lot of questions. Audrey, in turn, seemed grateful for the columnist's interest and answered with the confiding warmth of an old friend.

'Everything significant in my life has happened gloriously

and unexpectedly – like the trip I am making to Monte Carlo tomorrow,' she told Radie. 'I've always longed to go to the French Riviera, but could never afford it. Then this picture, *Monte Carlo Baby*, turned up. I play only a small supporting role, but I never thought I'd even get that.

'The day the producer interviewed me was one of those days when *everything* went wrong. I had a terrible time finding a stocking that didn't have a run in it. The zipper got caught in my dress and, when I finally arrived at my agent's office, the whole interview lasted exactly a minute and a half! I was sure I'd failed.

'I tried to comfort myself by telling mother that if I went to Monte Carlo for this small part, I might miss out on a larger role in London. And anyway, some day I'd make enough money so that we could both go to the Riviera on *my* expense account. Then suddenly the phone rang and I heard those four words that are the sweetest music in the world to every actress, "The job is yours!"'

Monte Carlo Baby, a frothy little musical comedy about high jinks on the Riviera, was steered by one of France's most prolific directors, Jean Boyer, who, the following year, would direct Brigitte Bardot in her first film role. It was dubbed in two versions, French and English, and starred the tall, sad-eyed American comedian, Jules Munshin, who had been one of the three sailors (the other two being Gene Kelly and Frank Sinatra) in MGM's *On the Town*, and the Brooklyn-born comedienne Cara Williams, then in the throes of marrying John Barrymore Jr.

Audrey played the part of a girl on her honeymoon. Although many reference books place her name at the head of the film's credits – and, therefore, by implication, make her the star – she appears in it, in fact, for only twelve minutes. It was another bit-part, though rather more 'featured' than her earlier bit-parts.

She was shooting a scene in the lobby of the Hôtel de Paris in Monte Carlo one afternoon when, during a camera line-up, she noticed an elderly woman being pushed in a bath-chair. The woman sported red corkscrew curls and a slash of lipstick. Ray Ventura, the producer, drew Audrey aside. 'Do you know who that is?' he said.

Audrey shook her head.

'Colette,' he volunteered, 'the French novelist.'

80

Colette, then aged seventy-eight and in the final lustrum of her life, was the foremost woman writer of her epoch. Now, in the burnished, autumnal months of 1951, she was practically immobilised, human arms and a wheelchair being her only means of locomotion. Her beloved husband, Maurice Goudeket, seventeen years her junior, had organised their winters in Monte Carlo for the five successive years. Thus it was, as she entered the hotel lobby while the film unit was there, that she asked Maurice to push her closer to the action – and to Audrey.

The novelist was so captivated by the actress that, after two days, she insisted on meeting her. Maurice ascertained where she was staying – the Hôtel de Paris! – and arranged a rendez-vous. Before doing so, he gave Audrey a piece of amazing information. He explained that Anita Loos, the American author of *Gentlemen Prefer Blondes*, had adapted *Gigi* for the New York stage and that Gilbert Miller, anxious to give it an early production, had ordered a team of talent-scouts to scour Broadway, Hollywood, London and Europe for a young, unknown actress sufficiently accomplished to make Colette's will-of-iron child-woman a believable creature and not a theatrical curiosity.

'We have had a lot of difficulty in finding a star for the Broadway production,' he told Audrey. 'For two years we have been searching. But my wife thinks that you might be the right person for it.'

Audrey could hardly believe that he was being serious. When she went along to see Madame Colette, however, the writer smiled at her: 'My dear, I have just sent a cable to New York to tell them to stop looking for a Gigi. I have found her.' She glanced at Maurice. 'When I saw you filming in the hotel lobby, I said at once to my husband, "There is our Gigi for America." I could not take my eyes off you, my dear.'

Audrey did not know whether to laugh or cry, because she honestly felt she was not the right person for the part.

'What is the matter, my child?' enquired the novelist, unable to ignore Audrey's obvious misgivings. 'Would you not like to do *Gigi* on Broadway?'

'I'm sorry, Madame, but I wouldn't be able to,' Audrey replied tremulously, 'because I can't act. I'm not equipped to play a leading role since I've never said more than one or two lines on stage in my life. I've done bits in films, of course, but I don't consider that acting.'

81

Colette was insistent. 'You've been a dancer,' she said positively, 'you've worked hard, and you can work hard and do this, too. I have faith in you, my dear.'

Audrey capitulated and returned to London that weekend.

But producer Miller and playwright Loos did not at first share Colette's enthusiasm. And yet, although both these veterans of the worlds of screen and stage were fully conscious of Audrey's dramatic limitations, they could not at the same time ignore the French novelist's awesome conviction that the girl possessed *something* – the divine spark which makes it easy to separate the stars from the players. In the end it made little difference how badly she read the play, for she still managed to hold everyone's rapt attention.

Miller signed her to a contract. He related later that 'we named her for our Gigi – a young actress whom we had never seen on a stage; indeed, a young actress whose two years' stage experience had been confined to dancing bits in topical revues.' The London press made so much of the fact that a practically unknown actress was about to star in a potentially important play, that two or three films in which Audrey had bit-parts were ballyhooed anew.

Suddenly, Audrey's life was in a whirl. There were newspaper interviews, three flying trips to Paris for dress-fittings, legal formalities to complete . . . plus further night-long discussions with Jimmy Hanson about marriage. But *that* would have to be postponed. Again. The publicity she was now receiving was turning her into a minor celebrity, and she was being asked to make the occasional 'personal appearance'. Her first P.A. job, for which she received a welcome nominal fee, consisted of opening a country fête. On the way there, she turned to her publicity agent, John Newnham, and exclaimed: 'Please let's work out what I've got to say. I'm terrified. I've never given a talk in public before!'

They rehearsed her speech.

Newnham was sitting close to her when she stood up to open the fête. After only a few seconds, he realised that the carefully rehearsed speech was going all wrong – she had missed out all the early parts. She caught her publicity agent's eye, who could see instantly that she knew what had happened.

'I don't think any of the people there could have known that Audrey was scared stiff,' Newnham reflected later. 'She recovered herself, improvised, and made the speech much more delightful than it would have been. What was even more remarkable was that, within a few months, Audrey was on her way to New York to become an overnight hit on Broadway in her first play. No one but Audrey would have dared to tackle such a tremendous job with so little experience – but Audrey was always game to try anything.'

Additionally, Hollywood beckoned. In July the American studios had started to take an active interest in her, though the negotiations would be prolonged for some time. She was still under contract to ABC.

In the mid-Forties, Ian McLellan Hunter and Dalton Trumbo wrote an original story about a pretty Ruritanian princess who, while visiting a foreign country, eludes her attendants for twenty-four hours while having a madcap spree with an American newspaperman. This property, *Roman Holiday*, was acquired by the Italian-American director Frank Capra for his Liberty Films company, and, when Liberty went to Paramount in 1948, it was arranged that the film would be made there by Capra. Elizabeth Taylor and Cary Grant were approached to star in it; but, because Paramount imposed so small a budget, Capra lost interest. Early in 1951 *Wuthering Heights* director William Wyler was told of the *Roman Holiday* script that was gathering dust on a shelf at Paramount, and subsequently expressed an interest in making the picture if it could be shot on location in Rome. The studio agreed – it had a lot of lira frozen in Italy – and so did Capra, who gladly released the story to his old friend Wyler.

Coincidentally, at this time, Gregory Peck was letting it be known that he now wished to try his hand at comedy. Peck read the script for *Roman Holiday* and announced that he liked the story, although he was not entirely happy at first over the fact that his part was not as big as the leading lady's. That consideration, however, could be remedied later. Elizabeth Taylor's name was again raised, plus that of Jean Simmons, although in the event neither actress was available.

'I don't need a stellar leading lady,' insisted Wyler. 'I want a girl without an American accent to play the princess, someone you can *believe* has been brought up as a princess. That's the main requirement – besides acting, looks, and personality.'

With such requirements in mind, Wyler set off for Europe to find his princess. In London he interviewed several girls, including Audrey (he had seen a rough-cut of *Secret People* and was immensely taken with the young actress), and then went on to Paris and Rome to continue his search. Before departing for the Continent, he conferred with Paramount's London production boss, Richard Mealand, who, in turn, in a letter dated 9 July 1951, despatched the following note to his New York office: 'I have another candidate for *Roman Holiday* – Audrey Hepburn. I was struck by her playing of a bit-part in *Laughter in Paradise*. . . .'

New York cabled: 'Please airmail report and photographs actress Audrey Hepburn.' Wyler, meanwhile, was sending back his own reports, and the New York cable added: 'Is French actress Colette Ripert practical possibility. . . ?'

Mealand lost no time in supplying details on Audrey. He explained: 'She is twenty-two years old, 5ft 5½in in height [she was one and a half inches taller!], darkish brown hair. She is a little on the thin side . . . but very appealing. There is no question of her ability and she dances very well. Her speaking voice is clear and youthful, with no extremes of accent. She looks more Continental than English.'

The return cable said: 'Studio very interested Hepburn. Anxious see her soonest on film.'

Paramount's appetite duly whetted, the cablegrams became more and more enthusiastic. A few days later, however, Mealand received this message: 'Ask Hepburn if OK change her last name to avoid conflict Katharine Hepburn.'

Audrey was adamant: 'Decidedly not. If you want me, you'll have to take the name too.'

The cables, letters and telephone messages continued to cross the Atlantic with increased regularity, but, at the end of the day, Paramount would not commit themselves until they saw Audrey's screen-test. The studio was determined not to have her unless they considered her good enough for a long-term contract. At length an inter-office memorandum was sent from London to New York saying: 'Test arranged Pinewood Studios, September 18, 1951. Thorold Dickinson directing. Other players – Lionel Murton and Cathleen Nesbitt. Two scenes from *Roman Holiday* script and an interview.'

When the subject of a screen-test came up, Audrey had asked specifically if it would be possible for Dickinson to direct it. She loved and admired the man and, professionally, had complete confidence in him. So had Wyler and, unknown to

Audrey, had already asked Dickinson to conduct the test. The British director would later explain: 'We made up a sequence from *Secret People* and did some scenes out of the script of *Roman Holiday*. And Paramount always wanted to know what a person was actually like, and so I did an interview with her . . . all through the war, all through the Arnhem raid, Audrey was in the town, hidden. So we talked about that. We loaded a thousand feet on to the camera and every foot of it went on this conversation. Most moving thing.'

'Thorold took many demanding close-ups of Audrey,' said Sidney Cole, who was present at the test, 'yet she was very relaxed throughout. In fact, she'd do anything that Thorold asked her to do in that moment – she had utter faith in him.'

For the test, Dickinson used more than one set-up, though all of them shot in the context of a bedroom scene. The test began with a wink and ended with a giggle. Her self-possession was fantastic. The wink came at that tense moment when Dickinson ordered the camera to focus on a close-up. Audrey's back was to the camera, she turned her head slowly to face it – as the script called for – and then came the unsolicited and impudent wink. 'The minute you saw it,' said Louis Berg, one of America's top movie writers, 'you knew that this girl was in.'

And the giggle? This came at the climax of a scene in which Audrey flung herself on a bed.

'That's it,' said a voice from behind the camera. 'You can get off the bed now.'

But Audrey, obviously luxuriating on the bed's sumptuous comfort, refused to move. 'I didn't hear anybody say "Cut!"' she argued.

'Cut,' said the voice.

'Only one man here has the right to say "Cut",' she said giggling. 'I won't move until I hear him.'

'Cut!' said Dickinson, grinning.

Although this verbal horseplay was conducted in the best of spirits, it would prove to be the first recorded instance in which Audrey laid down the law and asked to be treated according to 'the rules'. She treated other people with proper respect, and she expected to be accorded the same courtesy in return. And the one man she respected above all others on the set was Dickinson, and he was the only person from whom she would take commands.

'She was very thorough – word-perfect in rehearsal – and took direction extremely well,' confirmed Canadian actor Lionel Murton, who had just made *Monte Carlo Baby* (though he and Audrey had never met), and who had been asked by Dickinson, for the purpose of the test, to play the 'lean, earnest young man' role which would be portrayed eventually by Gregory Peck.

Wyler himself, though not present at the test, had meanwhile left specific instructions as to what he required on film *after* the final scene had been completed. By pre-arrangement with the crew, the camera and soundtrack would keep rolling when Dickinson called 'Cut!'

Accordingly, when the 'Cut!' call came, the camera kept rolling – and Audrey sat up in the royal bed, clasped her hands around her knees and grinned delightedly at the chorus of praise from studio hands. She then realised that everyone had gone quiet and surmised what was happening, that the camera was still running – and *that* reaction was caught on film, too.

Murton, positioned just behind and to one side of the camera, also found himself grinning. 'This little doe-eyed charmer is a very smart cookie,' he thought to himself. 'She knows perfectly well that the camera is still running – and is giving it the works.'

With the reel of test film secured safely in his suitcase, Don Hartman, Paramount's head of production, caught the next plane back to Hollywood, where Gregory Peck was one of the first to see the results. He was enthusiastic. Everybody was enthusiastic. A cable went off immediately to London. It said: 'Congratulations fine test Hepburn. All here, including Meiklejohn, think her great.'

Meiklejohn was then chief of Paramount's talent department. Following close on the heels of the cable was a letter in which, under the heading 'Audrey Hepburn' (underlined in red), Paramount proposed: 'Exercise the option on this lady. The test is certainly one of the best ever made in Hollywood, New York or London. Hearty congratulations on behalf of Paramount – New York and Hollywood. This includes Balaban, Freeman and Hartman. . . .'

The accolades could come from no loftier a plane. For with Barney Balaban as president, Frank Y. Freeman as vice-president and Don Hartman as production chief, the cable had been signed by Paramount's top three executives. Realising they might have a hot property on their hands, Paramount were eager to get Audrey to sign an exclusive contract, but she was still legally committed to her one-picture-a-year contract with ABC and so, while the niceties (and not-so-niceties) of the law were being ironed out, they negotiated a short-term, two-picture package deal.

Yet even the tantalising Hollywood deal was not without its difficulties. Audrey and her agent knew exactly what they were doing and refused to be brow-beaten by tough-talking, cigar-chewing movie moguls with leather-look suntans. They fought every inch of the way to gain what they wanted and Audrey got the financial deal that she demanded. She secured a clause in the contract allowing her to act in stage plays. But there were long arguments over her insistence that she should be permitted to do television work.

'No TV,' snorted the film chiefs during the negotiations.

'No TV?' queried Audrey. 'In that case, no Hollywood.'

She was very much aware of the big fees offered by the American television networks and she wanted a slice of the action. The film chiefs swallowed their cigars with indignation, but were forced to relent. Paramount, Wyler and Peck would nevertheless have to wait nearly a year before starting work on their two-million-dollar baby – until, that is, Audrey and *Gigi* finished their run on Broadway. Shrewdly, the studio decided not to publicise her subsequent contract until after *Gigi* had premièred.

In a letter to Richard Mealand, the film boss in London who helped her find her Hollywood feet, Audrey scrawled a few words in her large, bold handwriting. 'Heaven help me live up to all this,' she said.

11

'I never expected to be a star, never counted on it, never even wanted it. Not that I didn't enjoy it all when it happened.'

PROFFERING A GOODBYE kiss to Jimmy and the Baroness, Audrey sailed for New York at the beginning of October, little realising just how much the journey would transform her life. She would fall madly in love with the town, as it would with her.

Gilbert Miller had instructed her to take a slow boat to the United States and to spend the eighteen days at sea to learn her part for *Gigi*. She was at once elated and nervous at what lay ahead. But, on the eighteenth day, a schoolgirl excitement prevailed, and, at two in the morning, she stood freezing in a nylon nightie in front of her cabin porthole – looking for the famous Manhattan skyline.

Despite all the press ballyhoo in London, Audrey's arrival in New York went unnoticed by the newspapers. Miller was keeping his publicity trump-card for opening night. As soon as she had settled into her tiny room at the Blackstone Hotel, arranged for her by Miller's wife, Kitty, the young woman on whose shoulders so much hope had been piled began rehearsals in earnest.

Cathleen Nesbitt, a veteran English character player of the British and American stage, who would celebrate her sixty-third birthday on *Gigi*'s Broadway opening, had already guided the young actress through her Paramount screen-test and, for the next three years, would be as untiring in her devotion to Audrey's Thespian tutelage as Audrey would be in receiving it. In an all-British cast comprising Michael Evans,

Josephine Brown, Bertha Belmore, Francis Compton and Doris Patston, Miss Nesbitt played Gigi's lovely and rich great-aunt Alicia de St Ephlam, who taught her sixteen-year-old schoolgirl niece, Gigi, how to eat lobster, how to distinguish between canary and blue diamonds, and how to make a man comfortable.

Audrey worked hard, just as Colette said she should, and tried to meet every challenge presented, though Miller's faith in her talents rapidly deteriorated the more he saw of her work. To help heighten her stage illusion as a very young girl, Audrey, who was already (to quote Paramount again) 'a little on the thin side', decided she must lose weight. She embarked on a strict, almost ruinous dieting course and, within a fortnight, managed to shed fifteen pounds. Miller saw what was going on and, fearful that an under-fed actress would hardly give of her best – especially when, in his eyes, her best was mediocre – decided prompt action was called for.

'Kitty, dear,' he wailed on the phone one afternoon, 'I want you to come over and watch a rehearsal with little Audrey Hepburn. She seems to conk out in the afternoon.'

The producer's wife was there within a quarter of an hour. 'Come on, Audrey,' she said, 'I'm taking you to lunch. You're going to have a good square meal and don't let me hear any of this dieting nonsense! How about a fat, juicy steak?'

Audrey, always quick to detect when something was wrong, worked harder than ever to please producer and playwright. When the rehearsals were finished each day, she continued with her acting lessons; she would arrive back at her apartment at nine or ten in the evening, dog-tired and ready, literally, to drop. But she was consumed by a completely singular ambition: to be a success in the play and, by definition, be a credit to Miller. This was vitally important to her, and so she avoided directing her energies at anything but the job in hand.

All, however, was still not well. Just before the show's preview opening at the Walnut Theatre in Philadelphia, Gilbert Miller was so convinced that she was incompetent that he was considering firing her. It was only because he had no one to replace her at such short notice that Audrey was retained. But Miller was in for a big surprise.

The reviews for the play itself were cool, yet the Philadelphia critics – and they come no tougher in the whole of the United States – acclaimed Audrey as 'the acting find of the year'. Philadelphia is America's top try-out town for new Broadway shows and its critics seldom guess wrong. Henry P. Murdoch, of the *Philadelphia Inquirer*, reported: 'She gives a wonderfully buoyant performance which establishes her as an actress of the first rank.'

While her producer did an about-turn and talked to the press about the utter and complete confidence he had always had in his young star, the star herself cabled the Baroness: 'Come over – we'll get a little flat, because I hope to be here a long time.' Although everyone who saw her was predicting that a new star would soon be shining in the Broadway heavens, the backers of the show were acutely aware that such forecasts often turn New York reviewers sour. And no one, least of all Audrey, could forget that there was still one further hurdle to surmount – namely, the critics known, not without good reason, as the 'Seven Butchers of Broadway'.

Audrey returned with the rest of the cast to New York in readiness for the big evening. In a room next to hers at the Blackstone was lodged Britain's debonair David Niven and his beautiful wife Hjördis. Niven, who had already made more than thirty films, would remember this period with great fondness: 'We were both staying in an inexpensive hotel, inexpensive for obvious reasons – neither of us had any money. I had been suspended and virtually blackballed by my boss, Samuel Goldwyn, and was "out" as far as the movies went, and Audrey was an "unknown" in the United States getting her first big break in *Gigi*. I was doing a play called *Nina* with Gloria Swanson, and Audrey and I shook with fear as our opening nights on Broadway drew inexorably nearer.

'I think we met when a body crashed down from the eighteenth floor and bounced off Audrey's windowsill on its way to the ground. Anyway, she rushed into our room and we later discovered that some poor man had committed suicide. However, our grisly beginning ripened into a long, long friendship. I was there with my wife, newly married, and Audrey was alone and, I think, very lonely. But she was cosseted by the people who were producing the play and who obviously knew, because they'd been trying out the show out of town, as we had, that they had a great big potential hit on their hands, both with the play and, of course, with Audrey.

'She was far more relaxed than I was, probably because she knew that she was headed for an immense triumph and I knew that I was headed for an absolute disaster. However, we both had the maximum amount of first-night nerves and panic to compete with. She always seemed divine, of course, to look at – and gave the impression of being vulnerable. Mark you, I think she was, because she was a very beautiful girl alone for the first time in that particular city and obviously she was being made much of; but she was wise enough, and had the inbred common sense, to spot the phonies who were clustered around her.'

Directed by the sympathetic Brussels-born actor of innumerable French films, Raymond Rouleau, with scenery by Raymond Sovey, *Gigi* finally opened at the Fulton Theatre, on 46th Street, on 24 November 1951. A friend from London, newsman Logan Gourlay, went backstage before curtain-up to wish her luck. 'I'll need more than luck,' she replied. 'You'll have to pray for a miracle.'

As it happened, she was right. And, to add to her nervousness, she was suffering from a bad dose of influenza. 'On the final scene rested the whole reason for the play being a play,' Audrey would recount, 'and right at the climax I forgot my lines and everything stopped. A whole speech was missed out. But I managed to pull round and last out until the final curtain.'

She got very little sleep at the Blackstone that night. Convinced that she had ruined the whole play, as well as her chances of becoming a star, she awoke to find that she had captivated all the critics to a man with her radiant performance. Walking out of the hotel that morning, on her way to the nearest newsstand to buy up all the papers, she bumped into David Niven on his way back. He was clutching a copy of the *New York Times*.

'Congratulations, darling!' he said, planting a kiss on her cheek. 'You're a sensation! Have you read what they're saying about you?'

'I'm just about to,' she said with a cautious grin.

'They're comparing you to Maude Adams and Laurette Taylor and suggesting that you should revive *Peter Pan*. What do you think of that?'

'I'm stunned.'

But the best was yet to come. At the theatre, Gilbert Miller was jubilant. He had cut out all the reviews and had spread them out proudly on his office desk. 'Let me kiss you, Audrey!' he said, beaming.

She sat down with Kitty and re-read the reviews. 'Audrey

Hepburn is a young actress of charm, honesty and talent,' commented Brooks Atkinson in the *New York Times*. Walter Kerr, in the *New York Herald-Tribune*, wrote that 'Miss Hepburn is as fresh and frisky as a puppy out of a tub. She brings a candid innocence and a tomboy intelligence to a part that might have gone sticky, and her performance comes like a breath of fresh air in a stifling season.' In the *New York World-Telegram and Sun*, William Hawkins observed that 'Audrey Hepburn in the title-role has unquestionable beauty and talent . . . and acts with grace and authority, if in this case without much relaxation.' The public, too, were no less impressed by her unique facial structure, her vitality, and her radiant acting.

Gilbert Miller was so ecstatic at the critical, public, and financial reception accorded his protégé that, a week later, he put her name up in lights and changed the order of the wording on the marquee. On opening night it had read:

GIGI
with
Audrey Hepburn

A week later it became:

AUDREY HEPBURN
in
GIGI

When Miller informed Audrey that he had put her name up in lights, she darted across the street to see if he was telling the truth. She looked up at the evidence and sighed: 'Oh dear, and I still have to learn how to act.'

It would be easy to interpret this exclamation as a burst of girlish modesty. Yet it was no secret at the time that she felt it was a fact – had not Miller reminded her of it just a month earlier – and so she was determined to correct the situation. Her acting tuition continued. For all that, Audrey was not so dewy-eyed that she was unaware of her status as a star. Her highly developed business mind would not let her forget it. From that moment on, as one writer put it, she 'was solely interested in consolidating her foothold in a heaven strewn with fallen stars.'

And consolidating her status meant work, work, work while adhering to a Spartan and disciplined schedule that worried her friends and often annoyed her critics. Instead of doing the

92

expected and participating in some after-theatre party life, she continued taking acting lessons with Cathleen Nesbitt. 'This training thing is a pose', declared one of her critics.

Although her natural reserve sometimes resented it, she accepted with good grace the demands made upon her time for photographs and stories about herself in magazines and newspapers. She rightly saw it as part of any successful actress's career. And yet newspapermen and fellow performers regarded her as a snob.

She responded to such criticisms by replying: 'I can't allow all this public acclaim to turn my head or induce me to ease up in working towards my life's ambition – to become a truly great actress.' She considered her situation. 'Acting doesn't come easy to me,' she maintained. 'I put a tremendous amount of effort into every morsel that comes out. I don't yet feel that I have enough experience or store of knowledge to fall back upon.'

Accusations that she was a snob would continue, yet in most instances they seem to have been founded on an imperfect knowledge of the young woman in question; or based, at any rate, on a misunderstanding of her motives. If she was not 'doing the town' after the show, it was because she was engaging her free time in trying to remedy her dramatic abilities (for prior to *Gigi* she had never even carried a maid's tray in a straight play), and not for any reasons associated with being a snob.

Her life, though, had changed and was continuing to change. By the third performance of *Gigi* she had removed the framed picture of Jimmy Hanson from her dressing-table – not because her heart had in any way fluctuated in those three days but because her life had entered a new and more difficult phase. 'So many people whom I hardly knew asked me what was his name and when were we going to be married,' she explained to a receptive ear, 'that I simply had to put the picture into a drawer. My private life is my own. How can I laugh off these questions without appearing rude?'

By not trying to laugh them off, or, at the very least, by not talking about Jimmy to her colleagues and the newspapers, she was already being labelled as 'stand-offish'. She was regarded not so much 'difficult' as 'coy'. No doubt to allay these accusations, and to respond to the growing speculation regarding her relationship with the 'mysterious' boy-friend, the following announcement appeared in the 'Forthcoming Marriages' column of the London *Times* of 4 December 1951:

Mr J. E. Hanson and Miss A. Hepburn: The engagement is announced between James, son of Mr and Mrs Robert Hanson, of Norwood Grange, Huddersfield, Yorkshire, and Audrey Hepburn, daughter of Baroness Ella van Heemstra, of 65, South Audley Street, London, W.1.

The press were now more than ever intrigued about this certain Mr James E. Hanson. Who was he? Far from crushing the media's curiosity, the *Times* announcement simply accentuated it. Requests for interviews were suddenly turned down – 'because of Miss Hepburn's pressure of work'. On top of this, she was steadfastly refusing to break into her time for social engagements during the week; and her weekends were devoted to Jimmy, whose haulage business kept him in Canada a great deal. If he couldn't fly to New York to be with her, as was frequently the case, she would grab a plane after the Saturday night performance and fly to him.

Their marriage was scheduled for early 1952 and would be held in Huddersfield. Invitations were duly sent out to 200 guests and Sharman Douglas, daughter of a former US Ambassador to Britain, was invited to be bridesmaid.

If the conditions under which they conducted their romance were not exactly ideal, they none the less worked hard to make it appear so. Pictures of the happy, smiling couple continued to be published in newspapers and magazines on both sides of the Atlantic. Theirs would be the wedding of the year.

Audrey, as Gigi, had now firmly asserted her irrefutable position as the toast of Broadway. As a result, the American producer and screenwriter, Collier Young, secured the US rights to *Monte Carlo Baby* and, with commendable perspicacity, released it to the nation through his Filmakers Company. Numerous New York art houses also jumped on the bandwagon by importing some of Audrey's early films, which must have made those who had not seen *Gigi* wonder what all the fuss was about. But the British film industry, as so often where prodigious home talent was concerned, was behaving like so many half-baked amateurs in a race adjudicated by sharp-witted, hard-bitten professionals. Not for nothing were Cary Grant, Jean Simmons, Bob Hope, Stewart Granger, Charlie Chaplin, James Mason, Charles Laughton, Vivien Leigh, Boris

94

Karloff, Julie Andrews, Glynis Johns, Deborah Kerr, and David Niven lost to Hollywood early in their careers.

In the year that Audrey would be making her first film for Paramount, Hollywood's top 'glamour' actresses included Betty Grable, Ava Gardner, Janet Leigh, Jane Russell, Esther Williams, Marilyn Monroe, Virginia Mayo, Debra Paget, Lana Turner, Shelley Winters, Ann Sheridan, Vera-Ellen, and Rita Hayworth. In little over a year the list would be boosted by Audrey's quite different brand of 'pure glamour'. She would be unique among her contemporaries, however, in being one of the few stars who dared to dispense with 'cheesecake' poses. Her views were simple: 'I think sex is overrated.'

Broadway audiences, meanwhile, had noticed that Audrey somehow managed to put more 'oomph' into a single hand-shake than most women could do with a less-subtle wiggle of their hips. That indefinable 'oomph' had also not been lost on London impresarios. Alluring offers of stage roles crossed the waters with almost tedious regularity, but the Broadway star was compelled to turn them all down with the explanation that she was 'too busy'. British film offers poured in, too, including an invitation to play Polly Peachum to Sir Laurence Olivier's highwayman Macheath in *The Beggar's Opera*; the film role eventually went to Dorothy Tutin. Again, Audrey was 'too busy'.

It was precisely this 'busy-ness' in her private life which was beginning to prove incompatible with the interests of Audrey's future husband. Their plans for an early marriage consequently grew increasingly dimmer as Audrey's career took her further and further away from him.

With her Broadway run in *Gigi* almost at an end, she was set to fly to Italy to make *Roman Holiday*, following the completion of which she would be returning to America to star in a road tour of *Gigi* in the Mid-West. There would be little time for romance. The arrangements for a wedding in Huddersfield were postponed until the winding-up of the film later in the year. It would take place in America.

'When I marry Jimmy, I want to give up at least a year to just being a wife to him,' Audrey told Radie Harris during one of their tea sessions. 'I can't do that now with the *Roman Holiday* film on location in Italy ahead of me, and then the road tour of *Gigi*. Jimmy is being wonderfully understanding about it. He *knows* it would be impossible for me to give up my career completely. I just can't. I've worked too long to achieve something. And so many people have helped me along the way, I don't want to let them down.'

And yet although her days were literally devoted to pursuing fame, fortune and her career, the true Hepburn personality was a welcome and surprising combination of all these qualities plus a warm and willing heart, a rare sense of the comic and a truly unique gift for making others feel that whatever she chose to do was right for her – if not always for them. She was strong and firm in character, and seemed to be never swayed to do the foolish or unkind thing. She was eager, quick and alert. Once she had summed up every aspect of a situation she went into action. 'Only those people who are absolutely definite succeed,' she would tell people. She was thorough, yet thoughtful. She was quick to pull the stops on anything which didn't hold up under her analysis. She would brook no phonies. She recoiled from flattery: 'That's right. Flattery will get you nowhere.' She liked to be liked, yet she wouldn't make a deliberate effort to have people like her. She would do nothing by impulse. Almost every action she took, almost every remark she made, was carefully thought out beforehand. She was her own woman.

When *Gigi* closed on Broadway in June, Audrey returned to London where, albeit briefly, she suddenly found herself with the leisure and the money to go to the theatre. She was avid to see everything. Lynn Fontanne and Alfred Lunt, at the time the most formidable acting team in the history of the American theatre, were playing at the Phoenix in Noël Coward's *Quadrille*.

Radie Harris takes up the story: 'I knew Audrey had never seen this magnificent team, so when Noël graciously sent me his house seats, I invited her to go with me. Of course, she was enthralled by their magic spell, and later, when I took her with me to the Lunts' dressing-room to meet them, she was like a wide-eyed child meeting Santa Claus for the first time. When Alfred talked to her about *Roman Holiday*, she was flabbergasted that the great Alfred Lunt had even heard about her.'

Before catching a plane for Rome she was asked what fame in New York had meant. 'I thought being the "Toast of Broadway" might mean people standing up and raising champagne glasses,' she reflected. 'But no one has ever done that. I thought it might mean sailing into restaurants when they were full and getting a table with just a smile at the head waiter. But Jimmy didn't risk it – he booked in advance. I thought it would be heady and fun seeing my name in lights for the first time. But it is not like being a success in the chorus. The rest of the show can help you there. When you are the lead it is no longer happy-go-lucky. You feel everything depends on you.' The large Hepburn eyes twinkled. 'Another thing about being called a star,' added Audrey. 'You can never feel tired any more – ever.'

Fame could be a wonderful feeling.

PART THREE

Hollywood romance:
Mel, marriage and leading men

Audrey: 'There's nothing tough about Mel! He's sweet and sensitive!'
(cartoon by Emmwood, from the London *Evening Standard*,
22 September 1956).

12

*'If I'm honest I have to tell you I still read
fairy-tales and I like them best of all.'*

WHETHER AUDREY HEPBURN was chosen for *Roman Holiday* or it was chosen for her, is a moot point. But the result was an alliance made in some cinematic heaven. The story called for a young beauty who could play an authentic princess – not the haughty faked regality of a musical comedy soprano who does it with a stiff spine and a rhinestone tiara, but rather a creature displaying the never-failing, bred-in-the-bones serenity of the genuine article; and in Audrey, probably the most convincing member of a mythical Royal Family ever to romp through a fictional adventure, the story got exactly what it needed.

'You could *believe* her as a princess,' declared William Wyler. 'If you hadn't known otherwise, you'd have assumed she was one.'

The timelessness of the picture's scenario was also extraordinary. It was a year for royalty, modern-style, all over the world, but especially in the English-speaking countries, where the most independently democratic citizens on earth permitted themselves to enjoy every elaborate detail of the coronation of Queen Elizabeth II; and, as the picture opened, the British queen's sister, Princess Margaret, was rocking the world by falling for a commoner, Group Captain Peter Townsend, equerry first to George VI, then to the deceased monarch's daughter, Elizabeth. In the public mind, *Roman Holiday* – about a pretty little princess who, while visiting a foreign country, eludes her attendants for twenty-four hours while having a madcap spree with American newspaperman Gregory Peck – became linked as an exact parallel with the Princess Margaret headlines from London.

So, by the happiest of coincidences, a public obviously in the mood to peer behind the scenes in palaces was being presented with the delightful fable of a princess who became (by the time the picture was half over) as absolutely true-to-life as any royal lady ever shown in the newsreels. The picture also had Rome. It was filmed entirely on location there . . . the fountains, the statues, the *palazzi*, the wide avenues, the Spanish Steps, the monuments, the venerable ruins. Audrey was a creature inspired.

Booked into one of Rome's best hotels ('Way over my head – I could never afford them before'), she told the press on the first day of filming that she was grateful for the opportunity to do a picture with William Wyler 'so early in my career'. She was making her first big-budget American movie, and she was determined to learn – fast. 'She gives you the distinct impression that she can spell schizophrenia,' noted an impish Wyler.

Very early in the filming Audrey experienced a new twist to the old saying, 'If you can't stand the heat, get out of the kitchen.' She was shooting some of the interiors in the Palazzo Brancaccio, a magnificent eighteenth-century palace situated in the heart of the city and decorated in flamboyant rococo, with huge, glittering chandeliers hanging from frescoed ceilings and satin-lined walls crawling with plump cupids.

As Princess Ann, beautiful heir-apparent to an unnamed throne, she was ensconced in the royal boudoir. The temperature outside was a stifling ninety-five degrees, but under the arc lamps of the princess's private chamber it sizzled up to a hundred and four. Matters were not helped by the cosy woollen nightdress in pink that she was required to wear. Unable to stand the heat a minute longer, she escaped into an adjoining room and flung open a window.

'Now I know,' she said, 'what it's like to be a star – it's warmer, more uncomfortable, and the hours are longer.'

The previous day she had filmed several ballroom sequences surrounded by forty-three bona fide European princesses, countesses, baronesses, and one impoverished duke, each of whom were paid 20,000 lire a day for six days instead of the usual 'extra' rate per day of 2,000 lire. The reason for the increased rate, apart from the prestige of shooting a grand ball

102

with authentic nobility, was that they brought their own costumes and jewellery.

But Audrey had yet to film a scene with co-star Gregory Peck, who had rented an opulent villa overlooking the valley's of vineyards near Albano, fifteen miles from Rome. He was there with his Finnish-born wife Greta and their three sons, Jonathan, eight, Steven, just six, and three-year-old Carey Paul, all of whom shared the delights of the exotic gardens and the marble swimming-pool filled from the gaping mouth of a Roman lady in plaster.

Peck, idol of a hundred million women, was at first as doubtful of Audrey's ability as she was herself. Within a few days of working with the young actress, Peck telephoned his agent, George Chasin.

'What's my billing?' he asked.

The agent was astounded. His client was the one big-name movie star on his books who rarely bothered about such egotistical things as the size of his name on the credits. 'Greg, you've got top of the bill as usual. Nobody can be billed above you and nobody can be billed with you.'

'Well,' Peck continued, 'you know the real star of this picture is Audrey Hepburn. It would be pretentious of me to take the billing alone. Go to the studio and tell them I want Audrey Hepburn to be billed on the same line.'

On Peck's behalf, Chasin sent the following cable to Hollywood: 'Suggest Audrey Hepburn is given co-star billing in *Roman Holiday*.'

The reply from Paramount production chief Frank Freeman was swift and to the point – and conscious, as ever, of the box office. 'Absolutely not,' he said. 'This is an unknown girl. Our job is to sell Gregory Peck.'

'Mr Freeman,' responded Chasin, 'you're going to have a very unhappy actor.'

Acutely aware that an unhappy Gregory Peck could be a bad omen for the picture, Freeman said: 'Leave it with me. I'll get back.'

Later that day he rang Chasin again. 'I've discussed the whole thing with my publicity department,' said Freeman. 'They're on Greg's side. They've decided to go along with the idea of projecting a new star. Audrey Hepburn gets co-star billing.'

By any standards, it was a rare and unusual gesture on Greg-

103

ory Peck's part. For actors, even modest, level-headed actors like Peck, are notorious for guarding their billing as zealously as they preserve their hair-lines.

Audrey first met Peck at a little cocktail party that Paramount gave for the crew just before *Roman Holiday* started shooting. Her initial impression of the handsome $120,000-a-picture star was essentially that of a young fan for an idol. As the weeks passed, the professional rapport of the star and the showgirl was plain enough for all to see. They got on well together, shared an instinctive feel for what would 'work' and what would not, and laughed a lot between takes. They made a good team, and they knew it.

'I'm enchanted with Greg,' she confided, 'because he's so marvellously normal, so genuine, so downright *real*! There's nothing of the "making-like-a-star" routine, no phoneyness in him.' To another, she said simply: 'Greg's a dear.'

Peck, in turn, was noting that 'Audrey is not the type who, bit by bit, turns to granite until they are a walking career.' She was also 'modest', he said, and, more cryptically, 'as lovable as an overstrung tennis racquet.'

The nature and quality of their rapport was by now being talked about as being much more than merely professional. Undoubtedly helping to stoke the embers of their rumoured romance was the fact that, while making the film, Peck's marriage was 'splitting ever more wide open' and that he was going through a great deal of personal torment. Halfway through the shooting period, Peck's wife Greta packed her bags to visit her family in Finland. 'At times like that,' observed his biographer, Michael Freedland, 'both realised they were happier apart than they were or ever could be together.'

The gossip about the alleged Peck–Hepburn romance would percolate for more than a year. For a while, the question of Audrey's engagement to Jimmy Hanson remained very much in the background, certainly as far as the outside world was concerned . . . though her wedding gown hung in a closet in Rome while she made *Roman Holiday*. Jimmy, feeling intuitively that all was 'not right' with regard to his own romance with Audrey, flew out to America to discuss matters with her. He was patient, calm, loyal, laughing off as 'absolute rubbish' the merest suggestion of a romantic liaison between his fiancée and Peck. But it was an unhappy and disillusioned bachelor who returned to Huddersfield a few weeks later. His patience was not limitless – and neither, come to that, was Audrey's. On 15 December 1952, an announcement said: 'The engagement between Mr James Hanson and Miss Audrey Hepburn has been broken.'

They both insisted that there had been no violent quarrel or rift. They had grown apart – professionally and geographically rather than emotionally. 'It occurred to me when the *Gigi* tour started and we were trying to arrange the wedding,' she told a friend, 'that if it was difficult to find time for the actual ceremony, what would it be like later on? I decided it would be unfair to Jimmy to marry him when I was also in love with, and tied to, my work. He agreed.'

To another confidant she related, 'When I found out that I didn't even have time to attend the furnishings of our London flat, I suddenly knew that I would make a pretty bad wife. I would forever have to be studying parts, fitting costumes and giving interviews. What a humiliating spot to put my husband in – making him stand by, holding my coat while I signed autographs.'

She reflected that it would be very difficult for them to lead what she referred to as 'a normal married life'. Other people in her position had tried it but it had rarely worked. 'The business of running a house is a fulltime job,' she said. 'What happens if I've been so busy cooking my husband's supper that I don't know my lines at rehearsal next day? I lose my job – and probably lose my husband, too.'

Quite simply, Audrey and Jimmy had careers to make. 'When we've made them,' she intoned with renewed confidence, 'we might talk again.' She paused momentarily. 'The time *will* come,' she insisted, 'when I can afford the luxury of a husband. Just now, I haven't got the time.'

In the course of time, Audrey issued an ambiguous one-sentence statement about her change of heart. 'When I get married,' she said, 'I want to be *really* married.' It was generally agreed after that by Audrey's friends that when she did marry, it would have to be to somebody in the theatre. Somebody who would *understand*.

Back in Hollywood, Audrey was discovering that her sparkling spinsterhood was becoming a source of fascination to the pedlars of hot air and scandal. She was a challenge to Tinsel Town.

Bing Crosby escorted her to a party – and the next day it was reported that a new romance was blossoming between the 'Old Groaner' and the young Golden Girl. She denied the liaison with an explosive 'No'.

Groucho Marx extended another Hollywood invitation to Audrey, which she happily accepted. The reports next day had her more or less engaged to the sixty-two-year-old funny-man; she was described as his 'mate'. 'Just nonsense,' responded Groucho. 'I don't want to be ungallant, but Audrey's too old and wrinkled for me.'

An enterprising Hollywood scribe, noting Audrey's sudden popularity among the film capital's big-name males, asked her outright if she was afraid of Hollywood wolves. 'Look, if you really want to know,' she answered, 'I think all men, at least all the men I've met, are harmless. Actually, I've never yet had to fight off a man!'

The tattlers, meantime, were still clocking-up considerable mileage with the latest lowdown on Gregory Peck's purported love for Audrey.

'I know all about those stories,' she told a *Photoplay* reporter. 'Who starts them? And how could they be true, especially when I'm so friendly with Greta? I saw her coming out of Romanoff's the other day, and she asked me to spend next Sunday swimming in the pool at her home. Does *that* sound like I'm a home-breaker?'

Peck, having moved to Paris for his next film, was drawn into the debate. 'I believe in the old maxim, "Never complain or explain,"' he said guardedly. 'All I want to say is that my family have gone to America because they were homesick. I have to stay on here to work. That's all.'

When the publicity campaign for *Roman Holiday* got under way in France, a dark-haired, lissom Parisienne named Veronique Passani interviewed Gregory Peck for her newspaper. Into her notebook she scribbled, '*Dined with G. tonight. He likes me. We eat by candle-light and he takes my hand in his. The hairs prickle on the back of his hand. He has sex, this one. I laugh because they all talk about Audrey Hepburn. Studio talk. He says so. Why else would he be with me? I think I am beginning to fall in love. . . .*'

On his visits to London, Peck lived a quiet, respectable life in a rented Grosvenor Square apartment. He availed himself of a wonderful Hungarian cook, who not only dished up the most delectable food for her boss, but also for such friends as the Leo Genns, Ronald Neame, and the many other pals Peck had acquired in Britain since making *Captain Horatio Hornblower*. It was also 'home' for one of his closest friends, American actor Mel Ferrer, whenever he was in town.

Having completed her exhausting road tour of *Gigi*, ending in Los Angeles, where Paramount had given her a gala party, Audrey arrived in London for a well-earned break. Learning that she was back at her South Audley Street apartment with the Baroness, Peck threw a 'welcome home' cocktail shindig for his latest, yet-to-be-seen co-star. Also there was Mel Ferrer, who was filming *Knights of the Round Table* at Elstree with Audrey's old tutor, Felix Aylmer. Ferrer and Peck enjoyed a common burning passion. For years, in the company of Dorothy McGuire, Joseph Cotten and Jennifer Jones, they nursed an ambition to bring legitimate theatre to the California coast on an annual summer-season basis – a dream which by then had already become a remarkably dull reality at the La Jolla Playhouse.

'We began talking about the theatre,' Ferrer would fondly recall of his first meeting with Audrey. 'She knew all about the La Jolla Playhouse Summer Theatre, where Greg and I had been co-producing plays for years. She also said she'd seen me three times in the movie *Lili*. Finally, she said she'd like to do a play with me, and she asked me to send her a likely script if I found one.'

With Mel and Audrey, it was instant attraction. 'A sensitive man with a sensitive face,' she thought as she listened to him. 'I could love him.'

'Is it any wonder that Mel Ferrer fell head over heels in love with such a provocative, desirable creature?' Radie Harris asked herself. 'Mel has always been attracted to glamorous, successful women.' But the chemistry worked both ways. 'I can also understand why Audrey succumbed to Mel's charm,' continued the actress's old friend. 'Because Mel has that rare quality in an American male: he makes a woman feel like a woman.'

The next evening, Mel took Audrey to the theatre. Nobody attached any importance to it, because at that time there was no reason to do so. They were not openly 'in love'.

And so, for a while, Audrey's 'romance' with Peck still occupied the minds of the society gossips. It all came to a head when Greta gave a party for Audrey in Hollywood. Following the party, one tattle-tale murmured: 'I wonder if Greta knows about all those dinners Audrey and Greg had together in London?' Well, she had ears, and she could read.

107

By this time, Peck's patience had run out, and so had his belief in the 'Never complain or explain' maxim. It was time to talk. He said it was 'ridiculous' to connect him romantically with Audrey – 'unfair', indeed, to link her good name with a married man. But he would be a married man for not very much longer – and, indeed, when making the 'ridiculous' statement, he and Greta had been separated for eight months. Their divorce came through little more than a year later – Greta alleged that he 'stayed away from home nights' – and the following year, the actor married the French journalist who came to interview him in Paris, Veronique Passani, and she gave him two more lovely children.

Audrey, however, was adamant in repeating that *she* was much too career-minded to get married for some time. 'I dropped the idea of one marriage because it would have intruded on my acting,' she said, 'and there's little reason to suppose I'll change my mind until I really feel I'm a very good actress. I have a long way to go.'

13

'There's a very big division between what's in the public's eye and what you feel about yourself. I never saw in myself what other people saw in me.'

AUDREY, NEVER AN enthusiastic partygoer, now found in her brief London interlude that not only was she attending numerous shindigs, but she was also giving them. *Roman Holiday* had not yet been released, but that was only a few weeks away; she was being interviewed and photographed by magazines and newspapers, and appearing on radio and television. The publicity machine was set in motion. She was news.

Among the guests at one party held at her South Audley Street flat was the designer and photographer Cecil Beaton, who was welcomed at the door by the Baroness – 'a lady with a rather charming rolling accent'. Presently, Mel Ferrer arrived – 'a charming, gangling man,' perceived Beaton, 'who, no doubt as a result of his theatrical career, has developed a slightly professional charm of manner.' He described Audrey to Beaton as 'the biggest thing to come down the turnpike'.

At last, the room now filled with film people, Audrey made her entrance. The designer noted her 'huge mouth, flat Mongolian features, heavily painted eyes, a coconut coiffure, long nails without varnish, a wonderful lithe figure, a long neck, but perhaps too scraggy.'

'Today's stars are brought from a different stratum of life,' he entered in his diary the following morning. 'Audrey's enormous potential cinema success, with attendant salary, seem to have made little impression on this delightful human being. She appears to take wholesale adulation with a pinch of salt:

gratitude rather than puffed-up pride. Everything very simple about and around her: no maid to help her dress, or to answer the door to the guests.

'In a flash I discovered Audrey Hepburn is chock-a-block with spritelike charm, and she has a sort of waifish, poignant sympathy. Without any of the preliminaries I felt that she cut through to a basic understanding that makes people friends. Nothing had to be explained: we liked one another. A chord had been struck and I knew that, next time we met, we would continue straight from here with no recapitulation of formalities. This was a unique occasion.'

Their paths would indeed cross again, many times, but eventually with momentous consequence.

Audrey's biggest problem in life was that, at this stage, she was a 'publicity success'. The big men in show business were so confident of her appeal that they beat the big drum hard for her. 'She's the most exciting thing to hit Hollywood since Garbo and her namesake Katharine,' gushed Sam Goldwyn; and, predicted Sol Siegel, 'She'll be the biggest star in Hollywood within two years.'

It should be mentioned that independent producer Goldwyn and 20th Century-Fox's Siegel had no financial interest in the Hepburn future – unlike Don Hartman. 'The greatest we've had since Jean Harlow,' murmured the Paramount boss, as well he might. 'That girl is going to be the biggest star in all Hollywood,' concurred Wyler.

Back in Britain, executives at Associated British were smiling and rubbing their hands. It would have taken them years to build up Audrey to full star status in Britain; and now, by giving her Gregory Peck, William Wyler and a first-class film, those nice people at Paramount were doing it for them. The ABC gamble had come off. Her value was about to rocket. By the time Elstree found a part suitable for Audrey she would have made at least one more film for Paramount and – taking into account the great stock of attendant publicity – would be worth her weight in dollars and pounds in the States and Britain. The laymen of Elstree would then pluck her back to Britain and proceed to make use of her accrued talents and reputation.

While Hollywood fought to have her play the life story of Twenties revue star Gertrude Lawrence (which went to Julie Andrews fifteen years later), Audrey patiently read every script that ABC gave her. But, despite her eagerness to make a film in England, she would not chance something which she felt was not appropriate to her personality. It was precisely for this reason that she turned down a proposition by ABC to cast her in a bio-pic of Lancashire's inimitable singer-comedienne Gracie Fields.

A flop for her first major film in Britain would be disastrous, she said repeatedly; too many potential stars had slipped back into obscurity due to bad management and poor material. Audrey resolved it would not happen to her. She continued to turn down the scripts from Elstree who, to their credit, were letting her use her own judgement. The studio's own judgement, however, was another matter. It did not seem to occur to anybody that if Audrey was big enough for Hollywood she was good enough to have a script written especially for her. In many respects, ABC was still run by amateurs.

When *Roman Holiday* finally opened in August, on both sides of the Atlantic, it turned out to be exactly the right kind of tale for the launching of the Hepburn image on the screen. For a day, tired and endlessly shaking hands and replying to speeches, her princess does all the things princesses are not supposed to do. She drinks champagne at a pavement café, rides on the back of commoner Peck's motor-scooter, takes over the controls and faces a dangerous-driving charge, gazes in shop windows, licks an ice-cream cone, and goes dancing on a barge where she is involved in a fight. By the end of the day she and reporter Peck have fallen in love, but they kiss and part.

It is the oldest story in the world, but, with it, she exploded across the American consciousness like a beautiful skyrocket. Men found in her the combination of loveliness, perception and intensity that poets sang of, and women saw why. Young girls copied her hair-do and her shirt-waist and even attempted to imitate the way she used her eyes. This was no glossy product of the Hollywood glamour mill – no Galatea fashioned by hairdressers, voice coaches, masseurs, dentists and dieticians. She had imperfections. She was a modern royal princess, but, watching her, perceptive audiences knew with certainty that she could be Camille, or Juliet, or Peter Pan. She could have been Scarlett O'Hara – and, one day, she might be a strong and touching Joan of Arc.

Britain's reaction to the film, the only taste they had had of

111

the new Audrey Hepburn dish, was warm but controlled. The newspaper columnists noted that she had a face of remarkable mobility; also that she was now able to establish audience contact with the ease and rapidity of a baby.

But *Roman Holiday* achieved for Audrey what they all said it would: it made the whole world hers. And nowhere in the world was success worshipped more fervently than in Hollywood. Everyone wanted to meet her. The local and foreign newspapermen, all of them, wanted exclusive interviews. Paramount spread out the red velvet carpet for their new queen.

Adolph Zukor, founder of the Paramount empire, was the screen world's greatest single star-maker. He was the man who made Mary Pickford, Gloria Swanson, Douglas Fairbanks, Rudolph Valentino, Pola Negri, and Marlene Dietrich. And now he was confident he had made Audrey Hepburn. 'If Miss Hepburn gets the roles to suit her,' he maintained, 'she will be the greatest actress the screen has ever seen.'

And what did Audrey think? 'She was scared,' Radie Harris noted. 'She was grateful for the recognition of her work, of course – but she was *scared*. To begin with, she couldn't believe she was *that* good, and this was no false modesty. She was really petrified by the blaze of public interest in which she suddenly found herself.'

Yet despite all the ballyhoo surrounding her arrival on the international movie scene, the film itself was a financial disappointment to Paramount, which had shelled out nearly £750,000 and made a profit in the first eight months of only £300,000. The studio expected to do much better than that – had hoped, in fact, to make a clear two or three million pounds profit. 'We can't find out what went wrong,' Don Hartman lamented. 'Everyone liked the picture,but it just didn't make them go out and seize hold of their friends and force them to go in and see it too.'

But Hollywood, like Freud and all the salesmen of America, believed that sex was at the root of everything. A prominent bustline would break down the most stubborn sales resistance. There was only one answer, and it was the oldest Hollywood trick of all. It had just happened to Claire Bloom, and now it was Audrey's turn. She fell victim to The Poster Stunt. Her face was superimposed on the voluptuous contours of busty 'sexpot' starlet Terry Moore, whose undulating charms had recently been displayed in another Paramount film, *Come Back, Little Sheba*.

A small movie-house in Berkeley, California, hearing that *Roman Holiday* was manna for the critics and small oats for the box-office, gladly availed itself of the poster flaunting the 'doctored' pose of Audrey Hepburn. It paid off. Attendances that week broke a two-year record. The same thing happened wherever the poster was exhibited.

The Poster Stunt came to Audrey's attention by accident. She had bought a newspaper at an airport kiosk and, *en route* from Los Angeles to New York, saw an advertisement in the paper for *Roman Holiday*. She blinked. The face was hers – but the body? She was not amused. It was promptly withdrawn. But Terry Moore did not mind. 'Gee,' she said, 'I feel flattered. Hope it does as much for me as it did for Audrey.'

What *Roman Holiday* achieved for Audrey's career, in fact, could be likened to the prime accomplishment of a rollercoaster: it gained momentum. In Britain, the *Sunday Express* dubbed her the 'Golden Girl of the Year'; another national newspaper chose her as 'Star of the Year', and yet another named her 'Woman of the Year'. Additionally, *Life*, the American picture weekly, devoted its cover and eight inside pages to Audrey Hepburn, again the 'Golden Girl of the Year'.

Jean Simmons, who was the original choice for the role of Princess Ann, and who vowed she would never go to see the film, none the less sneaked into a cinema where it was showing. Later that day she telephoned Audrey: 'Miss Hepburn, my name is Jean Simmons.' Pause. 'Thank you, Miss Hepburn. I've just seen *Roman Holiday* and, although I wanted to hate you, I have to tell you I wouldn't have been half as good. You were just wonderful.'

She hung up, and realizing that her husband, Stewart Granger, had been listening, sat down beside him. 'I meant it, darling,' she told him. 'She was better than I could have been and I wanted to tell her so. D'you know she told me she'd been a fan of mine for years. Wasn't that sweet?'

When Oscar-time came round, London and Hollywood held their ceremonies on the same night for the first time ever – and Audrey swept the board in both. The British Film Academy in London and the Academy of Motion Picture Arts and Sciences in Los Angeles each named her the best actress of 1953. Similar honours were bestowed on her by British movie-goers (the *Pic-*

turegoer Annual Award), by the New York film critics, and by the film critics of the whole of America: the year's leading film actress.

'This means more to me than any other award I could hope to attain,' she said of her British Academy citation. But this was a few hours before learning that she had also run off with a Hollywood Oscar. What could top that?

Someone at the Oscar awards asked her what she would do next.

'I still have the same goal,' she replied with a smile.

'To be a great actress?' she was prompted.

'Yes, to be a really *good* one.' She then declared: 'It's the second big film which will prove if I was really worthy of the first.'

14

'I could become lyrical about Mr Bogart. I admire him tremendously.'

'*B*OGIE' WENT AROUND acting like Humphrey Bogart and possessed a great faculty for getting people embarrassed, upset and downright angry. You could say it was his 'trade mark'. Jack L. Warner, of Warner Bros, was adamant: 'Bogart's a tough guy, not a lady's man.' And Paramount had chosen him to be Audrey's next leading man. It was like casting Tom with Jerry. Two more dissimilar types would have been difficult to find: the veteran screen hoodlum with the rasping voice set against the innocent new screen goddess with the sweet-sounding vowels. It was mixing black with white, rough with refined, serenity with perturbation. Bogie with Audrey.

It might have been laudable if, for *Sabrina*, the studio had deliberately concocted a plot to bring together such an unlikely co-starring combination for the sheer hell of seeing sparks fly. Yet the film, known as *Sabrina Fair* in Britain, had been conceived initially as a vehicle for Cary Grant, the script specifically tailored for his debonair personality. When Grant had to pull out at the last minute, the only big-name star currently available was Bogart, and debonair was never an adjective which sat easily on his shoulders. No amount of frantic rewrites, either, could accommodate the replacement star, who was an actor more familiar as a private eye or an idealistic recluse than as a business magnate in a frothy screen comedy. 'He was in totally unfamiliar territory,' said Wilder, 'and very uncomfortable.'

It was Bogart's least-happy film and, because of it, he

seemed hell-bent on making life miserable for everyone around him. His open hostility toward director-writer Billy Wilder and co-stars William Holden and Audrey spelled a bad omen for the screen adaptation of Samuel Taylor's hit stage comedy.

Up to a point, Bogart's unhappiness with the film was well-founded, since every single piece of wit which the stage version possessed had been ruthlessly cut by Wilder – Bogart, indeed, is said to have accused Wilder's three-year-old offspring of being responsible for the script. What remained of the original was Audrey, as the daughter of a chauffeur to a millionaire Long Island family, playing out a limp Cinderella story in which she got, in the end, not the younger playboy son (Holden), but the older and much richer one, played by Bogart with a tired but efficient despair which suggested that he was bored with the whole picture.

The one consolation was that Audrey was condemned to sparkle alone, which she did, like soda water. She was photographed from every conceivable angle, wearing Paris fashions with the awkward, unfeminine grace of any popular, sharp-hipped fashion model. All things considered, she played her sadly unrewarding part with great care, like a gazelle put into a circus and made to do tricks.

What did little to help the mood on the set, at least as far as Bogart was concerned, was that Audrey, Holden and Wilder had all won Oscars that year, and, he felt, illogically, that they were all behaving like juvenile 'smarty pants'. Audrey, anyway, immediately wrote her way into his 'bad book' when she commented that he seemed to be extremely nervous during their romantic scenes. His pride was hurt.

'He was always touchy about his pride, not in his artistry but in his competence,' said Alistair Cooke, an old friend, 'and competence was something he greatly admired in any field . . . he measured all his fellow workers by the test of professionalism.'

'He had the occupational insecurity of most actors,' added Lauren Bacall, the last of his four wives. 'He was never sure when he would work again.'

So Audrey, having inadvertently touched a couple of sensitive nerve-ends, labelled 'pride' and 'insecurity', became a ready-made target for Bogart's missiles.

'How do you like working with that dream girl?' the waspish Clifton Webb asked him one day.

116

'She's okay,' he replied morosely, 'if you like to do thirty-six takes.'

The question was asked on a bad day. Although Audrey still benefited from a certain amount of careful directorial attention in what, after all, was only her first Hollywood-based film, she never required more takes than her more celebrated co-stars. 'In my case,' director Fred Zinnemann would note five years later, 'she never needed more than one or two takes; but with *Sabrina* she was still learning.'

But Wilder had such a high opinion of Audrey's intelligent judgement that he consulted his young star on which takes to select after each day's work on the set. He became not just her mentor but her great friend who, in a moment of inspired foresight, would predict: 'This girl, single-handed, will make bust measurements a thing of the past.'

Audrey herself felt she was ideally suited for the part: 'Sabrina was a dreamer who lived a fairy tale and she was a *romantic*, an incorrigible romantic, which I am. I could never be cynical. I wouldn't dare. I'd roll over and *die* before that.'

Audrey, who was still green when it came to on-set feuds, found herself caught inextricably in the crossfire between Bogie's bitter quarrels with Wilder on the one hand, and Bogie's even more lethal battles with Holden on the other. Bogart was convinced that Wilder was trying to make it Holden's picture, and so the offended party began claiming that Holden 'mugged' in scenes and that he was at best a mediocre actor; and behind his back, he referred to him mockingly as 'Smiling Jim' – an allusion to all the 'useless, juvenile parts' on which Holden had cut his movie-acting teeth. The two actors had fallen out fourteen years earlier while making *Invisible Stripes*; but these new gibes and accusations incensed Holden so intensely that he threatened to kill Bogart, and it was only by being physically restrained by Wilder that he was prevented from carrying out the threat. From that day, Holden used every opportunity to malign Bogart's name in the press.

Trapped in the thick of so much verbal and physical animosity, Audrey went to work each day with a heavy heart. At Paramount she usually travelled around the lot on a green bicycle – a present from Wilder – which she propped up outside her dressing-room (previously Dorothy Lamour's exclusive property): dressing-rooms at Paramount opened straight on to the road. On one side she had Dean Martin and Jerry Lewis as

117

neighbours, while on the other there was Danny Kaye, all of whom parked their big chesty Californian cars right outside.

'It's just as well that bicycles don't suffer from inferiority complexes!' cracked Audrey.

A movie journalist who visited her at the studios noted that she moved round her dressing-room like a cat – 'gracefully, proudly, a trifle arrogantly'. He could not know, of course, that the 'arrogance' was simply a bi-product stemming from a lack of belief in her own stature as a 'celebrity'. 'You sit up and take notice,' he went on, 'because her arrival is like a blare of trumpets. This is an actress in the grand manner: another Garbo, Bette Davis, Katie Hepburn, Greer Garson, Joan Crawford, or who-have-you. This is *it!*'

Off the set, Audrey lived alone in a little two-room apartment on Wilshire Boulevard, which could be classified as the Hollywood equivalent of a Kensington bedsitter. But it boasted rather better plumbing, plus a few extra mod. cons – like a dining alcove with Regency décor and an inviting sun patio where she learned her lines at night. At $120 a month, the rental was low for those parts, though it was all she could afford; her salary was still not much above $800 a week – but that was about to change. 'It's fun to unlock my door and find the new record that the store down the street has delivered during the afternoon,' said Audrey. 'I get into old, soft, comfy clothes and then I play the new music while I cook' – her tastes in music ranged from modern jazz to *Rigoletto* and Brahms' Second Symphony. 'Oh, I love to cook,' she continued. 'I'm into steaks. Boy, those Californian sirloin steaks!' Another speciality was cheese soufflé.

In Hollywood, as in New York, Audrey resisted invitations by being determinedly aloof. At home, she told everybody, she liked to have most of her time to herself. 'I have to be alone very often,' she told her disappointed hosts. 'I'd be quite happy if I spent Saturday night to Monday morning alone in my apartment. That's how I refuel.'

A friend who visited her one evening at the apartment found her to be 'a confusing but captivating amalgam of adolescent gaiety and adult gravity'. She did her own cooking and housework – but she did not know how to mix her guest's requested Martini. Eventually having prepared the drink 'with the enthusiasm of a deb. uncorking her first bottle of champagne,' she retreated to her small kitchen 'with the self-conscious air of a young spinster experimenting in the role of hostess.'

118

Despite all outward appearances to the contrary, Audrey was still very much the little-girl-lost in the dark, dangerous forest that was Hollywood. She had yet to acquire the confident persona of The Star; and working with Bogart was not the environment to generate such self-confidence. She seemed to irritate him like a flea irritates a dog; he scratched occasionally, but she was always there. 'I was rather terrified of Humphrey Bogart – and he knew it,' she would confess many years later.

Bogart, in turn, when forced to voice an opinion of his leading lady for publicity purposes, was inspired to heights of unaccustomed coyness by pronouncing her 'elfin' and 'bird-like'. 'Audrey is like a good tennis player,' said Bogart. 'She is unpredictable, interesting and varies her shots.'

William Holden, who adored Audrey with even more fervour than he hated Bogart, watched over her like a guardian angel. 'Before I even met her, I had a crush on her,' Holden said later, 'and after I met her, just a day later, I felt as if we were old friends, and I was rather fiercely protective of her, though not in a possessive way. Most men who worked with her felt both fatherly or brotherly towards her, while harbouring romantic feelings about her. She may be more classy than the girl next door,' he then added, 'but she's always been a dish. I think people love her off the screen for the same reason they love her performances – a kind of orderliness and formality.'

The film was constantly in the throes of script re-writes. One night, while working late on some new dialogue for the following day's filming, scriptwriter Ernie Lehman strolled unannounced into Holden's dressing-room – to find Holden and Audrey 'standing a foot apart, facing each other, their eyes meeting'. An embarrassed scriptwriter, apologising for the intrusion and bidding goodnight, did a quick about-turn and departed, noting that 'something profound was happening between the two of them'.

Holden was not a free-wheeling Hollywood stud. He liked his women, and his women invariably liked him, but he possessed very definite ideas about what he looked for and expected in his lady-loves. Audrey embodied the lot and, besides, she was a young woman, eleven years his junior – a very important consideration in his list of priorities.

With Audrey he had found his match: beauty allied with intelligence and sensitivity. A powerful, irresistible combina-

119

tion. As his marriage to Ardis Holden was on the verge of splitting wide open, his mind turned increasingly to his latest leading lady. She, it seems, was receptive and even reflected, says Holden's biographer, Bob Thomas, 'that they could make beautiful babies together'. But in that direction there would be a fundamental problem. It would be impossible for Holden to sire any further babies. At twenty-nine, after he had given Ardis two sons, he underwent a vasectomy operation.

But still he pursued Audrey, and would continue to do so long after work ceased on *Sabrina*. In the course of time, however, Audrey's admiration would be directed towards another leading man, and he would become her husband. Holden eventually got the message that, as far as Audrey was concerned, she was out of his life for ever.

Many years later, while at work in Mexico on *The Wild Bunch*, he confessed openly for the first time about how Audrey's love for another man drove him to despair. 'I was really in love with Audrey but she wouldn't marry me. So I set out around the world with the idea of making love to a woman in every country I visited. My plan succeeded. When I got back to Hollywood, I went to Audrey's dressing-room and told her what I had done. You know what she said? "Oh, Bill!" That's all. "Oh, Bill!" Just as though I were some naughty boy. What a waste!'

In spite of the off-camera shenanigans, *Sabrina* was generally regarded as a successful comedy-romance, though *Films and Filming* magazine was less than happy with Audrey's performance. 'Surely the vogue for asexuality can go no further than this weird hybrid with butchered hair,' it said of her. 'Of course, none of this would really matter if the charm and grace were sincere, but she is letting her calculation show. The toothy grins are pure Ann Blyth and the coo-ings are a direct borrowing from Joan Greenwood.'

But Audrey's efforts were otherwise well received, Bosley Crowther of the *New York Times* perceiving that 'her fragile, bewitching charm and grace flows beautifully into the character of the chauffeur's lovely daughter'. And Edith Head, then doyenne of Hollywood's costume designers, who won an Oscar for *Roman Holiday* – and who would do so again with *Sabrina* – designed a dress for Audrey which would influence the world. Its distinguishing factor was what became known as the 'Sabrina Neckline' – 'but only because it was designed for a *chic* woman like Audrey,' insisted Miss Head. 'If it had been worn by somebody with no *chic* it would never have become a style.'

Audrey, too, was again nominated for an Academy Award, though she was up against four particularly strong contenders: Judy Garland for *A Star is Born*, Dorothy Dandridge for *Carmen Jones*, Jane Wyman for *Magnificent Obsession,* and Grace Kelly for *The Country Girl* – and Monaco's future Princess Grace ran off with the prize.

While her greatest weakness was still a tendency to cuteness, Audrey's greatest asset was unquestionably her magnetism. It refused to be ignored. In the inner circles of the film world, consequently, she was causing more talk than Marilyn Monroe. Of course, the skies over Hollywood had exploded with new stars time and time again – *femmes fatales* like Pola Negri, sturdy peasants like Anna Sten, calendar girls like La Monroe, and dignified actresses like Deborah Kerr – but Audrey could not be accommodated by any of the clichés. She was both waif and woman of the world. She was disarmingly friendly and strangely aloof. She was all queen and all commoner. You could imagine her lifting a *lorgnette* at a ball or milking a cow in a barn. In New York they called her *soignée* and *ravissante* and a lot of other fancy French names. In Hollywood they called her a 'slick chick'. The truth, perhaps, was that Audrey had brought to the screen and the stage a quality that was not dependent on being a symbol of sin, sex or purity. Like all great actresses she had the consummate ability to bridge the gap between herself and her audiences and make her inner feelings instantly known and shared.

The part which Fate played in bringing Audrey to international stardom may partially have accounted for her ultimate philosophy that it was silly to worry about the future – beyond being ready to meet the challenge. She was certain that if you did your best every day, and learned all you could about your profession, big things were bound to come your way. She recognised that a star *must* be a consistently good performer who knew all the angles of her craft. So she continued to work and study, with perfection as her goal. There were those, however, who felt that that very perfection could work against her.

Billy Wilder was such a person. 'Audrey may be too good for some people,' he said. 'Or she may get lost in the whirling technical revolution going on in the movies just now. That would be too bad. There is no one like her.' He chewed on his cigar: 'After so many drive-in waitresses in movies, here is class.'

15

*'My first dream was to be a ballet dancer. I
didn't know about success at all. You can only
hope to get a combination of happy work and a
happy life.'*

*A*UDREY SEEMED TO glow as she drafted a wire to
Radie Harris: 'Darling Radie, now that the play is all set, I'm able to
give you the good news. It's *Ondine*, and guess who is going to direct
me – Alfred Lunt! Needless to say, I am happy beyond words,
especially at being given the opportunity to work for, and learn from
him. How wonderful that you introduced me to him in London.
Much love, Audrey.'

While still at work on *Sabrina*, Mel Ferrer had sent Audrey a copy
of Jean Giraudoux's romantic fantasy play, *Ondine*, about a man
who is engaged to a girl to whom he is devoted, a girl of the social
world and the comfortable world. Yet he is distracted by another
girl, who comes from the spirit world, the world of excitement. His
commonsense takes him to Bertha, the dark girl, but his heart drives
him to Ondine, the light girl. And between the two he is destroyed.

Mel had seen *Ondine* in Paris, and it did not take long to persuade
Audrey that she would be the perfect heroine to his 'knight errant'.
She became tremendously excited, in fact, and agreed to appear in it
immediately after *Sabrina* was completed. Actor-director Alfred
Lunt, unknown to Audrey, had consented to direct the play on the
sole condition that she could be got for the lead. With Audrey in the
role, any management would have grabbed the property, and the
fabulously successful Playwrights' Company of Broadway were the
lucky winners. In appreciation of Mel's 'package deal', Audrey said
she would not only share co-star billing with him, but would insist
on splitting her percentage of the profits with him.

For all his handsomeness, charm and intelligence, Mel Ferrer had

had a curiously chequered career. Once called 'the nerve in perpetual motion', for reasons which will become apparent, he had arrived in Hollywood after stints as a writer of children's books, a publisher's editor, a radio commentator and disc-jockey, a film producer and director, and a dancer on Broadway.

Born in Elberon, New Jersey, on 25 August 1917 – Audrey's senior by almost twelve years – Mel was the son of a prominent Cuban-born New York City surgeon and a Manhattan-Newport socialite, attending prep school and Princeton University but dropping out in his sophomore year to become, after winning a playwright's award, an actor in summer stock. He was a movie actor when he met Audrey, having played a black physician who passes for a white in *Lost Boundaries*, a toreador in *The Brave Bulls* and a lame, morose puppeteer to Leslie Caron's French orphan in *Lili*.

He and his first wife, the sculptress Frances Pilchard, had loved so deeply that after divorcing, they remarried. He had a son and daughter by that marriage, a son and daughter and another divorce by his second to Barbara Tripp. When Mel first met Audrey at Gregory Peck's London apartment, he was again estranged from Frances, who then had no immediate plans for a second divorce. Word soon reached her, however, that a certain 'rapport' had developed between her husband and the leading lady of *Roman Holiday*. She wasted no time in suing for divorce.

Audrey had found an apartment in Westwood Village, which she shared with her newly acquired secretary, Helen Goodman, plus a few cage birds and two poodles. According to William Fields, press representative for the *Ondine* company, Audrey 'did not profess to be a housekeeper'. She was 'fascinated by the displays of pottery' in the New York stores and still found it 'exciting to buy food'.

As Audrey and Mel plunged into rehearsals in New York, they became more and more inseparable, on-stage and off, though they would repeatedly deny all rumours of a romance. It was not difficult to understand the bond that had brought them together. There was first of all the question of the attraction of opposites: he was as outward-going as she was shy, as strongly masculine as she was softly feminine. And then, besides Audrey's undeniable allure and innate breeding, and Mel's well-practised charm which had hit Cecil Beaton so forcibly between the eyes, they were both fired in their careers by a relentless ambition.

Unlike Audrey, however, Mel was driven by ambition the way a shark is driven by its stomach acids to eat everything in sight. Long before meeting Audrey he had become known in Hollywood as the man who could not sit still. While others were having a hard time assuring themselves of one career, he was propelling himself in all directions: actor, director, theatre manager, businessman. His telephonitis was worse than a teenager's, and at nightclubs he was always waving to somebody across the room or getting up to table-hop. He was the nerve in perpetual motion. 'I often wonder,' mused one of his early associates, 'what Mel finds to keep himself busy while he's asleep.'

The answer, perhaps, was dreams – and in Audrey he evidently saw his dream, walking. She was ambition incarnate – *his* ambition. Through Audrey he saw his way to the stars, to the heady glittering solar system that always, somehow, seemed to elude his particular orbit. But it had to be *his* way. When they first met at Peck's party, Mel was still basking in the glow of his modest success in *Lili* – but Audrey's subsequent triumph in *Roman Holiday* suddenly pushed his career, by comparison, two rungs below hers. 'As so often happens,' surmised their mutual friend at that time, Robert Flemyng, 'Mel's success in *Lili* didn't quite bear the fruits which he might have hoped for and, in the course of time, he was not pleased to be Mr Hepburn.'

In the past, as a director, Mel had made his colleagues dizzy with his acrobatic gyrations; as an actor, upstaged them into fury. His talent for inducing rage and rancour among his fellow workers reached new heights during rehearsals for *Ondine*.

'Alfred Lunt was fairly discreet about everything,' said a fellow actor, 'but his wife, Lynn Fontanne, was outraged by Mel's behaviour and – as she always did – expressed her disapproval with considerable candour. Both Lynn and Alfred felt that Audrey had been (not surprisingly) influenced too profoundly by him, an influence they clearly thought was not to her advantage.'

But the play itself, despite the backstage arguments, was a triumph. At its dignified, upper-crust Boston preview, first-nighters applauded and shouted 'Bravo' for twenty minutes. One critic telephoned his newspaper: 'This show will probably be known from now on as *The Audrey Hepburn Show.*' The Boston *Globe* added: 'Audrey Hepburn is all magic in her ballet dancer's body and in the music of her voice.'

The most distinguished ermine-and-white-tie gathering of 1954 flocked to New York's 46th Street Theatre the night *Ondine* opened, on 18 February. Waiting in the wings for her entrance, Audrey experienced a terrible attack of first-night nerves. During the days leading up to the Broadway opening a stubborn cold had plagued her, and now she was petrified that she might lose her voice altogether. But Audrey, as usual, underrated her powers of reserve, that same willpower and tenacity that had steered her safely through the siege of Arnhem – underrated, too, her special magic.

That night she was the water-nymph who magically ascended from the sea and fell in love with a handsome German knight, played by Mel. Suddenly she appeared on stage wearing a costume that consisted of little more than some green fishnet with bits of synthetic seaweed strewn casually here and there. The asexual Audrey Hepburn of *Sabrina* had promptly become The Figure Beautiful.

A Paramount executive, attending the opening night performance, commented about the audience reaction to Audrey's costume. They approved. 'Any other actress,' he concluded, 'would have been censored from here to Timbuctoo for this Minsky outfit. But what censor would dare point a finger at Audrey Hepburn?'

On curtain-down, the crowd went wild: rhapsodic. Audrey felt a great weight had been lifted from her shoulders, but there were still the reviews to come. A constellation of show-business celebrities packed her dressing-room after the show, among them Marlene Dietrich, Leueen MacGrath and Dolores Gray; and there were so many flowers they had to be stacked on the floor against the walls. Later, that evening, accompanied by Mel and the Baroness (who had flown in for Christmas), Audrey attended a supper party sponsored by the cultural attaché of the French Embassy.

The drama critics embraced her with the kind of glowing notices that every actress dreams of. The *New York Times*' Brooks Atkinson, usually a man to be feared on opening nights, discarded his pen of vitriol for one of syrup. 'She is tremulously lovely,' he purred. 'She gives a pulsing performance that is all grace and enchantment, disciplined by an instinct for the realities of the stage.' While the *New York Post* and the *Herald Tribune* generally shared these views, the latter was obliged to point out that 'To look at *Ondine* is a jewel box. To listen to it is rather a trial.' Still, the critics were more than kind to Audrey herself. One, carried away, said she had 'the body of a Minoan princess and the eyes of a wise, virgin owl'.

One of the things that surprised veterans of show business, most of whom were prepared for any kind of behaviour among their own members, was Audrey's ability to brush aside yesterday's accolades. It happened with *Gigi* and *Roman Holiday*, and now it was happening with *Ondine*. She had little respect for the past, was concerned only lightly with the present, and was totally serious about her professional and personal future. Her capacity to shrug off such ego-boosters as Oscars and Tonys brought Audrey more enemies than admirers, many of whom interpreted her behaviour not in terms of modesty, but as light-headed ingratitude. Her severest critics labelled her 'bad-mannered'. Other adjectives were 'inconsiderate' and 'thoughtless'.

At the party after the first night, Audrey was asked, 'What is your idea of success?' This question – and she was noted for her gift for giving evasive replies – was one she didn't mind answering. 'Success,' said Audrey, thoughtfully, 'is like reaching an important birthday and finding out you're exactly the same. All I feel is the responsibility to live up to it. And even, with luck, survive it.'

All, however, was not favourable for Mel – of his own making. On the first night, and thereafter, the audience roared its approval and demanded, at the end, to see Audrey – again and again. What the audience got, instead, was Audrey and Mel – again and again. His behaviour was instantly noted by the American press by way of some pretty acid statements. One annoyed critic said Mel was 'churlish' to share Audrey's curtain calls. Mel, clearly, had no intention of being excluded from the warming glow that surrounded Audrey at the hour of her new triumph.

His unfavourable effect on theatre-goers in general quickly came to the notice of Audrey herself, who, as always from now on, would come promptly to his defence. He was her man and, in her eyes, could do no wrong. 'Why shouldn't Mel share my curtain-calls?' she asked everyone. 'After all, it's his play, too, isn't it?'

A month later, Audrey was taking solo curtain calls. And with good reason. She had won an Oscar award (for *Roman Holiday*) and a Tony award (for *Ondine*) in the same week. She was not just the best actress in the cinema, but also the best actress on Broadway. In the entire history of these awards, only one other actress had ever managed to capture both of them in the same year, and Shirley Booth had claimed that distinction just the previous year.

Automatically, Audrey became the hottest star in show business. She also became the highest-paid woman performer on Broadway – $2500 a week, plus a percentage of the box-office earnings. All of which explained why Mel reluctantly agreed to let Audrey take her curtain calls alone. Yet from that day forward he would be by her side at almost every other opportunity.

In a novel by George du Maurier, published in 1894, a Hungarian musician and hypnotist named Svengali mesmerises an artist's model, Trilby O'Ferrall, into becoming a famous singer. When he dies the spell is broken, she loses her voice, and herself dies broken-hearted. Audrey became Trilby to Mel's Svengali.

Few who knew them would dispute it, then or now. 'It was pretty obvious almost from the outset that Audrey and Mel had a crush off-stage as well as on,' remarked a contact whose job it was to pick up snippets of gossip backstage on Broadway theatres. 'Mel used to take her on sightseeing expeditions around New York. After the show each night he would squire her home. But boy! That fellow certainly knew how to take command.'

Certainly, unlike the evenings spent alone after performances of *Gigi*, Audrey now usually left the theatre on Mel's arm, and would frequently be spotted in the early hours 'doing the town'. Few nighteries escaped their presence. One night they were discovered at a jazz emporium on Broadway called The Metropole, 'Lindying' between the tables. They hot-rumba'd at Ciro's, shared plates of ice-cream in downtown restaurants, roamed the streets hand-in-hand, both intent on each other. On some occasions when they were together people remarked that they seemed even closer than lovers – more like brother and sister, anticipating each other's thoughts and gestures.

'You have to be a bit in love with your leading man,' Audrey would tell people.

Away from the theatre Audrey was still that piquant mixture of adolescent bounce and womanly dignity. One night she might be giving a hilarious imitation of movie clown Jerry Lewis.

127

The next could find her paying a duty call with all the poise of Queen Juliana of the Netherlands. She spoke gently of her private affairs but she would squash questions that pried too deep. Those around her, at least, observed a distinct change in her personality. She was in love.

Robert Flemyng and his wife, together with Audrey and Mel, occasionally dined with their mutual friend, Cathleen Nesbitt. 'It was plain that Audrey adored Mel,' Flemyng would later record. 'In fact, she was very much influenced by him, to put it mildly.'

The hold which Mel now exerted over his leading lady was all but total – a fact which an ardent Eddie Fisher would discover all too painfully for himself. Fisher, then approaching the vertex of his popularity as a teen-idol crooner, had yet to marry and divorce Debbie Reynolds, Elizabeth Taylor, and Connie Stevens; but, if all had gone according to plan, Audrey might have become wife number one. It happened one night after he had seen *Ondine*.

'I fell hopelessly in love with everything about her,' said the singer. 'The next day I sat down and wrote her a letter, printing it out carefully like a schoolboy and sending it to her with some flowers. I have no idea what I said – something about being her number one fan, hoping she would suggest we meet.'

But all he received in return was 'a very formal and ladylike' 'thank you' note. The door to Audrey's heart was now firmly closed to all outsiders, with Mel's foot pressed hard against it.

When someone asked Audrey how her romance started, she blushed and nervously fingered a pearl earring. 'It was quite simple,' she replied. 'I saw him, liked, him, loved him. . . .'

'She's quite astonishing,' Mel then said affectionately. 'I just fell for her simplicity, her candour, her directness and her honesty. But, believe me,' he went on, 'she has her own "Yes" and "No" – she certainly doesn't need *me* to speak for her.'

No one believed him. If he was deluding anybody, it was himself.

16

*'I had so many complexes about my looks I
thought no one would ever marry me and I'd
be left on the shelf. Well, I'm delighted I have
a husband and I'm off the shelf.'*

*B*ECOMING ONE OF the biggest stars in the world
suddenly made even the minutiae of Audrey's life important
news. When she and Mel finally admitted their love for one
another, it was avidly reported and voraciously consumed. So
was the opposition from Audrey's family. After arriving in
New York, the Baroness was at pains to avoid public attention
and was even careful to deny that her daughter was romantically involved with Mel.

Such a tactic suited her own purposes. The romance, however, which had long been blossoming, now suddenly turned
'serious'. It could no longer be brushed aside as 'nonsense'.
How could it be otherwise when the two lovebirds talked
openly of their undying mutual adoration?

The Baroness's objection to Mel was based initially not on
their wide age-gap but on the fact that he had been married
three times before and had four children. But Audrey's mother
was using the wrong strategy. She was reminded, rather tactfully, of her own marital record.

Another crisis was also simmering. Two months into the run
of *Ondine* and newspaper headlines on both sides of the Atlantic were declaring to an alarmed public: 'Audrey Hepburn ill'
and 'Audrey Hepburn rests between shows'. She was suffering
from anaemia, loss of weight and severe emotional exhaustion.
On her doctor's advice, who reported that she was fifteen
pounds underweight, she cancelled all social engagements and
spent most of her free time at health resorts accompanied by Mel.

By the middle of June her doctor was so concerned about his patient's rapidly deteriorating health that he ordered her to abandon the show and sit on top of a deserted Swiss mountain for a month. Typically, Audrey tried to make light of it. 'It's not really serious,' she endeavoured to reassure everybody. 'It's just that I've been worrying too much, not getting enough sleep, and feeling the New York heat dreadfully.'

As a top Hollywood and Broadway actress Audrey should have been the happiest girl in the world, but, her love for Mel apart, she was far from happy. Those closest to her said her trouble was that she tried to please too many people – the producers of *Ondine* by not missing one performance despite her tiredness and ill-health, and the thousands of people who showered her with letters and invitations.

The producers strove to persuade her to stay with *Ondine* through the summer, arguing that if she left the play it would have to close, and the rest of the cast would be thrown out of work. But with her health as it was, and with other commitments, Audrey had no choice.

So she pulled out of the show, and *Ondine* closed at the end of June. 'I tried awfully hard to fulfil my obligations,' said Audrey. 'I'm sorry if some people are mad at me.'

Before leaving for Switzerland, Audrey was committed to a date in Manhattan with Robert Clark, the shrewd, soft-speaking Scottish chief of Associated British Pictures. He arrived from Elstree with two film scripts, a romantic comedy specially written by Graham Greene, and an emotional drama, one of which he hoped Audrey would choose as the vehicle for her next movie, to be made in Britain before the summer was out. He also hoped to secure Gregory Peck as her leading man, since he would be working at Elstree during that summer on *Moby Dick*.

Paramount had already offered to buy out the remainder of Audrey's Elstree contract. They had put in a bid of one million dollars, to be inaugurated with an immediate down-payment of $200,000. But Clark, noting that Audrey was far too valuable an asset to be auctioned, flatly declined the Paramount offer. By so doing, he made it the most expensive reject of a Hollywood bid for a British star.

Audrey was momentarily happy. To be owned contractually, whether to an individual or to an organisation, never appealed to her all-abiding sense of freedom from despotic control, a

130

deep-seated hangover of her formative years under the sway of Nazi domination. 'Contracts scare me,' she said candidly. 'It's unhealthy to be completely under contract, to have no life of your own. The idea of a telephone jangling, calling you to Hollywood – or anywhere – leaves me cold.'

Instead, she came to an astute compromise. While continuing to honour her existing contract with Associated British, she would also agree to make seven pictures for Paramount, with up to twelve months off between pictures to permit her to do stage work. 'My bosses at Paramount realise I am very sincere about the stage,' said Audrey. 'I feel I wouldn't last long if I were to do pictures only. I have learned the little I know about acting from my stage work, and I think I'll continue to learn from the theatre. I adore the stage and would be very unhappy to leave it altogether.'

But, unknown to her at that time, and having already bid farewell to Broadway, she would never again set foot on another stage professionally. Just before opening in *Ondine*, it was suggested that she might star at Stratford-on-Avon as Juliet, but the Avon Memorial Theatre directors did not press the point. The part, they reminded her gently, was difficult, exacting, with 500 lines. She offered to throw up every other offer if they would consider her for the role. The decision was left in abeyance.

Among other projects being considered at this time, but ultimately never taken up, was a proposition from BBC Television to star her in *Broken Doll* (the story of musical comedy star Clarice Mayne), and a make-or-break deal from director Otto Preminger to put her in the lead of a screen version of Shaw's *Doctor's Dilemma* (in the event, the part went to Leslie Caron – and Anthony Asquith directed). That was show business.

With the finer details of her film career more or less settled, Audrey said goodbye to New York and left for the recuperative ambience of Switzerland. Here, under strict medical care, she was promptly cooped up in a second-floor hotel bedroom at the jet-set ski resort of Gstaad and was told that she must not see anybody, not even her closest friends, for one month. She was not even allowed to go down for meals. Her doctors and her English secretary laid down the law: no visitors, no telephone calls, no interviews. After the month was up, they said, she could then perhaps consider her future.

Audrey arrived at the Alpine resort in pouring rain to find

131

posters advertising her arrival plastered all over the town. The local cinema had even put on *Roman Holiday* in the hope that she would appear on the stage; and an enterprising hotel manager hoped she would attend a champagne gala dinner – precisely the sort of public engagements she had fled to Switzerland to get away from.

For days she lay in bed, half crazy with incessant migraine, and with what she herself so aptly described as 'the agony of recharging the battery'. She was unimaginably miserable. People were left with the impression that what Audrey lacked most of all during this 'medical exile' was inner sunshine: that the girl who had given pleasure and joy to millions through her disarmingly sensitive manner had not yet succeeded in acquiring happiness for herself.

Just over a week later, complaining that it was impossible at Gstaad to secure the peace she needed, she retreated to a picturesque two-bedroom chalet on top of Burgenstock, a lofty mountain overlooking Lake Lucerne. Here, she insisted, she *really* wanted to be alone. She had certainly gone to the right place. Apart from three hotels (five today) and a few farms in the valley below, Audrey had the mountain very much to herself.

The location was literally what the doctor ordered. 'It has a healing power,' she would later explain, 'without which I just cannot seem to survive too well.' The secluded locale and beneficial atmosphere, in fact, were so compatible to mind and body that, although she would subsequently acquire other properties elsewhere, she would never desert her Burgenstock hideaway. For one thing, the remoteness of the mountain top prohibited droppers-in, sightseers and autograph-hunters.

Switzerland, traditionally, has always offered asylum to the restless wanderers of other lands, and Audrey felt instinctively 'at home' the moment she arrived at her Swiss retreat. The country's first famous exile was Voltaire. Byron, the German poet Rainer Maria Rilke, James Joyce, Thomas Mann, Bertolt Brecht, Brahms, Wagner, Stravinsky and Paul Hindemith all lived and worked there. Exiled kings chose to live there, and, concurrent with Audrey's arrival, a colony of American and British cinema stars found Switzerland a haven from devastating income taxes. Audrey soon found she had such neighbours as Van Johnson, Sophia Loren, David Niven, William Holden, Deborah Kerr, Richard Burton, and Charlie Chaplin.

Here, as her doctor advised, Audrey seldom strayed far from her chalet, except for cruises on the lake or for golf and tennis lessons. At meals, too, she remembered the medical man's instructions – devour to her heart's content those famous Swiss cakes: oh-so-small, oh-so-delicious but oh-so-fattening.

Audrey deliberately chose this particular chalet, the 'Villa Bethiana', because it was relatively small and compact for adequate heating. Big picture windows, too, overlooked the Alps, the lake and the valley below. Outside, in an exquisite walled garden filled with ferns and brightly coloured Alpine flowers, she could take in the views and enjoy the clear, edifying highland climate. As a tonic, it suited her admirably. 'I love to wake up in the early morning, to throw open the shutters and drink in the sight of the tall mountain peaks and the lake down below,' she enthused. 'It's the greatest view in the world.'

In such an environment Audrey gradually rallied from the verge of a nervous breakdown to something bordering near-perfect health. Her health, in fact, would never be classified as 'perfect'; a lifelong asthma problem would strike from time to time, usually when she was visiting less-favourable climes.

Her thoughts were now turning more and more towards Mel, who was about to start filming *La Madre* in Rome. It was to Rome that, on the occasion of his thirty-seventh birthday in August, she despatched a small, neat package wrapped in black tissue-paper. Inside was a very special and a very precious gift: a platinum watch inscribed 'Mad about that Man'.

Mel, elated by the changed circumstances in his relationship with Audrey, caught the first weekend plane out of Rome and, in the warm, scented garden overlooking Lake Lucerne, held Audrey in his arms – and proposed. They sealed their engagement with a kiss rather than a ring. 'When I fell in love with Mel,' said Audrey, 'I knew an engagement ring wasn't necessary.'

Audrey had always said that when she married, it would be as secret as she could make it, and so it was. Well, almost. Few friends would be there, and even fewer would be at the civil ceremony the day before, at Buochs, on the shores of Lake Lucerne. She was furious, however, when a photographer found them at Buochs for the civil ceremony, conducted by the local mayor, M. Eduard Wyrsch, in his back parlour, which had been turned into a reception room for the occasion. She refused

133

to leave by the front door and was hurried out through the kitchen and washing-room into the back courtyard.

The religious ceremony which Audrey had always dreamed about took place on 25 September below the snow-tipped mountain at Burgenstock where, prayer-book in hand, she went to a tiny thirteenth-century chapel which had been decorated with white carnations, her favourite flowers. She was clad in an alluring Pierre Balmain white organdie robe without a train, a small crown of white roses (recalling Ophelia), white gloves, silver and white shoes. Waiting for her was her husband-to-be, his six-foot-two frame towering over her.

Outsiders were kept at bay by a small posse of policemen, and the chapel doors were locked as soon as the small party had disappeared inside. Among the twenty-five guests, who had flown from all over Europe to be there, were two of Mel's children, Pepa and Mark; Terry Ferrer (Mel's sister); Paramount's London chief, Richard Mealand; and the man who gave Audrey away, Sir Neville Bland, a former British Ambassador to the Netherlands. The Baroness made ample use of an embroidered white handkerchief.

Following the ceremony, performed by Pastor Endiguer, the couple went to a country club, where the doors were again securely locked, and a small celebration party was held. The toasts were simple. The party was short. And then the couple scurried away.

They departed immediately for a honeymoon in Italy . . . that, at least, was what they wanted all their friends to believe. Decoys were even hired to complete the deception. They stayed, in fact, at the luxurious chalet of Swiss hotel millionaire Fritz Frey – their best man – not far from the tiny chapel where they were married only a few hours earlier.

Mel had been given four days' leave of absence from the Italian studios where he was making *La Madre*. Audrey would then return with him to Rome. In the meantime a ceaseless stream of telegrams and flowers were delivered to the newly-weds from all parts of the world. But well-wishers, even close personal friends, who wanted to speak to them on the telephone – there were calls from New York, Hollywood, London, Paris and Rome – were solemnly informed that 'Mr and Mrs Ferrer have left for Italy.'

The couple, comfortably seated before a large open log fire, spent the second day of their brief clandestine honeymoon writing postcards to their friends. In a letter to the Baroness, whom she had left at the country club in tears, Audrey said: 'This is by far the happiest day in my life. I have never been so excited before.'

Strictly speaking, she should not have been happy at all, for few weddings had attracted more dire predictions. Audrey's friends sobbed in a body, and some of Mel's own supporters, such as they were, gave the marriage little chance. The prophets of gloom not only deplored the age difference, but also what they termed 'the tremendous difference in temperament'. These glum views would not only persist after several years, but would grow even darker.

As far as Audrey was concerned, however, such prognoses fell on deaf ears. 'I've been restless, but that's over,' she said immediately after the wedding. 'I didn't know where or what I wanted to be. Now I do. Wherever Mel is I'm home.'

Their actual departure from Switzerland was as conspiratory as their fictional one. As the train pulled into Lucerne's main railway station, Audrey's secretary first walked along the platform to ensure there were no crowds or photographers in sight. Only after she had waved a white handkerchief, their pre-arranged signal for the 'all clear', did Audrey and Mel emerge from their station hide-out and, pushing fifteen pieces of matching light-grey luggage, walk briskly to their compartment. Porters then quickly passed the luggage through an adjoining compartment's open window. All this took place behind drawn blinds, which were let up only when the train moved slowly out of the station.

But a surprise awaited them in Rome, where they were besieged by photographers at the railway terminus.

'No pictures!' demanded Mel, holding up a warning hand. 'We want to be alone.'

They escaped by a fast car to Cinecitta, the centre of Rome's film industry, where Mel was engaged on *La Madre*. He was told that the studio had re-arranged the schedule to permit him to enjoy a further week's honeymoon. He and Audrey meanwhile locked themselves into a studio office until they were told a villa had been secured for them, in Albano. At an opportune moment, their car, a big Mercedes-Benz, whisked them off up the Appian Way at speeds touching more than a hundred miles an hour. Five car-loads of photographers followed.

The couple eventually leapt from their car, dashed into the

twenty-room stone villa, and bolted the door. The photographers, undeterred, sprinted across the grounds and pounded the doors and rapped the windows. Eventually, for the sake of peace and quiet, the honeymooners came out to pose for pictures – Audrey understandably sullen and not in the best of moods. From that dramatic beginning to the present day, Audrey would not know a moment when a photographer, somewhere, was not peering at her through a camera viewfinder.

The villa farm, high above the sea in the Alban Hills, overlooking the beach at Anzio, would be their amply protected sanctuary for several weeks. It was here that Augustus was proclaimed 'father of the Roman nation', here that Caligula and Nero were born. Hired guards patrolled the farmhouse grounds day and night to discourage uninvited guests. The Ferrers were big news, and the *paparazzi* hid for days within the vicinity to secure 'off guard' pictures of the honeymoon couple.

But their security arrangements were generally adequate to enable them to laze beneath the shade of a fruit-laden quince tree, drinking iced cocktails among the voluptuous flowers, the ripening grapevines and the six languorous cats, the donkeys, chickens and assorted livestock that went with the villa. Here, too, they nibbled the last fragments of their everlasting wedding cake, and bathed in the swimming pool.

They talked about bringing *Ondine* to London and, while there, to film the play. Having declined Associated British Pictures' latest two scripts, Mel was optimistic that Elstree might accept the *Ondine* project as part of Audrey's commitment to them.

The British studio did not. Water-sprites spelt death at the box office. Through her Hollywood agent, Kurt Frings, Paramount offered Audrey a property called *House of Mist*. It came to nothing. There would be time for movies; but now, mused Audrey, was not the time.

17

*'I lack self-confidence. I don't know whether
I shall ever get it. Perhaps it is better to be
unsure of yourself, as I am. But it is very
tiring.'*

TOWARDS THE END of October, while Mel completed filming in Rome, Audrey flew to the Netherlands to embark upon a five-day charity tour. One of the shows was televised by Dutch television. She was the local girl made good and the esteem with which the Dutch regarded her bordered on pop-style mass hysteria. When she arrived in Amsterdam a fortnight later, this time accompanied by Mel, the police had to be called in to protect her against the thousands of fans who besieged her at the airport.

The following day a crowd of ten thousand screaming teenagers stormed an Amsterdam department store where Audrey was signing photographs of herself in aid of Dutch war invalids. The mob shattered showcases and overturned counters in the surge to catch a glimpse of their idol. When the fracas got out of hand, scores of police with batons were called in to try to control the excitable horde.

A few days after Christmas, Mel and Audrey flew to London, their luggage including their Christmas presents to each other: blue and yellow cashmere sweaters for him, household linen for her. They moved into a third-floor flat in Portman Square, near Marble Arch, which belonged to Louise Morris, a friend of the Baroness's. For their £30-a-week rent they were accorded two reception rooms, two bedrooms, and two bathrooms. The main bedroom was furnished in green, with concealed lighting and a full-length mirror at one side of the double bed. A well-stocked bar waylaid visitors in the entrance hall.

The Baroness, now back in South Audley Street, had seen neither Audrey nor Mel since they left for their honeymoon three months earlier. When asked, prior to the couple's arrival in London, if she felt any trepidation at the thought of meeting the son-in-law with whom she was apparently at daggers drawn, the Baroness replied unreservedly: 'Certainly not. I know him very well and we have spoken a number of times over the long-distance phone since Audrey's marriage.'

There could be no doubt, however, that in Mel and the Baroness there were two strong-minded individuals each of whom, where Audrey was concerned, enjoyed being the boss. In matters touching Audrey's present and future life, the son-in-law and the mother-in-law would rarely find a common meeting-ground. At best, they would agree to differ; at worst, they would either avoid each other or maintain 'a wall of silence'.

For the most part, the Baroness chose to remain discreetly but ineffaceable in the background – always fiercely proud of her daughter, in whom she saw her own ambitions fulfilled. But not, she insisted, by coercion. 'I can really take no credit for any talent that Audrey may have,' she was fond of telling people. 'If it's real talent, it's God-given. I might as well be proud of a blue sky, or the paintings in the Flemish exhibition at the Royal Academy.'

Significantly, though, there were more pictures of Audrey in the Baroness's flat than of Flemish masters. Pictures of Audrey at every stage of her career, in fact, dominated the décor. 'Don't misunderstand about my mother,' said Audrey in her defence. 'She is anything but the "typical stage mother". Would you believe, she has never been to a ballet class or rehearsal of mine! She has never even been on a movie set where I've been working. She has never been on location with me – except once, and that was only after I *begged* her to come and fetch me.'

The Baroness may not have been the usual dominating, interfering, insufferably possessive stage mother, but neither was she quite the passive, free-and-easy Momma that Audrey wanted the world to believe. Discreet she may have been; meek, docile, soft – never. 'My mother taught me to stand straight, sit erect, use discipline with wine and sweets, and to smoke only six cigarettes a day,' is how Audrey put it.

For her return to London, Audrey held a cocktail reception in the elegant Oliver Messel penthouse of the Dorchester Hotel.

Cameramen clambered on chairs to get pictures, while Mel tried calmly to answer questions – he was already the official spokesman for his apparently less-worldly wife.

'Just look at him!' Audrey said excitedly as Mel chatted to an intimate knot of women. 'His qualities are so enormous, I just can't put them into the right words. Gosh, I'm jealous of the way women ogle him. I intend to keep on the same side of the ocean with him – and to keep my man!'

This was an era when women were attracted to the lean and hungry look in the opposite sex. Mel certainly came into that category: the semi-emaciated face, the death-like pallor, the sunken eyes, the skinny frame of a man who apparently had not enjoyed a good square meal in months. 'He's a man you feel you *must* mother,' noted London's top stage and society photographer, Vivienne, whose camera had clicked everybody from Sir Laurence to Sir Winston. 'He certainly brought out the maternal in me.'

Audrey's career, she decided, would from now on be placed second to the strict domestic obligations she had imposed on herself. Throughout her career in films, Audrey would never make more than two films a year: usually it would be one a year, and sometimes – always by design – an interval of two years would separate one production from the next. For Audrey, film-making was the perfect means to an ideal end: it brought her sufficient funds to permit her to spend, on average, seven or eight months of the year exclusively with her family. Herself the product of a broken marriage, she was obsessed with the fear that, improperly managed, her own life might follow the same pattern as the Baroness's and, indeed, as Mel's. Never did a woman more obediently obey her marriage pledges of loving, honouring and obeying than the spritely Mrs Ferrer the Third. Her master-plan was formed the moment she walked from the little chapel in the Swiss Alps: she would build a cosy nest for the cock bird and, in time, for their fledglings. Audrey nursed strong maternal feelings the way others nursed ambitions to win a million.

And so she talked about babies. 'If and when one comes along,' she said, 'it will be the greatest thing in my life – greater even than my success. Every woman knows what a baby means.'

Meanwhile, the Foreign Press Association, from a poll conducted in fifty countries, voted Audrey Hepburn and Gregory

Peck the world's favourite film players for 1954. Pier Angeli and June Allyson were second and third to Audrey.

Audrey's extended winter honeymoon suited her fine. She was in no immediate hurry to return to films, to the acute irritation of her dual employers, Associated British and Paramount. The former was still trying to persuade her (by means of some thirty prospective scripts) to honour her commitment to the Elstree studio, while the latter was showering her agent in Hollywood with several no-less-tantalising offers – including an intriguing proposition from William Wyler to cast her in *L'Aiglon*, about Napoleon and Marie Louise's frail son, who died very young of tuberculosis; Audrey would play the boy, a part immortalised on stage by the great Sarah Bernhardt.

But she declined the offer, as she did all the other scripts, one of which came from 20th Century-Fox for the title role in *Jane Eyre* – though actor-turned-producer James Mason was not unduly hurt by the turn-down, since he was not keen on the casting in the first place. 'Useless to point out,' said Mason, 'that Audrey Hepburn just happened to be the most beautiful woman in movies. A head-turner. The whole point about Jane was that no one noticed her when she came into a room or left it.'

Another role to which she said 'No' was that of the Maid of Orleans in Otto Preminger's cinematic realisation of George Bernard Shaw's *Saint Joan*; the part went to a stage-struck small-town eighteen-year-old named Jean Seberg.

Was Audrey *really* so difficult to please when it came to finding the right film part? The short answer must be 'No'. She and Mel were still endeavouring to cajole Associated British into putting *Ondine* before the cameras, and Audrey reasoned (with a little gentle persuasion from Mel) that, by making herself 'scarce', the studios would eventually agree to anything – even, for goodness sake, to *Ondine* – just as long as she made a film for them. But Elstree refused to play that sort of game; and so, for the time being, no scripts interested her.

While Mel worked on a straight, romantic, light-hearted role in *Oh, Rosalinda!* at Elstree, he began to put substance into the rumours that he was lord and master in his relationship with Audrey. This came to a head one day when she visited him on the set.

'Would you mind posing for a picture?' asked the photographer who handled the studio's publicity.

'Certainly,' said Audrey, smiling.

A hand stretched out from behind a piece of scenery.

'I don't think so – not now,' said the voice of her husband.

'I don't think so – not now,' said Audrey to the photographer, inclining her head obediently.

Before people knew otherwise, it was assumed that Audrey's charm was due to a type of helplessness which men associated with femininity – that she *wanted* Mel to run her life and make all the decisions. Even her *Sabrina* co-star and self-appointed guardian, Bill Holden, was fooled into disbelieving Mel's overriding dominance in the Ferrer household. 'I think Audrey allows Mel to *think* he influences her,' Holden suggested.

But few people really believed that statement, and neither did Holden in later years. 'Mel had an enormous influence over her in the early days following their marriage,' observed Fred Zinnemann. 'And Audrey, as a young girl madly in love with a much older man, was probably more than happy to do as Mel said.'

The time would come, however, when Audrey's judgement would mature – when, indeed, she would tell Mel to shut up. But for the moment he was the Boss and she did as she was told. 'She was madly in love with him,' her old friend David Niven would affirm. 'He was a good deal older, of course, and I think she was rather awed, in fact over-awed, by Mel for a long part of their marriage. Audrey, in fact, was perfectly happy to subjugate her career to his, which was nothing like so brilliant.'

However, fine, sensitive actor that he was, Mel simply did not set the film salesmen dancing with delight. As one movie chief in London told *Photoplay*: 'You know what it is, old boy, the young cinemagoers simply don't go for drawn looks and thin hair. Ferrer isn't a star the way that Hepburn is a star.' But, with a little bit of help from Audrey, perhaps that situation could easily be arranged. He and Audrey, after all, had made a pact to work out their film plans so that they could keep together as often as possible. A working relationship in every sense of the term.

So when, in the summer of 1955, she was signed to star in the Carlo Ponti–Dino de Laurentiis company's six-million-dollar film version of Tolstoy's epic *War and Peace*, a wish was expressed by Audrey that Mel should be included in the cast. That was not the original plan of the veteran director, King

Vidor, but Mel got the part – of Prince Andrey. And then there was the question of a leading man for Audrey. 'How about Gregory Peck or Marlon Brando or Peter Ustinov?' suggested Vidor. 'Fine actors. Right on top of the poll.'

But Mel secretly felt that Greg, great old friend that he was, still had 'romantic' connotations which, as far as his wife was concerned, were not yet completely erased. Actor-manager-decision-maker Mel frowned and pondered over the list. He said: 'Henry Fonda'. Fonda became the tormented, idealistic, stumbling Pierre to her tender and vivacious Natasha, the Russian novelist's 'personification of youth' and the most lovable teenager in all literature.

The casting of Audrey and Mel in *War and Peace*, a gargantuan wedge of vice on the ice, and sex on the Steppes, with half of Moscow and most of Siberia spread magnificently across Rome's Cinecitta studios, more than ever convinced visitors to the set who was the Boss. Audrey's part in the epic, for which she received a then record salary of $130,000 – three times Mel's fee – was made under her contract to, or rather in arrangement with, Associated British, who were delighted to procure the film's UK distribution rights.

Because of her frailty during the filming – she had suffered a miscarriage earlier in the year – Mel continued to act as her off-screen liaison officer when they felt changes, advantageous to Audrey's best interests, seemed necessary. There was a problem with the Italian assistant director: Audrey found it difficult to understand his English. The assistant director duly 'resigned'.

Jack Cardiff, the film's director of photography, complained: 'Mel is like a manager with her as well as a husband. "Is the car ready for Miss Hepburn?". . . "The costume is wrong for Miss Hepburn.". . . "It is too hot (or too cold) for Miss Hepburn."'

In conveying Audrey's wishes on such matters, Mel did not endear himself to the gritty Texan director, although to his dying day Vidor would maintain that, of all the actresses he had directed, Audrey was his favourite. Audrey, however, took exception to something Vidor uttered one day within earshot – that his leading lady was 'an innocent waif in need of protection'.

'Protection from what?' asked Audrey incredulously. 'I'd been in films a long time before I met Mel and nobody ever took advantage of me. Of course, Mel has had a lot more experience than me and as a husband he naturally advises his wife. But that's all. I assure you I don't need protection.'

Mel, the man who supposedly never gave an opinion unless asked, was himself beginning to get a bit hot under the collar. 'Of course I wear the pants,' he wailed. 'I'd look pretty daft wearing skirts. It's true that we're moving heaven and earth to stay together and, if possible, work together. What's wrong with that after one year of marriage? We dread the thought of separation. Look what it's done to so many Hollywood marriages. . . .'

But the separation inevitably came. When Mel finished work on *War and Peace*, some time before Audrey concluded her own scenes, he flew to France to star opposite Ingrid Bergman in *Paris Does Strange Things*. It was the first time they had been apart since their marriage more than a year earlier.

Audrey took it badly. But they were reunited, briefly, a couple of days later. 'Oh, darling!' cried Audrey as she clung to him at the airport. 'We've been apart nearly two whole days!'

Their let's-try-to-be-together-always pact brought with it certain self-destructive elements. It was common knowledge in the film world that the offers which Audrey deemed the most attractive were those which would also exercise the talents of her husband – if necessary, on a concurrent production, should the script she selected have nothing for him. Because the director George Stevens would not, or perhaps could not, agree to these terms, Audrey would later turn down the title-role in *The Diary of Anne Frank*, based on the famous journals of a Dutch girl who died in Auschwitz. It seems that for similar reasons Mel's studio, MGM, declined to have Audrey repeat her *Gigi* stage triumph when it was turned into a screen musical by Alan Jay Lerner and Frederick Loewe.

In *War and Peace*, a film lasting three and a half hours, calling on the services of six scriptwriters, nearly 5000 guns, as many rifles, 7000 authentic costumes, 100,000 buttons, and tons of artificial snow flown in from England, Audrey found herself engaged to a prince, seduced by a count, and pursued hopelessly by a Henry Fonda resembling a spaniel in rimless glasses. While Audrey and Fonda won almost universal approval from the critics, and while the spectacle itself sensitively re-created quite a bit of the mood and philosophy of Leo Tolstoy's 650,000-word classic, the film as a whole was not a success financially, despite the critics' lavish praise. One critic, noting that every minute brimmed over with love and hate, life and death, blood and sweat, perhaps spoke for many movie-goers when he concluded that in the film there was too much peace, too little war.

'One thing is certain,' insisted Vidor. 'Audrey *is* Natasha. She is fresh out of the book. I know of no other actress who could have played the part.'

The *New York Herald-Tribune* apparently agreed. 'Certainly,' proclaimed the newspaper, 'hers is the best feminine performance of the year.' But there were one or two dissenters, who complained that Audrey did not sufficiently submerge her own distinctive personality into the role she was playing. For the purpose of the argument they brought up Vivien Leigh's Scarlett O'Hara in *Gone with the Wind*, saying that while Vivien Leigh *was* Scarlett, Natasha was mostly Audrey.

Vidor, however, stuck to his guns. 'I used to see her wonderful performance over and over again in the dubbing and music-cutting,' he pointed out, 'and I never tired of it. I always found something new that she did.'

When filming on *War and Peace* was completed, Audrey's agent, Kurt Frings, arranged with Paramount that Hollywood's top publicist, Henry Rogers, should start the ballyhoo campaign as soon as possible. Rogers, an old friend of Mel's, arrived in Rome with his wife, Roz. Mel insisted that they stay with Audrey and him at their farmhouse overlooking the beach at Anzio rather than at an hotel. As the Rogers' hired car drove into the little courtyard of the house, Audrey, dressed in a black turtleneck sweater, and black slacks and loafers – her favourite colour combination for many years – ran out to meet the guests. 'I'm so glad you're here,' she called out, and, instead of the usual handshakes and 'How do you do?', she embraced them both warmly, while Mel looked on smiling.

'We had never met Audrey before,' said Rogers later, 'and Roz and I were both enchanted. She was warm, bubbly, enthusiastic and genuinely happy to entertain her husband's friends.'

Rogers and Audrey would form a special relationship that would endure many years and many crises. While Mel would continue to be her off-screen alter ego, Rogers, as her 'official spokesman', would smooth and soothe her life in a professional capacity, guiding the way and generally protecting her from ill-winds. He would mould her public persona. It would not be a pushover.

144

18

'Truly, I've never been concerned with any public image. It would drive me around the bend if I worried about the pedestal others have put me on. And also I don't believe it.'

CHRISTMAS AT BURGENSTOCK, where the Ferrers roasted chestnuts in the embers of their Alpine retreat, was a momentous occasion. As they sat before the big open fire, their pale faces bathed in a flickering redness, they made plans. Audrey, whose roots as an actress lay in the musical theatre, mulled over the possibility of making a film musical. It would be a thrilling new departure for her, the next obvious step in her career. Mel, after all, had been urging her to undertake such a project for some considerable time.

'And so,' she sighed, 'I suppose this will start all those stories again about Mel directing my career. Of course, he occasionally gives me advice, as does every husband to his wife, but I always make the final decision myself.' Her delicately-pointed chin tilted defiantly: 'I, too, felt that I needed something light and gay to follow my serious role in *War and Peace.*'

Audrey usually took about three days to read and consider a script. This one she finished in two hours. 'This is it!' she cried, bursting into the room where Mel was working. 'I don't sing well enough, and I'm not a good enough dancer, but, oh, if I can only do this with Fred Astaire!'

Paramount reasoned that a film musical starring Audrey Hepburn would make a million or three. With this in mind it acquired a property called *Wedding Day*, retitled it *Funny Face*, brought in Audrey and Astaire, and hired top director Stanley Donen – an ex-dancer who had earlier collaborated with Gene Kelly as choreographer on *Cover Girl* and *Anchors Aweigh*, co-directed *On the Town,* and directed *Royal Wedding* and *Seven Brides for Seven Brothers.* The studio also agreed to let Mel direct Audrey in a forthcoming film at MGM. The Ferrers had bargained well.

'Coming from *War and Peace* to this,' groaned producer Roger Edens, 'Miss Hepburn was all shrewd businesswoman till the deal was signed – a long, drawn-out process, believe me. But once it was set, she was all for it.'

She certainly was. 'This is the part,' cooed Audrey, 'I've waited twenty-seven years for – to dance with Fred Astaire at last.'

There was a deeper significance to that remark. Audrey was twenty-seven years old, and Astaire was fifty-seven – a veteran of some thirty movie musicals with such leading ladies as Ginger Rogers, Rita Hayworth, Eleanor Powell, Judy Garland and Cyd Charisse. Hollywood was more than aware that if the dapper but ageing hoofer was still to appeal to the teenage audience which made up most of the movie-goers in America and Britain, then he would have go be cast alongside a young, attractive woman.

Pairing him with Audrey, however, merely drew further attention to the dilemma: that Hollywood's top male stars were growing grey while the audience was getting younger. In *Funny Face,* in which Audrey plays a studious Greenwich Village bookseller kissed abruptly into life by fashion photographer Astaire (said to be based on Richard Avedon), who whisks her to Paris to transform her into a glamorous model, Audrey comes across as little more than a teenager. While she looks as fresh as a rose, with eyes that sparkle like polished diamonds, Astaire looks time-worn and weary.

Talking to an interviewer three years later about his decision to abandon screen dancing, Astaire explained: 'I was determined not to become a dancing freak at sixty.I knew the time had come to quit when one critic said of *Funny Face* that it had "something old, something new." I was the "something old."'

But in making a Hollywood musical at that time there was one problem even greater than the dilemma of finding a suitable girl for an ageing leading man. And that was money. 'By the time we'd bought the rights of *Funny Face* and made all the deals,' said Donen, 'it had cost a million dollars – and that was before a single foot of the film was even shot.'

146

For Astaire, the film was a happy reunion. Back in 1928, after he and his sister Adele had won rave notices for their roles in George Gershwin's stage version of *Funny Face*, they were subsequently tested by Paramount for a proposed film of the show. But the studio's adverse (now classic) evaluation of Astaire's screen-test – 'Can't act, can sing, balding, can dance a little' – quickly scotched any film plans. Under happier circumstances, it would have gone before the cameras in May 1929 – the month Audrey drew her first breath.

More than half a century later, at a gala celebration in Hollywood on the occasion of eighty-two-year-old Astaire's Lifetime Achievement Award for his unique contribution to film, Audrey gave an eloquent speech in which she described her first meeting with Astaire at rehearsal for *Funny Face*: 'I remember he was wearing a yellow shirt, grey flannels, a red scarf knotted around his waist instead of a belt, and the famous feet were clad in soft moccasins and pink socks. He was also wearing that irresistible smile.

'One look at this most debonair, elegant and distinguished of legends and I could feel myself turn to solid lead, while my heart sank into my two left feet. Then suddenly I felt a hand around my waist and, with his inimitable grace and lightness, Fred literally swept me off my feet. I experienced the thrill that all women at some point in their lives have dreamed of – to dance just once with Fred Astaire.'

Astaire, for his part, was captivated by Audrey's lambent charm. 'She's a show-business phenomenon,' he was fond of telling people. 'She can do anything and do it with spirit and verve. Her capacity for hard work is amazing.'

'We've formed a sort of mutual admiration society,' Audrey admitted with obvious pride. 'I must say it's rather flattering when Fred asks me what I think about steps and movements in dance numbers.'

The Paris couturier, Hubert de Givenchy, who sketched all Audrey's dresses for *Funny Face* and who designed her personal wardrobe, called her 'the perfect model'. 'I'm always inspired by Miss Hepburn when I look for my own mannequins,' he told a visitor to the set. 'She has the ideal face and figure, with her long, slim body and swan-like neck. It's a real pleasure to make clothes for her.'

That pleasure had begun just a few years earlier, in 1951, when 'a tall, slim young woman in a tee-shirt and check trousers' (to quote Givenchy), arrived at the showing of his first collection. At first she modelled his wears and then, when she had more money, she bought them – and would continue to buy them. At that first historic meeting, the young couturier – then just twenty-three, a year older than his tall, slim model – had been expecting Hollywood's other Miss Hepburn, the older and more forceful Katharine. But rapport was instant. 'I loved him – and his clothes – instantly,' recalled Audrey some years later. 'He's been my closest friend ever since.'

Givenchy made the first dresses she ever bought from a good fashion house. He designed the sensational ball gown she wore in *Sabrina*; he was now working on *Funny Face* – since 1953, in fact, a clause specifying that he designs her clothes had been written into all her film contracts. His clothes for Audrey's private use, too, would promote her into a permanent fixture on the 'best-dressed' lists. By 1956 she would be buying half a dozen outfits from Givenchy each season. 'His are the only clothes in which I am myself,' she explained. She admired his spare, simple lines, but also the fact that his finery possessed a 'delicate, romantic quality'.

Audrey's shape, of course, was – and would remain – the opposite of Rubenesque. Not a bulge, not a curve; and the Givenchy line was made for it. Waists rose high in front on suits and dresses – so high, in fact, that his models appeared to keep their bosoms where most people's collar-bones would be. Audrey, for her part, helped popularise Givenchy, for all the women who admired the Audrey Hepburn Look flocked to his Paris salon.

The way he dressed her could be keynoted as simplicity, a plainness that hovered just above dullness, and a single-minded devotion to her favourite colours: black and white, navy and white ('I can't wear anything sludgy or grey-toned'). The Hepburn Look was described as 'waif-like, fragile, and feminine'. There was no doubt that her size and weight made her any couturier's dream package. Additionally, not many women could claim they inspired a couturier to create a perfume.

Her fashion sense was also lauded by Gladys de Segonzac, *Funny Face* wardrobe supervisor. 'Audrey can wear anything, with taste and dignity,' she mused. 'And her patience in fittings is extraordinary. She can stand for hours at a time, never fidgets, never squirms. You know how tired she must

148

be, but she never mentions it. She makes her changes with amazing rapidity, with never a wasted motion.'

Interior scenes for *Funny Face* were begun in Hollywood, and Audrey and Mel rented the exotic Malibu Beach house of movie director Anatole Litvak, with whom they would shortly be working. It was the first time in her career that Audrey did not have to work on Saturdays. 'Those long weekends did wonders for me,' she later told a friend.

But all that ended when the unit moved to France for outdoor location shooting and adopted a seven-day week. Here, the wondrous sight of Audrey Hepburn and Fred Astaire dancing in the streets of Paris became one of the city's major tourist attractions. Sometimes an early-bird would be amply rewarded, as when the two stars filmed a dazzling dance sequence on the steps of the Paris Opéra – at five in the morning.

During the filming, Audrey's Paramount colleagues noticed a distinct change in her personality. The word being used was that she was much more 'open'. When she left Paramount after making *Sabrina*, she had not yet found herself, not yet established the woman she would become. Her life was singularly intense and one-dimensional. She loved her work, as she loved it now, but she did not have much aside from work.

In France, engaged on the film, she still took her career with utmost seriousness, but now it constituted only one dimension in her life. The perspective had shifted and widened since she fell in love and married. In the process, Audrey became a woman. 'Two years ago, she was a pixie,' said one of her friends at that time. 'You didn't know but what she'd suddenly climb a tree or hurdle a hedge or just vanish in a spiral of smoke. Now you're reasonably sure she'll eat a ham sandwich and go to a ball game, or whatever.'

When asked about the 'old' Audrey Hepburn, the actress grew thoughtful. 'I've often been depressed and deeply disappointed in myself,' she confessed. 'I hated myself at certain periods. I was too tall, or maybe just plain too ugly. I couldn't seem to handle any of my problems or cope with people I met. If you want to get psychological, you can say my determination and "definiteness" stems from underlying feelings of insecurity and inferiority. I found the only way to get the better of them was by putting my foot down, by adopting a forceful, concentrated drive.'

Even in later years, when she had been acknowledged as one

of the entertainment greats of our time, she would profess that one of her chief aims in life was to have security – and she was not just referring to dollars and cents. Considering the early traumatic years of her home life, and a tense and often fear-packed childhood and adolescence, this was understandable. A few years ago, while talking to a woman friend about the capriciousness of youth and beauty, she pulled out a lipstick and fluffed a comb through her curls. 'I'm much more insecure,' she opined, 'about somebody continuing to love me, to want me, than I am about my age.' To another she declared: 'I don't think your insecurity ever disappears. Sometimes I think the more successful you become the less secure you feel. This is kind of frightening, really.'

Her lifelong search for security found its most touching expression not in front of the camera but at home with Mel. Hotels and boarding-houses had been the rule for Audrey since she was a girl. Until she married Mel, it mattered little; she was young and ambitious and dedicated to her work. But when she became Mrs Ferrer, she wanted to make a home for her husband under whatever circumstances they had to live. And since they did not own a permanent home anywhere, except the rented accommodation in Portman Square and Burgenstock, she learned to make the best of life in an hotel room.

The means by which she created her own security in such an artificial, inevitably heartless environment was clearly illustrated when the Ferrers moved into the Hotel Rafael in Paris for the filming of *Funny Face*. Within an hour of their arrival, Audrey had cleared from their suite all standard hotel items and then unpacked the personal belongings which she and Mel had collected, including four silver candlesticks, matching salt and pepper shakers, records, books, pictures, ashtrays, bed linen, and tablecloths, so that she could give meals that did not look like hotel meals. To accommodate these precious home-making treasures, she and Mel would often travel with as many as fifty-five pieces of luggage.

Audrey always did the packing. The logistics of the operation appealed to her inherent orderliness. On one occasion, when she left the packing to someone else, Mel had needed his cuff-links on the night of their arrival and she had to go through six huge trunks before she located them. 'I didn't think this was fair to Mel,' she said later. 'I considered it my responsibility not to let it happen again.'

Having done what she could to make their rented home seem more like a real home, Audrey would then set about re-arranging the furniture, usually when Mel was out, to make it a surprise for him. She would call in help from the hotel, personally giving a hand to move heavy pieces around until everything was placed exactly where she wanted it.

On this last occasion, while making *Funny Face*, she remembered a little table that had been in their suite during their previous visit. The concierge was asked to get it for her.

'I'm sorry, Mrs Ferrer,' he apologised, 'that piece is in another suite.'

'I'm afraid the other suite will just have to do without it,' she said politely but firmly.

She got the table.

When Mel walked into their suite later that night, a big grin formed on his face. 'I see you've done it again,' he said, and then kissed Audrey on the cheek.

The same routine would be repeated wherever the Ferrers came down to roost. It was an essential ritual, for it served more than Audrey's basic need for instant, consummate security: it was an extension of a lifelong practical nature. At home in Holland it was Audrey and not her half-brothers who mended the fuse or changed the tap-washer.

On one occasion, while giving a magazine interview in her suite at the Hotel Rafael, the wire-recorder being used by the journalist broke down halfway through their session. Almost without thinking, Audrey took hold of the machine and, squatting on the floor in the middle of the room, set about remedying the fault. It was promptly fixed.

Another time, while appearing on Broadway in *Gigi*, a famous photographer took her out to do a photo layout, and his camera started to malfunction. After attempting to put it right, without success, the photographer was in the process of packing up when Audrey interceded. She pressed here, fumbled there, and five minutes later handed back a repaired camera to an astonished photographer.

And Audrey's practical streak was not confined to mechanical contrivances. Her *savoir faire* came to the fore one evening while dining with France's great screen lover, Charles Boyer, at Lucas-Carton on the Place de la Madeleine. When crêpes Suzette were served for the dessert, she insisted on taking over from the *maître d'hotel* and flambé-ed them herself. She was duly applauded.

As those who knew her best were beginning to discover, this was a formidable young woman, one of whose prime concerns was the cultivation of self-control. She devoted hours on end to it and, through it, controlled others: audiences, movie moguls, *maîtres d'hotel*, journalists, horses – and eventually Mel. 'You won't believe this,' a friend of Mel's said wonderingly one day, 'but he has actually begun to sit still.'

So who had most influenced whom? If Audrey controlled Mel's home life, Mel still had much to offer when it came to Audrey's career. He was still the Boss. Audrey had always been, and would continue to be, attracted to tall, strong, self-motivated men. Whatever else they lacked, it would not be force of character.

Within a few months of completing *Funny Face*, Audrey speculated: 'I think I know when this talk of Mel's "domination" really started. It was towards the end of my "big year", the year I won an Oscar for *Roman Holiday* and a Tony for *Ondine*. These awards are wonderful, but you have to be physically very strong to keep up with the publicity which goes with them on top of the usual demands on your time.'

There was the occasion when she and Mel had to appear at a big charity affair in New York. They had to ride round the arena on black horses. 'I was at exhaustion point,' Audrey went on. 'My doctor had told me to give up everything. We arrived, after two strenuous performances of our play, round about midnight, to be greeted by a tremendous battery of cameras. They went on and on, and in the end I said: "Could that be enough? I must sit down before I get on that horse." And that was the first time that Mel said: "Stop! That's enough!" He took me away, put me in a room, locked the door and stood guard outside.

'And,' she added with determination, 'he's done it plenty of times since. Surely it's a natural reaction for him to steer me through the crowds and look after me? It's the natural reaction of a man, and my husband is a *man* and not a Svengali.'

Later, to an associate who knew her intimately, she mused aloud: 'Even if it were true that Mel dominates my life, hasn't my life changed for the better?' The companion agreed that it had. 'Today,' Audrey underlined, 'I have more friends than I have ever had before. Today I know more about my work and enjoy it more. I read better books, I've come to appreciate the finest in art and music.'

Audrey (as Eve) in her third British film, *Young Wives' Tale* (1951), with Joan Greenwood and Helen Cherry and, behind them, Guy Middleton, Nigel Patrick and Derek Farr *(Associated British/Allied Artists)*

For lovelier skin

Lacto-Calamine is the safest, surest protection for your skin against sun and wind. It's effective, too, for all those minor blemishes and skin ailments. Use Lacto-Calamine as a powder base by day, as a skin food by night.

CROOKES *Lacto-Calamine*

The nameless face which, between 1949 and 1951, helped to promote a popular beauty preparation *(Zenka Woodward Picture Library)*

Guest artist Audrey, as a balletic Cossack, in *Christmas Party* (Cambridge Theatre, 1949), a matinée show for — and performed mainly by — children
(Keystone)

As hat-and-cloak girl Chiquita, resting between
scenes for *The Lavender Hill Mob* (1951)
(Ealing/Rank/Universal)

A bemused cigarette girl, with an equally bewildered Guy Middleton,
in *Laughter in Paradise* (1951)
(Associated British/Pathé)

Audrey, as the ballet student Nora, is watched by Valentina Cortesa,
who plays her older sister, in *The Secret People* (1952)
(Ealing/Lippert)

The
PLAYBILL
for the Fulton Theatre

GIGI

In the title role of the Broadway stage version
of Colette's *Gigi,* Fulton Theatre, 1951
*(Playbill, a registered trade mark of American
Theatre Press, Inc., NYC, USA. All rights
reserved. Used by permission)*

With Eddie Albert and Gregory Peck in a scene from Audrey's
Oscar-winning performance in *Roman Holiday* (1953)
(Paramount)

In Rome with fiancé James Hanson during
filming in 1952 of *Roman Holiday* — her
engagement ring proudly displayed for all the
world to see
(Popperfoto)

Three nights after the Oscar ceremony Audrey receives a Broadway 'Tony' for her role in *Ondine*. She is pictured with fellow Tony recipients (in different categories) Dolores Gray and Jo Van Fleet *(Popperfoto)*

Audrey with Mel, on the programme for the Broadway production of *Ondine* *(Playbill, a registered trade mark of American Theatre Press, Inc., NYC, USA. All rights reserved. Used by permission)*

The 1953 Academy Awards presentations at the Centre Theatre, New York. Actor Jean Hersholt presents Audrey with her Oscar for her portrayal of Princess Ann in *Roman Holiday* *(Popperfoto)*

With Humphrey Bogart, with whom Audrey
co-starred in *Sabrina* (1954)
(Paramount)

On the set of *War and Peace* with director
King Vidor and co-star Henry Fonda
(Pictorial Press)

Audrey (as Natasha) and Mel (Prince Andrey) in a scene from
War and Peace (1956)
(Paramount)

Sandwiched between co-stars Gary Cooper and Maurice Chevalier
in a moment of tomfoolery between takes on the Paris set of
Love in the Afternoon (1957) *(Popperfoto)*

As the disillusioned Sister Luke in
The Nun's Story (1959)
(Warner Bros)

In Holland in 1954 for the unveiling
of the avenue named after her in Doorn
(Associated Press)

A tense moment in *The Unforgiven* (1960), with co-star Burt Lancaster
(United Artists)

Coffee break, with co-star George Peppard,
during location shooting in Park Avenue, New
York, for *Breakfast at Tiffany's* (1961)
(Popperfoto)

Her love for Mel was absolute, and her love was returned. 'But heaven help her if love ever lets her down,' a friend observed. 'I think it would devastate Audrey, who is one of those who believes once-in-a-lifetime for true love.'

As a result of her thorough training in classical ballet, and her early experience as a dancer on the London stage, Audrey was quick to learn the steps of the dance routines in *Funny Face*. The movie was a natural crystallisation of her girlhood ambitions and schooling. Not only did she dance with Fred Astaire, but sang with him, too.

With a score that included such imperishable tunes as 'S'Wonderful', 'He Loves and She Loves', 'Bonjour Paris!', 'Clap Yo' Hands', 'Let's Kiss and Make Up', and the title song, 'Funny Face', it was a musical which really sang. And, in 'How Long Has This Been Going On?', Audrey's glorious rendition made this classic ballad uniquely intimate, lyrical and affecting. Here, as in her other numbers, Audrey staked her claim to be considered the most entrancing 'non-singer' in the history of the art.

Probably the most difficult aspect of producing the film was trying to make Audrey, as the studious bookseller, seem unattractive. Dressed like Miss Potato-Sack of the Year, in sackcloth and black stockings, her piquant beauty still defied the make-up man. She was a gorgeous butterfly from beginning to end.

While *Funny Face* owed a great deal to its setting and its satire, aimed at phoney intellectuals and the fashion elite, it was Audrey, slim, spry and lithe as an urban elf, who added the dimension of charm to a hard-boiled plot. But a seven-day working week left her exhausted, and she counted the hours until she and Mel could return to their Alpine hideout to recuperate.

The gruelling schedule, however, was cushioned for Audrey whenever she saw the Baroness, who flew to Paris several times during the shooting of the film. Yet the visitor was not averse to telling her daughter a few home truths: 'When I think I look well, my mother says: "You've got rings under your eyes," or "You really don't have a healthy colour." But even she agrees that I'm now in top form.'

So did the company. She would think nothing of lending her sheepskin-lined ski jacket to the young assistant choreographer as protection against the chilly location weather, while she herself conducted her outdoor routines in the flimsy costumes of her part, without a quiver. 'I think we should all work in our shirt sleeves,' one French crew member was inspired to comment. 'Audrey's not cold – why should we be?'

Work on *Funny Face* was completed in the first week of July. The Ferrers flew to London on a lightning shopping spree before retreating to Burgenstock and a brief vacation. In four weeks' time Audrey would have to be back in Paris to make a movie with Gary Cooper.

19

'There is a Dutch saying, "Don't fret; it will happen differently anyway." I believe that.'

IN THE WOODS of Landru, near Paris, where the French Bluebeard did away with ten women, the trees parted . . . and there in the clearing was Gary Cooper with a daisy in one ear. He was a man enjoying himself, a man kissing Audrey Hepburn – well, not so much kissing her as eating her hand, wrist, elbow, shoulder, neck. His lips were working overtime. And Audrey was laughing.

'What's with you, Aud?' enquired Billy Wilder, scratching his balding pate.

'Coop's tickling my funny-bone,' she protested.

'Shucks, honey,' drawled Coop, 'ah haven't started yet.'

For Gary Cooper, shy, long and lanky, whose conversation was normally confined to 'Yup' and 'Nope', this was a very long speech indeed. But, to repeat, the Oscar-winning star of *High Noon* was a man enjoying himself; and so, it transpired, was Audrey, reunited with *Sabrina* director Wilder for a romantic sex comedy, *Love in the Afternoon*, the third attempt to bring Claude Anet's witty novel, *Ariane*, to the cinema screen.

The plot concerned the infatuation of French teenaged 'cello student Audrey for American middle-aged millionaire playboy Cooper, whose activities were being investigated by Audrey's private-eye father, Maurice Chevalier. He was unaware of his daughter's affections.

Coop's enthusiasm for his role in the Landru woods was not the only problem confronting Wilder. On each occasion that Coop took a taste of Audrey, something happened to ruin the

155

scene. Planes flew overhead, visitors intruded, somebody sneezed. It was supposed to be a picnic scene and standing by were a score of cooked chickens and a dozen bottles of champagne.

Billy got wilder and wilder. Audrey laughed and laughed. Coop picked out a chicken leg from the succulent array and droned: 'Ah never noo a seducer's work could be so tough.' He turned to Audrey and disclosed: 'Ah'm only in films because ah have a family and we all like to eat.'

'Action!' commanded Wilder, and Coop went into another seductive bear-like hug. Audrey, wearing candy-striped tapered pants, squirmed and turned away her lips. A jet then whistled overhead. She giggled.

'Cut!' moaned Wilder, adding a few choice words. Coop went back to his chicken bone. Audrey entertained him by performing a mock-Flamenco *zapateado*. Where *Sabrina* was all electricity on the set, *Love in the Afternoon* was all party-time; but then Bogart and Holden were nowhere to be seen.

Much of Coop's youthful camaraderie stemmed from a complex. He was deeply conscious that Audrey was 'in trouble' again for being teamed up with an elderly leading man. Audiences would feel uneasy and embarrassed, the accusers said, over a romance between a supposedly eighteen-year-old Audrey Hepburn and a fifty-six-year-old Gary Cooper. And so Coop tried to adopt a more 'youthful' form of behaviour – hence the tomfoolery in the clearing. In reality he could not quite understand why people should find such a story distasteful. 'Is it impossible,' he asked a friend, 'to believe that a young girl could fall in love with a man like me?'

Gary Cooper was idolised and admired. But he was also greatly beloved as perhaps no other contemporary screen actor was beloved. John Wayne called him 'the world's best man'. He was hero-worshipped by his fans, and adored by his leading ladies. Lauren Bacall declared that 'Coop was one of the most attractive men I've ever seen, with his cornflower-blue eyes', and Audrey could not look at his still-handsome features without something dark and profound stirring within her. Her giggles were a convenient release in the romantic scenes.

She would certainly not listen to the 'cradle-snatching' allegations that had been made about the film without some form of intervention. 'The charge is particularly unfair to Coop,' she rebuked. 'In *Love in the Afternoon* he's not trying to fool anyone.

He's supposed to be a man of fifty – that's the whole point of the story.' Indeed. But *she* was also supposed to be eighteen; and that, allied to Coop's maturity, was the spark that ignited so much moral indignation.

The disparity in their ages, however, outraged Audrey's American admirers and the upholders of virtue. They caused such an outcry that a commentary had to be added to the United States version of the film, explaining that the couple would be married some time in the future. But in Britain the picture was screened without the 'explanation'. A London film official pointed out, 'The British audience can believe they might marry some time, or not – just as they choose.' And yet, as a distinguished university professor in America reflected, 'Were the male lead Hepburn's age and the female that of Cooper, it would hardly be romantic.'

Strangely, in view of her valiant words in Coop's defence, Audrey would also go on record as saying that the picture might have been more believable had Cooper and Chevalier switched roles. She was not alone in that sentiment. Not only did most critics agree that Chevalier's acting attained a buoyant youthfulness more striking than that of Cooper, but Chevalier himself wished that Cooper had not played that part. 'It was ridiculous,' he said afterwards. 'He was supposed to be in love with Audrey. He looked as old as I did and people did not like it.'

Chevalier, however, who was then sixty-eight, had his own problems. Regarding *Love in the Afternoon* as a decisive landmark on his road back to Hollywood after a break of twenty years, he was more than usually apprehensive. When Wilder held a first run-through of his early scenes with Audrey, he was as nervous as a tyro, to such an extent that he wondered how he would ever overcome the ordeal. The part was more or less tailor-made for him, yet the English lines had a paralysing and disastrous effect on his lips. Audrey then informed him that she, too, was worried about working with him for the first time, that she was practically knocked off balance by the awful prospect of somehow not 'jelling'. Cooper also appeared to be in the same state.

Attempting to verbalise that first traumatic run-through with Audrey and Cooper, Chevalier wrote in his diary that night: 'We are like musicians tuning their instruments. Actors exchange more than words when they rehearse. Shades of feel-

157

ing emerge which will in time produce the speeches, or the music – and, on occasion, a good deal else besides.'

Later, their nerves disentangled, Audrey put her arms around Chevalier's neck and kissed him gently on the cheek. 'I can't tell you, Maurice, what an absolute joy and privilege it is to be acting with you,' she eulogised.

'Well, what about me?' replied the international artist, once the world's highest-paid. 'You don't know how much this means to me. For sixty years I have worked – for this. This is my big break. This part, in this picture, could be, for me, the beginning. If I could get two parts like this a year, as an actor – not as Chevalier – maybe I wouldn't have to work so hard on the stage . . . and I find that tiring. In this picture, though, I work hard. I want so much to be good in it – with none of the old Chevalier tricks.'

This child of the Paris slums, the epitome of easy-going Gallic charm with his ready smile, rakishly tilted straw hat and the delectable, fractured English, had already conveyed a tribute to Audrey. It hung in her dressing-room. The first-day-of-shooting telegram said quite simply: *How proud I would be, and full of love I would be, if I really had a daughter like you.*

Even the Baroness was not forgotten. Hearing from Audrey that her mother derived a great thrill from receiving autographed pictures of celebrities for her 'collection', Chevalier despatched her a photograph inscribed: 'To Audrey's *real* mother from her *reel* father.'

Audrey had made a definite speciality of captivating some of Hollywood's greatest senior citizens (Bogart, Fonda, Astaire), and was continuing the trend with Cooper; Grant and Harrison would follow. Their domination of her dazzling wide-eyed looks and velvet voice was equalled by her propensity for revealing their vulnerability. Gary Cooper was hooked. 'I've been in pictures over thirty years,' he said, 'but I've never had a more exciting leading lady than Audrey. She puts more life and energy into her acting than anyone I've ever met.'

Although the public's reception for the picture was mild, *Love in the Afternoon* remains one of Billy Wilder's richest and most personal films; and just as Jack Lemmon was the ideal Wilderian hero, so Audrey was Wilder's perfect heroine, 'combining innocence and fragility with a sure sense of purpose and playfulness.'

Only one thing marred Audrey's sure sense of purpose in

real life, during the shooting of *Love in the Afternoon,* and that was the fact that Mel was not around and she therefore had to spend her off-duty weekday hours alone at the Hotel Rafael, while Mel was filming MGM's *The Vintage* in the South of France. It was their first prolonged separation. Away from the cameras, Audrey felt miserable in her solitude. But all was different at weekends. Every Friday night, over six weeks, Mel would leap into the white Thunderbird he and Audrey had brought from Hollywood and speed to Nice airport to pick up his wife. At St Tropez they would spend two relaxing days basking in the sun, swimming, playing tennis, taking excursions on *pedalos,* and searching out little country inns in which to hide out.

Although on the set Audrey was warm and friendly, she unintentionally surrounded herself with an aura of unapproachability. But then Audrey was always keen on privacy, and during her long film career would manage, like few others, to defend her private life. It became an accepted formula that 'Miss Hepburn gives interviews only when she works on a film – never in between.' These interviews were always terribly polite, often terribly boring, and left the world with the impression that there was an Audrey Hepburn that no one would ever know. She seemed always so constrained, always so perfect, so disciplined . . . and so *sad.*

Movie composer Henry Mancini, stimulated by Audrey to write 'Moon River' and 'Charade' and 'Two for the Road', always maintained that if you listened carefully to these three songs you could almost determine who inspired them. They were all imbued, he said, with Audrey's inimitable wistfulness – 'a kind of slight sadness'.

'There was a modesty and a sadness about her,' one of her future leading men, Peter O'Toole, would affirm. Henry Rogers, her one-time American publicist, would be even more emphatic. 'Rarely,' he said, 'did I ever see her happy.'

When she laughed, she laughed so loudly that everybody was carried away – people were compelled to laugh with her. When she cried, she crumpled up, disappeared and cried in complete secrecy.

For the moment, the Ferrers' personal and professional interests dovetailed neatly. Being cultured, sensitive, intelligent individuals, they found enjoyment in the same pursuits, and each learned – persevered – to like the other's hobbies. Mel, having begun his career as a dancer, shared Audrey's fondness for ballet. Audrey, for her part, boned up on the finer points of jazz from Mel, who was a fervent jazz enthusiast; their portable record-player and records were always a part of their luggage. Mel's zest for sports also rubbed off a little on Audrey, and she proved an apt if unexceptional pupil in tennis and golf. Both accomplished linguists, they enjoyed good literature and stimulating conversation in any country in which they happened to find themselves. Above all, they enjoyed each other's company, though friends who knew them well were divided on how long this idyll could last. Some said forever. A less-naïve faction wondered, particularly in the case of Audrey, whether or not she was not *too* coolly intellectual, *too* calculating in her dealings with herself and the world about her. These friends said she would never really be able to fulfil herself as a woman or as an actress until she *did* throw caution to the wind and permit herself to be guided by her heart.

All that was up to Audrey. Previously, there had been friends and critics to help her find her way. But now she stood alone on the threshold of what promised to be the turning-point in her career: the chance to fulfil herself as a great actress. Only a few doubted that she could accomplish it.

20

'People learn to accept unhappiness, I think.
It's a painful lesson of living.'

NEWSPAPER HEADLINES AT the beginning of
1957 – 'Audrey Hepburn Quits Films for a Year' – started the
rumours. Something was in the air. Could it be true that one of
the cinema's most sought-after stars was really turning down
all offers of work *just* to remain with Mel?

Twentieth Century-Fox wanted her to star in the screen version of Françoise Sagan's novella, *A Certain Smile,* and to take
the title role in *The Diary of Anne Frank.* She turned her back on
both offers. Paramount approached her to portray Maria, the
real-life postulant nun in Austria who was sent to be governess
to the seven children of the widowed, retired sea captain, Baron
von Trapp. In the event, Rodgers and Hammerstein turned the
story into a stage musical for Mary Martin, and *The Sound of
Music* opened on Broadway in 1959, with Julie Andrews subsequently playing the screen role.

Additionally, she was asked to replace Diane Cilento in the
London musical show, *Zuleika,* which was about to transfer to
Broadway. But Audrey wanted Laurence Harvey to be her
leading man, and when he said 'No', she bowed out.

On top of everything else, Associated British Pictures were
still knocking on the door. Criticisms that she had turned her
back on British films started to infuriate her. 'I'll return to Britain when they offer me a good script,' she lashed out. 'Anyway,' she said, 'why should I howl my eyes out because I can't
be in Britain? I only lived there for three years.'

Her only professional commitment that year was to honour a

161

long-standing promise to co-star with Mel in a ninety-minute colour production of *Mayerling*, presented as one of NBC's 'Producer's Showcase' specials and directed by the Ferrers' old friend Anatole Litvak. It was later released theatrically in Europe. Mel played Crown Prince Rudolf of the Habsburg Empire who, in 1889, carried out a double suicide pact with his baroness mistress, Mary Vetsera, portrayed here by Audrey.

Although it was one of the most expensive and ambitious television presentations ever mounted in the United States, complete with thirty lavish sets, ten costume-changes for Audrey, and a cast of more than a hundred, including Raymond Massey and Diana Wynyard, the enterprise was a failure. 'The lovers seemed more fated to bore each other to death than to end their illicit alliance in a murder-suicide pact,' commented one TV critic.

Paramount also agreed with that assessment and, noting that Audrey Hepburn *and* Mel Ferrer did not spell instant screen magic, declined to take up the option on three other projects Audrey was willing to undertake with Mel under its auspices: co-starring with him in Thomas Wolfe's *Look Homeward, Angel* and in Jean Anouilh's *The Lark,* and being directed by him (and not Wyler) in *L'Aiglon.* For once, Svengali was influencing no one.

Mayerling, in February, occupied just two weeks and four days of her time. And so Audrey, voted 'Our Girl of the Year' by Britain's *Picturegoer Film Annual, 1957–58,* by deciding to abandon all other work for a year, invoked the gossip-mongers into full battle-cry: 'Why? Why? Why?' More precisely, was she going to have a baby?

The rumours started because, when Audrey told friends 'I must rest', they remembered what she had confessed to them the previous autumn, after completing *Love in the Afternoon.* It was: 'I very much want to have a baby.' She and Mel were still very keen to start a family of their own, but Audrey was not letting on . . . not, at least, to the outside world. Her declarations had a hollow ring about them. 'A baby? No,' she said. 'After all, one wouldn't go to a way-off place like Mexico in such a case.'

While Mel joined Tyrone Power, Ava Gardner and Errol Flynn in Mexico City for location shooting for the screen adaptation of Hemingway's *The Sun Also Rises,* Audrey reasoned that the tropical air would do wonders for her health. If she wanted that baby, the doctors had told her, she would have to take things easy for a while. She obeyed the doctors. Mexico agreed with her.

Apart from a brief visit to New York, she spent the remaining part of the year at 'our honeymoon cottage' in Burgenstock. There she learned that New York columnist Cholly Knickerbocker had named her one of the ten most fascinating women in the world, that English society photographer Antony Beauchamp had idolised her in his Ten Loveliest Women citation ('I am always entranced by her eyes filled with wonderment'), and that the New York Dress Institute had voted her the sixth best-dressed woman in the world. The human race also learned that her Yorkshire terrier, Famous, was taking tranquilliser pills because he got so nervous crossing the roads. If her pet goldfish had died, no doubt that would have made the news, too.

No-pictures-this-year-Audrey had literally starved the media of Hepburn stories – though she more than compensated with her next film, *The Nun's Story*, Warner Bros' screen adaptation of Kathryn C. Hulme's best-selling novel. Audrey's portrayal of the real-life Belgian girl who joins a strict order, endures hardship in the Congo, breaks her vows and returns to ordinary life as a nurse, would become generally regarded as the finest performance of her career.

America's *Films in Review* magazine would echo the sentiments of most when it trumpeted, 'Her portrayal of Sister Luke is one of the great performances of the screen.' It had noted earlier: 'Miss Hepburn reveals the kind of acting talent that can project inner feelings, of both depth and complexity, so skilfully you must scrutinise her intently on a second and third viewing of *The Nun's Story* to perceive how she does it.' Audrey was no longer playing Audrey. She was now an actress.

The opportunity came about because, as always, the advice of Mel carried great weight with Audrey. He had read the book and commended it to her. About that time she learned that Fred Zinnemann, who had recently directed three commercial blockbusters (*High Noon, From Here To Eternity, Oklahoma!*), was interested in directing a movie based on the book. He asked her if she would consider playing Sister Luke, and she said 'Yes'. What he did not tell her was that, until she agreed to do the picture, every studio in Hollywood had turned down the proposition. 'Who,' they asked, 'will want to see a documentary about a nun?' But as soon as Audrey's name was mentioned, they were all queueing up with offers. Warner Bros won the deal. 'It was Audrey's name alone which made it possible,' said Zinnemann.

'It wasn't just that I wanted to play a nun,' declared Audrey. 'The book appealed to me, the movie had a good director, and the part was suited to my nature.'

Many of her colleagues feared that the role suited her nature too snugly for comfort. But while most movie stars played their roles only in front of the camera, Audrey lived her part around the clock. She never looked at herself in a mirror, because mirrors were forbidden to Sister Luke's order. She ate and lived simply, avoiding ostentation and unseemly entertainment.

A make-up man in Rome thought it would lighten the tedium for her during a camera line-up by playing a gramophone record. 'Please turn that off,' Audrey requested promptly. 'Sister Luke wouldn't be allowed to listen to it.'

On another occasion the official photographer on the set tried to give Audrey a beautiful doll to express his thanks for her co-operation. She jumped back dramatically in alarm, breaking the doll and screaming, 'Take it away – I hate dolls. They look like dead children.' The photographer could not have known that, from childhood, Audrey had abhorred dolls, regarding them as 'silly' and 'unreal'. But now her hatred of dolls had a darker, deeper significance, and Mel became worried over her emotional health.

No one but her husband knew that she was inconsolable over the fact that, despite the Mexican sojourn, she was still childless. Friends noted that she treated her little dog, Famous, as a child, hugging and kissing him and changing the ribbon round his neck every day. 'I just couldn't part with him,' she told people. 'She loved that dog dearly,' observed Zinnemann. 'He went everywhere with her. She even got him into Sweden, which has similar quarantine laws to Britain.'

One day, passing the dressing-room of Rosalie Crutchley, who played Sister Eleanor, Audrey decided to drop in for a chat. She had seen the British actress's ten-year-old son and six-year-old daughter at the studios the previous day, and the conversation quickly turned to children.

'How fortunate you are to have such a lovely son and daughter,' said Audrey, a tone of despondency in the voice. 'I do terribly want to have a child – more than anything else in the world. How have you managed to have children *and* maintain a career?'

'Unlike you, Audrey,' answered the striking, lean-featured mother of two, 'I am not a globe-trotting film star.'

'Yes, that *is* the stumbling block,' the film star concluded gravely.

Even before filming got under way in Rome and on location in Africa and Belgium, colleagues were commenting on the fact that she was more than usually timorous and taciturn. When Zinnemann took her to meet the Belgian woman whose life-story was the basis of the book, she behaved very 'strangely'. 'Miss Hepburn didn't really want to meet me,' the woman said later. 'She felt the story was too much of my private life. She just sat there and looked at me, and didn't ask any questions.'

While Audrey's child-craving depression continued to chew remorselessly into her emotional life, one more obstacle occupied her mind. She had yet to meet Peter Finch. The prospect of her co-star's hell-raising, womanising ways filled an already troubled soul with terror. What did not help matters was the very nature of the role he was due to play – a boozing, womanising doctor without morals who would play havoc with her heart. At what point, she asked herself, would terrible fiction blend with awful reality?

Yolande Finch, the actor's lover, mistress, second wife and friend, who was with him as he struggled to the top and who watched helplessly as the man she loved began to crumble, later affirmed as well as allayed Audrey's fears. 'His public image,' said Yolande, 'was no myth. He was a piss-pot and a hell-raiser, but he was also a happy drunk, a gigglebum and very, very good company . . . for a beach bum from Australia, Finchy had a lot of class, more class than he liked to admit.'

Audrey did not have to wait long to evaluate Finch the womaniser. On his way to the Congo for location filming, he developed a terrible attack of flying fear, in response to which a beautiful Belgian air hostess administered to him. A mutual infatuation developed and they saw a great deal of each other during the shooting of the film as she was always flying in and out of the Congo. Finch told everyone that she came over for 'dental treatment'.

'If she keeps up appearances at the present rate,' Audrey told the assembled film unit, 'she'll be giving her Finchy a very gummy smile!'

To everybody's amazement, Finch kept his hands off

Audrey. He always respected class; it had an inhibiting effect on him. 'There was a lot of rapport between them,' Zinnemann would later recall. 'Being both very giving people, they responded magnificently to each other without becoming too "familiar".'

'They were such total opposites,' added Rosalie Crutchley. 'But where Audrey was concerned, Finch was always on his best behaviour, no racketing or banging around. He bowed to her sheer professionalism.'

Audrey's reclusive behaviour, however, endured erratic fits and starts. Some days were worse than others. But Lionel Jeffries, the great English character player, who took the part of Dr Goovaerts, saw a different side to Audrey's oscillatory nature. 'She was so tolerant with me in one scene where I was having trouble with the pronunciation of "Quinine",' he would remember. 'I was giving the English emphasis, and Fred Zinnemann insisted on "Qui-*nine*". I was holding up the shooting, but I shall never forget a big wink from Audrey – and at last I got it.'

Her depression finally lifted, observed friends and colleagues, soon after some scenes were filmed in a leper colony, and following a visit to a mental institution. So she was childless, she mused, but how could that compare to the misery that these people were enduring? 'After looking inside an insane asylum, visiting a leper colony, talking to missionary workers, and watching operations, I felt very enriched,' said Audrey. 'I developed a new kind of inner peacefulness. A calmness. Things that once seemed so important weren't important any longer.'

Her composure was consolidated when she arrived back in Rome for interior shooting and received a surprise visit from her elder half-brother, Ian, there with his wife and baby daughter. Ian was now a soap company official living in The Hague, but when Zinnemann met him he decided he would be exactly right to play a Belgian friend of Audrey's in the film – a part he happily undertook with relish six weeks later even though he nursed no acting ambitions.

The interiors were shot in Rome concurrently with the interiors for William Wyler's production of *Ben Hur*, on adjacent sound stages. Rumour had it, though it was never officially substantiated, that, while visiting the backlot set for the Roman epic, Audrey became one of the extras in a crowd sequence as a gag. It no doubt boosted an ailing spirit.

166

Throughout the filming on *The Nun's Story*, a seemingly inherent quality of Audrey's – her vulnerability – constantly impressed itself on those with whom she came into contact. Outwardly she could be all warmth and femininity, the kind of helpless, cuddly creature that appealed to the protective instinct in every man and woman. Yet beneath that fragile exterior she nurtured the impenetrable emotional reserve of an introvert, intensified by the stolidness of her Dutch heritage. 'Audrey's vulnerability was her greatest asset as an actress,' a future co-star, Richard Crenna, would recall. 'Everybody wanted to take her under their wing and shield her and protect her. But,' he would then add, 'she was not at all a person who could be manipulated beyond her desires.'

An interviewer, finding her curled up on a tangerine sofa in her dressing-room, thought to himself, 'A very smart cookie . . . with an air of untouchableness about her. A fellow will think twice before he grabs hold of Audrey and tries to kiss her. She's the kind of girl you want to protect – and yet she gives the impression that she can take care of herself in almost any kind of tight squeeze. She'll either talk herself out of it or slither out of it.'

Audrey always had that effect on men, and its potency would never dim. As her old friend Van Johnson explained, 'I always, always felt a need to protect her; I didn't even want her to be alone.' But Cary Grant was more perceptive. 'Audrey is an extremely female female,' he would reflect after working with her, 'but she has the strength of steel in that little sinewy body.'

On location in the Congo, she was always crisp and fresh where strong men wilted under the humidity and hard work. A newsman reported that she had 'the appearance of delicate china and the endurance of stainless steel'. Said Audrey: 'One of the men told me I had an indestructible frailness. It isn't so.'

'I don't think for one second she put on an act,' said her lifelong friend David Niven, 'but Audrey was certainly never stupid enough, when she realised that she had been blessed with giving the impression of someone in need of protection, not to appreciate the dividends that came naturally to her because of it. And I don't mean financial dividends. But never could you say that Audrey was far tougher than she seemed on the surface. She was full of resilience and I think her child-

167

hood, under the German occupation in Holland, was tough and very unpleasant, but never was *she* tough.'

Rosalie Crutchley considered the proposition. 'Audrey, vulnerable? Yes, maybe, but I think that also stemmed from innocence and a self-effacing nature – but you can't be totally self-effacing if you're a film star. The one thing that is rather unpleasant about acting is that you have to reveal certain things about yourself through a character, and I don't think Audrey liked doing that.'

When Christopher Reeve first met Audrey at one of the Oscar ceremonies in Hollywood, and sat with her all evening as a dinner partner, he was immediately struck by her many-faceted personality. 'In an old Katharine Hepburn movie called *Bringing Up Baby*, with Cary Grant, she talks about the boat that they used to sail together when they were married,' Reeve would subsequently relate. 'She was a grand boat – she was "*yar*". It's an indefinable word, but it somehow says everything about Audrey: the grace, strength, dignity, the beauty and appropriateness, a beautiful boat being well sailed.

'You see those big brown eyes and the little nose, somebody who looks very vulnerable and crushable, but who has such a sense of rightness that she will challenge people who are failing in a certain way. Katharine Hepburn has the same quality, though hers is much more steak and ice-cream, fresh air, open windows, eight hours sleep. Audrey has a more European grace and elegance. It's that combination in a woman where femininity and courage mix in a captivating way.'

Although Fred Zinnemann had heard, before working with her, that Audrey was enormously independent in her opinions, he was unprepared for the enigmatic duality of her personality. It stemmed from a sensitivity that would result in an exciting, poignant performance on celluloid. But how much, he wondered, would this be achieved at the expense of Audrey's obviously delicate emotions?

'She may have been well-oriented when it came to knowing what she wanted from life,' mused the Austrian-born director, 'but in her private life she was emotionally vulnerable to certain people, the people she had a personal relationship with – her mother, her brothers, and Mel. She was very much influenced by them. On the surface she could be witty, gay, sparkling, but who can look into a person's heart? I think Audrey has probably been unhappy at times. Mel had an enormous

168

influence on her in the early days following their marriage. But as the marriage went on, that influence became less crucial and some friction – perhaps quite a bit of friction – developed. We had few problems while making *The Nun's Story*, because he was working in America and she was working either in the Congo or in Rome, which meant that Mel wasn't around very much. Sometimes he'd come over for a few days, but then he'd go again, so basically Audrey always seemed very relaxed.'

Perhaps the extraordinary effect Sister Luke had on Audrey, especially at the beginning of filming, was due in part to her own harrowing wartime background in Holland, when so many members of her family, and so many close, dear friends, died at the hands of the Nazis. Kathryn C. Hulme's novel, based on an article by Emmet McLaughlin in *People's Padre*, told the true story of Gabrielle Van Der Mal, the daughter of a distinguished Belgian surgeon who entered a convent in order to become a nursing nun in the Congo. But she soon discovered that there was more to being a nun than chastity and faith and, in the end, she smashed every individual feeling inside herself except the power to hate the Nazis who, during the war, killed her father. Back in Belgium, she worked for the resistance movement.

The parallel between Gabrielle's life and Audrey's was so overwhelmingly obvious that perhaps it would have been exceptional if the role had not affected Audrey in the way that it subsequently did. Audrey, certainly, brought her own special quality of wilfulness locked in fragile innocence to Sister Luke, making her struggle real and moving – and it earned her another Oscar nomination. There were also Oscar nominations for Fred Zinnemann's direction, Robert Anderson's screenplay, Franz Planer's photography, Franz Waxman's score, and one for best picture. In the event, the film did not receive a single Oscar. *Ben Hur* swept the board, and Simone Signoret was named best actress for her role in *Room at the Top*.

But *The Nun's Story* made more money for Warner Bros than any film in its history; and, in a poll conducted by *Film Daily* among more than 1,800 representatives of America's press critics, reviewers and film commentators, Audrey was voted Best Actress of the Year. The New York film critics also gave her the best actress award, as did the jury of the San Sebastian Film Festival, the Variety Club of Great Britain, and the British Film

169

Academy, so 'one of the great screen creations of the past decade' did not go unnoticed.

Lionel Jeffries, contemplating Audrey's success, verbalised it for millions. 'Like the great Katie Hepburn,' he proclaimed, 'she's a *listener*. She *re*-acts, and, above all, she's exclusive. Needless to say, I love her.'

21

*'It's tough for me when I see myself on the
screen. I suffer. It's hard to be objective.'*

*I*T HAPPENED TO all of them . . . all those un-
employed discoveries from Britain's sex-starved studios who
journeyed to Hollywood and became international stars. In the
process they matured. They became aware. They became
women. But people never thought it would happen to Audrey
Hepburn, the frightened fawn of Elstree. While making her last
picture in the Congo she had even confessed, in an off-guard
moment, 'I am happy to make this film because it's a story
without sex, a film in which I don't have to give either a kiss or
an embrace.'

Her next movie changed all that. *Green Mansions* was a watershed, the moment in her career which marked the transition
from a purely asexual screen image to one of full-blooded sex-
uality. Directed by Mel and based on W. H. Hudson's powerful
love story set in a South American jungle, Audrey indulged in
such an orgy of kissing, cuddling and sensual romping with
co-star Anthony Perkins that voyeurs could be excused for
thinking that she was determined to make up for lost time and,
indeed, for lost opportunities.

Audrey's admirers were shocked. Some, pleasantly. Never
for one moment had they thought of frail, elfin Audrey in
terms of a female Tarzan-like jungle goddess awakened to full
womanhood by handsome adventurer Perkins. Never had they
expected to see her gallivanting so scantily dressed among the
giant snakes and prowling jaguars of some tropical paradise,
and, as the 'bird girl' Rima, frolicking and gasping in the Ama-

171

zonian undergrowth with all the frantic fervour of a convent schoolgirl let loose on sex for the first time.

It was all Mel's idea. He had experienced a rare flash of inspiration. He had decided that Audrey was just the girl to play Rima, a role that had defied casting for nearly thirty years. MGM backed his inspiration with three million dollars and got Anthony Perkins, the leading young heart-throb of the day, to play the young man who loses his heart (and once or twice his clothes) to Audrey's jungle sprite.

While Audrey had been engaged on *The Nun's Story*, Mel and a film unit had spent three months photographing the jungle backgrounds on a location trip that entailed travelling some 25,000 miles into the hinterlands of Venezuela, Colombia and British Guiana by light plane, dugout canoe and machete. More than 250 tons of materials and props, and a veritable Noah's Ark of birds, plants and animals, were also shipped back from South America on the S.S. *Vesuvius* for use at MGM's Hollywood studios, where replicas of the native village and Rima's hut were completed and, on Lot 3, more than twenty-five acres converted into a river area.

Mel's three earlier efforts as a film director, *Girl of the Limberlost*, *The Secret Fury* and *Vendetta*, possessed individually about as much charm as a used Kleenex. He made no secret of the fact that he wanted to become a director of stature in the eyes of the world. Would *Green Mansions* change his directorial fortunes? It certainly would: for the worse. Yet he could not be faulted in his effort to secure, in one dramatic gesture, a more exciting and more sexy screen image for his wife. It was a stroke of inspiration in every sense of the word.

The truth of that statement could be found in Audrey's answer to a question which every visitor to the set asked her. As she extricated herself from Tony Perkins' passionate clutches, someone would invariably enquire: 'How does it feel to have your husband tell another man how to make love to you?' Her reply was always: 'Uninhibited.'

She meant every five syllables of it. Without Mel at the helm, the world would certainly never have seen the new, sexier Audrey Hepburn. Svengalis had their place. 'For the first time in my career,' she confessed to a confidant, 'I've lost my shyness. Everything seems to be going more smoothly, perhaps because I'm more relaxed. Love scenes have always been difficult for me. But with Mel directing and leading Tony and me

172

through the emotional passages, everything's fallen into place. I can see the love scenes in their true perspective.'

Audrey had been constantly reminded that many casting directors and producers did not look too approvingly on an elfin-like actress whose only attribute, apart from acting talent and charisma, was (as Audrey herself was inclined to quip) 'a fine line in bone structure'. She even overheard one studio tycoon turn her down for a part with the words, 'Heck, if I wanted to look at bones, I could always have my own foot X-rayed.'

Slights such as these were always taken with great equanimity by Audrey, who believed, and proved, that there was much more to sex-appeal than a top-heavy bust and a well-shaped bottom. 'Sex appeal is something that you feel deep down inside,' is the way she once explained it. 'It's suggested rather than shown. I'll admit that I'm not as well-stacked as Sophia Loren or Gina Lollobrigida, but there is more to sex appeal than just measurements. Those curvy screen sirens don't even know what it is, let alone how to use it. I don't need a bedroom to prove my womanliness. I can convey just as much appeal fully clothed, picking apples off a tree or standing in the rain, as some of those stars think they do wearing practically nothing.'

Audrey once conducted an impromptu 'consumer test' on her sex appeal. She was a fairly young starlet, at a studio party, and she found herself in a room full of beautiful girls, 'with absolutely gorgeous figures', and they were all surrounded by very attentive men. 'I picked up a drink,' she said, 'wandered into a corner away from the rest and decided to see just how much man-appeal I could generate from within myself. I just stood there for a while, whispering to myself that I was the most desirable creature in the world, that I was somebody men just couldn't resist – and it worked! Before the party was half-way over I had more men around me than I'd ever thought possible.'

It was her eyes that did it, large, clear, innocently bewitching – described once by Cecil Beaton as like 'enormous heron's eyes', topped by 'dark eyebrows slanted towards the Far East'. Those eyes, too, helped Audrey put more 'oomph' into a simple greeting than most actresses could manage with a plunging neckline.

When the Australian actor John McCallum spotted Audrey

173

dancing at Ciro's, his first impression was that 'Audrey Hepburn's attractiveness radiates from her eyes.' Said McCallum: 'Sex starts in the eyes. A film close-up of an attractive woman's face is far sexier than a close-up of naked breasts. There is an expression to the effect that men make love to women's faces, and I think there is a good deal of truth in it.'

Audrey was quite clear on the dynamic effectiveness of the eyes with which she had been blessed, especially as it applied to their impact on the opposite sex. 'There's never any need for any woman to ogle any man,' she maintained with certainty. 'Ogling only puts the men off. It scares them away. In fact, the faintest flutter of an eyelash should be enough.' She then went on to apply the clincher. 'The truth is that I know I have more sex appeal on the tip of my nose than many women have in their entire bodies. It doesn't stand out a mile, but it's there.'

A motoring accident during filming, however, disoriented her sufficiently to take her mind off all matters concerning sex appeal. Audrey was driving her hired car in Beverly Hills one afternoon when an oncoming vehicle approached rapidly 'from nowhere'. In an attempt to get out of the way, she ran straight into a parked car. She was greatly shaken, though not physically hurt.

But, this being Hollywood, a twenty-two-year-old actress-dancer named Joan Lora happened to be sitting in the parked car at the time of the collision, causing her 'severe' back and neck injuries. Miss Lora subsequently took Audrey to court, claiming that the injuries made her lose important acting jobs: she specialised in dancing and horse-riding roles in Western films. In her suit, she claimed damages amounting to $45,000. (She was eventually awarded $4,500.)

The incident had such a traumatic effect on Audrey that she vowed she would never drive a car again – certainly not for several months, and definitely not for the duration of filming. Fortunately, at this time, she was immensely consoled by a friendly fawn named Ip, which became her film co-star as well as pet and, like Mary and her little lamb, followed Audrey everywhere. So that the deer would be genuinely devoted to her in front of the cameras, Audrey raised the animal herself. It was just four weeks old when it came into her life; Famous's nose was severely put out of joint.

As Ip grew larger, life with a deer in the house became more and more adventurous for the Ferrers and, one evening, while it was scampering in the garden, it just disappeared. Without Ip – so named because of the noise it made when hungry – the film was doomed. A frantic search of the grounds and the immediate neighbourhood proved unsuccessful. Finally, it was found – dozing beneath a tree. Because of the adventure, however, the Ferrers arrived late that night for a movie première and an announcer at the door asked Mel what had delayed them.

'Deer was lost,' Mel explained crisply.

'You mean,' asked the puzzled announcer, 'your wife?'

Audrey and Mel rushed into the theatre, leaving the question unanswered.

Green Mansions, in the meantime, assumed an importance for reasons quite unconnected with its artistic merits. It helped to put Panavision on the international map. Panavision is the trade name for a group of wide-screen processes, outdistancing CinemaScope, Todd-AO and Paramount's VistaVision because of its improved anamorphic lens. Panavision came about, in fact, because of Audrey's rather square face. It could have happened with any other actress who had a very square face, but it was Audrey who precipitated the crisis.

President, chief operating officer, and guiding genius of Panavision, Inc., with its large, sprawling plant on Pontius Avenue in Santa Monica, was Robert E. Gottschalk. As he told it: 'The industry stood still technologically between the advent of sound (Vitaphone) and Fox's CinemaScope, which was a great step forward. But we had to find a new process when we starred Audrey in *Green Mansions*. A test had confirmed our worst fears: her square face looked too fat in CinemaScope. So we tackled our own process. Our camera, in the course of time, dollied into a big close-up of Audrey peeking from behind some foliage – and her face didn't expand! I remember the people in the projection room – executive Eddie Mannix, sound boss Doug Shearer, Audrey and Mel among them – all broke out in spontaneous applause.'

Gottschalk subsequently proceeded on his own – and Panavision evolved. MGM used it at about the same time in the filming of *Ben Hur*, the Mirisches used it on *The Magnificent Seven*, and more and more thereafter . . . and all because of Audrey's square face! *Green Mansions*, however, received with complete public indifference, was a box-office disaster. 'There were parts in it that I liked,' argued Mel to the bitter end. 'It wasn't a complete flop in my mind.'

There were no awards.

175

22

'It frightens me to think that so much is
expected of me. With Roman Holiday *it*
wasn't so bad. People didn't know me then,
so what could they expect?'

THE STATION WAGON bumped along the dusty
road at high speed, leaving behind the picturesque and fertile
valley formed by the eastern spurs of the Sierra Madre. Some
Mexican women waved by the roadside as the vehicle sped
downhill to a remote Mexican Indian settlement, and then suddenly it was out again, heading towards the parched open
desert of Guadiana.

'Journey's end; return trip at six this evening,' the driver
cracked as the station wagon pulled up by a multitude of boxes,
huts, generator trucks, caravans and cameras which made up
the film set. One by one they tumbled out of the vehicle,
Audrey, Burt Lancaster, Audie Murphy, Lillian Gish, Doug
McClure and John Saxon for another day of work.

By midday tempers were frayed as the cruel Mexican sun
beat down on the company from a cloudless sky. Difficult
scenes proved to be that much more difficult to shoot under
such sweltering conditions. More than once Audrey thought
she must be mad: first the Congo, now *this*. Why had she not
taken the holiday she had promised herself after winding up
the final scene in *Green Mansions*? The question was pointless.
She had read Ben Maddow's script for *The Unforgiven*, and she
knew immediately that its heroine was a part she simply had to
play.

The rambling and unlikely film hinged on the revelation that
comely young Audrey, sister of lusty Texan cattle-drovers Lancaster, Murphy and McClure, turned out to be a Red Indian.

176

She had been rescued by their late father as a baby and mother Gish had hitherto been able to keep the secret. But then a sabre-flourishing maniac recognised her one day and spread the word around the cattle country about her origins – and in this scattered area of Texas soon after the Civil War, prejudice against Indians ran high. 'You squaw – you red nigger!' shouted one of her step-brothers. Thus the seeds were sown for a Cowboys and Indians adventure described by one critic as 'the thinkingest Western I've seen for some time.'

Guadiana's remoteness was chosen in preference to Texas itself because of its numerous precious advantages: untramelled sky-lines, no aircraft vapours, no telegraph poles and intermittent highway traffic, absolute dead silence, and clear blue skies. Above all, the location site offered a 360° vista of untouched, unspoiled horizon and terrain, ideal for a picture dealing with the experiences of early settlers in the Texas panhandle.

John Huston agreed to direct the film because he saw in Maddow's script the potential for a more serious and better film than the producers had originally contemplated. He wanted to turn it into a story of racial intolerance in a frontier town, a comment on the real nature of community 'morality'. The producers disagreed. What they wanted was what Huston had signed on to make when he accepted the project in the first place – a swashbuckler about larger-than-life frontiersman Burt Lancaster. In the end he violated his own conviction that a picture-maker should undertake nothing that he did not believe in. The picture turned sour on him. 'Everything went to hell,' Huston would confess. 'It was as if some celestial vengeance had been loosed upon me for infidelity to my principles. Some of the things that happened are painful to remember. . . .'

For her part as Rachel Zachary, for which she received a fee of $200,000, Audrey was required to ride bareback on a tall, white stallion they called Diabolo, a horse which once belonged to Batista, one-time strong man of Cuba. She had not ridden a horse since childhood, and certainly not bareback, but she was determined to ride in every scene in her long-skirted Red Indian-girl costume, refusing all help of a stand-in. She usually practised at lunchtime under the heat of the noon sun; it was her only free time.

After one such practice ride, Huston called for the after-

177

noon's shooting to commence. While the camera was being set up, Audrey re-mounted the white stallion and cantered out to a spot by a riverbank and, without recourse to either saddle or bridle, sat alone waiting for her cue. As she waited, she noticed an unusual amount of confusion coming from the vicinity of the film crew; and then suddenly, from the knot of movie-makers, a horseman galloped towards her. Diabolo pricked his ears forward, became very tense, whinnied, and bolted towards the camera. A member of the crew, attempting to halt the runaway horse, threw up his arms. Diabolo stopped suddenly and hurled a petrified, screaming Audrey over his head on to the concrete-hard crusty earth. There was a sickening crunch. Audrey lay still, unconscious.

The scene was watched by the entire company in stunned silence. And then panic broke out. Huston and Lancaster dashed to the spot with three wranglers, shouting to the others to keep back.

'Call the doctor,' screamed Huston as he ran; and a few minutes later up rushed Dr Hernandez, a Mexican physician assigned to the unit.

The doctor knelt down beside Audrey. She opened her eyes and tried to move, but yelled out as a knife-like pain lashed out across her back. 'Lie still,' he said gently, and, turning to a man standing behind him, added abruptly, 'A stretcher – quick!' There was an urgent tone in his voice.

'. . . Mel . . . please don't tell Mel,' she murmured. 'Don't tell anyone . . . I want to tell Mel. He worries . . . he worries so much. . . .'

As she spoke, three men arrived with a stretcher and gently they lifted her onto it. They carried her to the station wagon and placed the stretcher in the back, where Dr Hernandez made a brief examination. Over Audrey's head and through the window, the doctor could see John Huston, Burt Lancaster and Audie Murphy talking earnestly together.

'He was telling me he believes a vertebra may be fractured,' Huston was informing them. 'She must be in terrible pain.'

The three of them walked towards the station wagon. 'I'm taking a vacation,' quipped Audrey as they peeped inside. 'Want to join me?' They laughed.

'Say, that's a great idea,' joked Audie Murphy. 'What about a place called Durango? Heard the weather's great over there. . . .'

The sedative began to take effect; she yawned.

Her personal physician, Dr Howard Mendelson, flew into Durango from Hollywood with Mel and, after examination, reported four broken bones and a badly sprained foot: the muscles in her lower back were also badly torn and there was some haemorrhaging. But the fractures were clean breaks, so no surgery would be needed. With this news, Audrey sent a note to be posted at Durango's Casa Blanca Hotel, where most of the actors, actresses and members of the crew were staying: 'Dear Folks, *maravillosos* friends, with all my heart I thank you. For you I would do it again!'

As Audrey recuperated at her rented Beverly Hills villa, the film was put on the shelf at an estimated loss to United Artists of $250,000. Three weeks later she made her first tentative steps since the accident, and the picture resumed production in Mexico a further three weeks after that. For the remainder of the two-month shooting schedule Audrey wore an orthopaedic brace, and was forced to travel lying down on mattresses in a station wagon over rough fields (not roads) to the set, and had to continue resting in a horizontal position when not working. She found it too painful to sit.

Mel did not hide his anger over the fact that Audrey was having to work while in such poor health. 'Actually,' he fumed, 'I think it's a bad idea to go on with the picture, but Audrey's pretty strong-willed.'

'Her fall was on my conscience,' Huston admitted later. Contemplating her fragility, he then sighed – 'oh, those thin arms, those thin legs and that wonderful face.'

'I'll ride that horse again,' Audrey pledged; but the scene in which she was thrown was a crucial one, and therefore had to be re-filmed, so Huston wisely scheduled the shot for the last day of the picture. This time Diabolo behaved impeccably.

Although Huston's career probably hit its critical nadir with this hysterical Western, most reviewers seemed to enjoy it, though some were bored and irritated by it too. Several critics noted that Audrey's ability and potential had been sorely used by the director, an assessment with which Lillian Gish was in complete accord. 'Audrey played my daughter and I loved her as a daughter,' said the great actress of the American silent film era, 'but her talent was never used properly in the film. When I saw the completed version of *The Unforgiven* I knew that if they had used her gifts completely the film would have been a much greater success.'

179

But it is doubtful that Huston would have agreed. He felt all the performances but Burt Lancaster's were doomed from the outset. Sensitivity, at which Audrey excelled, was not called for. The veteran director of *The Maltese Falcon* and *The African Queen* confessed later, 'Some of my pictures I don't care for, but *The Unforgiven* is the only one I actually dislike. Despite some good performances, the overall tone is bombastic and over-inflated. Everybody in it is bigger than life. I watched it on television one night recently, and after about half a reel I had to turn the damned thing off. I couldn't bear it.'

PART FOUR

Motherhood and other diversions:
the agony, the ecstasy, the tragedy

23

*'It's so nice being an expectant mother for
the first time.'*

To BECOME A mother was still a dominant fac-
tor in Audrey's life, and when she discovered, while shooting
The Unforgiven, that she was pregnant, she was frantically
excited. Back at the Alpine chalet she went into Garbo-like rus-
tication. Being able to tell friends she was expecting a baby lifted her to the heights of happiness. Forgotten were the dark
thoughts she had wept out to intimate friends: 'I don't understand why I can't have children. Mel and I are so much in love.'

Only the previous Christmas she had told close acquaint-
ances, 'I must work to forget. Only work can help me; holidays
give me time to think, and that's bad for me.' Always prone to
crises and near-breakdowns, Audrey had to watch her emotional state like others had to watch their weight. Another confidant said, just before the news of the impending birth,
'Audrey is a mental wreck who, in pursuit of happiness she
cannot find, makes herself ill.' But now she was ecstatically
happy. She began knitting baby clothes.

And then her world, a world so often as fragile as she was,
collapsed around her. She was shattered when she suffered a
miscarriage soon after, shattered when she learnt that
motherhood had once again been denied her. The repercussions of her fall from the white stallion were far-reaching. 'This
is a tragedy,' said Mel, his voice choked with emotion. 'It has
broken her heart and mine.'

She went into what she herself would refer to as 'a black de-
cline' and, once again, found herself fighting a nervous break-

down. At one stage she weighed exactly seven stones and smoked a steady sixty cigarettes a day: she usually smoked only moderately. She was engulfed by depression. The patient kindness of Mel was her only anchor. Time and the adoration of her husband healed the emptiness in her heart, and she started to live once more; but a film she was to have made that year with Alfred Hitchcock, *No Bail for the Judge*, opposite Laurence Harvey, which had already been postponed because of her pregnancy, was later abandoned. She would have played a London prostitute.

For a period that summer she was also in the running for the title role in what would prove to be the most expensive film ever made, *Cleopatra*. Her agent, Kurt Frings, had also sent a first-draft script to another of his clients, Elizabeth Taylor. Audrey and Taylor, then the world's two highest-paid film actresses, expressed more than a passing interest. But Paramount refused to release Audrey for the film, and Taylor ended up with the famous contract that gave her one million dollars outright, plus $50,000 a week for overtime, plus $3,000 a week living allowance, plus a big percentage of the picture's gross earnings. The intriguing question remains: What if . . . ?

One of the more agreeable moments for Audrey before the year was out, and one which filled her with immense pride, was an invitation to return to the family 'seat' at Doorn, the little town in the Netherlands where the Baroness had been raised in the ancestral castle. Audrey, already one of the district's favourite characters, now found herself unveiling a lane renamed in her honour – Audrey Hepburnlaan. The whole town came out in force for the occasion. If there was an extra depth and richness to the obvious joy that radiated from Audrey's eyes, then the Dutch townfolk would have to wait another month for the full revelation of her happiness. It would then be told to the world: seven months after her miscarriage, Audrey Hepburn was again expecting a baby.

This time round she resolved there would be no mishaps. She would take care of herself and, with this strategy in mind, she took the doctor's advice to accept no more film roles during the pregnancy. She accompanied Mel to Rome while he worked on Roger Vadim's *Blood and Roses*, and then flew to the South of France while he made *The Hands of Orlac*, but mostly she spent her days in the lovely garden at Burgenstock, contemplating the great day. 'There is not a second in the day

184

when I am not thinking of the little one,' she enthused. 'I am like a cloistered woman, counting the hours.'

She refused all invitations and was in bed by nine every night. Periodically she was haunted by old memories, and became obsessed by the maternal misfortunes of film stars. She thought constantly of Marilyn Monroe (two accidents) and Maria Schell. But she knitted no more; she had done enough already, and feared that more would bring ill luck.

As the weeks slipped by, she entertained Mel's four children and collected as many youngsters around her as she could. She borrowed them from their mothers, surrounding herself with young, happy laughter, squabbles, fights, rowdy friendliness. She wanted her baby to know right from the beginning how wonderful a young world could be. She wanted her baby to know about this young world, to long to be a part of it.

When they were gone, she waited.

After a rainstorm on a brilliant Sunday morning, 17 January 1960, at Lucerne's Municipal Maternity Clinic, Audrey gave birth to a sturdy, well-made son. He weighed nine and a half pounds, and they called him Sean. The Christian name was chosen because it was the Irish version of Audrey's half-brother's name, Ian, and because it meant 'Gift of God', the significance of which was not lost on all who knew the baby's mother.

Five minutes after the birth, Audrey's nerve broke. 'Let me see the baby, let me see it at once,' she cried, tears streaming down her pale cheeks. 'Is it all right? Is it *really* all right?' Her secret fear all along was that the baby might be born with a physical defect. Only when she had been reassured did a wan smile appear on her tired face as she kissed Mel.

'I'm the happiest man on this earth at the moment,' said Mel standing by Audrey's bed and wearing a long white doctor's coat over a collarless shirt. 'We both so much wanted a baby, whether a boy or a girl. It happens to be a boy, so we're just that much happier.'

When Audrey returned to the chalet ten days later, she found that Mel had had the nursery decorated in blue – to match Sean's light-blue eyes. He was now an American citizen but, having been born on Swiss soil, he would, on his twenty-first birthday, have the choice to remain American or become Swiss.

Two months later, in the little French–Swiss Protestant chapel

185

where Audrey and Mel were united in wedlock, Sean was baptised by Pastor Endiguer, who had married his parents six years earlier. The godparents were Audrey's half-brother, Ian, and Mel's sister, Terry. Sean cried briefly during the ceremony, prompting his grandmother, the Baroness, to remark: 'A good cry at a christening lets the Devil out.' His robe had been made by Givenchy, and so had Audrey's. The American ambassador to Switzerland, Henry Taylor, Jr., brought the baby two presents: his American passport and a fifty-star American flag. It was a small, family affair, all very chic and glorious, and Audrey disclosed that she hoped to have many more children just like Sean. Mel, now a father five times over, simply beamed.

Audrey spent the remainder of the summer at Burgenstock, with the Baroness and an Italian nanny on hand when needed. Motherhood was a great tonic; friends remarked that they had never seen her so happy and radiant. She reflected occasionally on some of the films she had been asked to do that year, including Otto Preminger's *The Cardinal* and the musical *West Side Story* – roles which finally went to Carol Lynley and Natalie Wood – but she felt confident that she had done the right thing in declining them. She was firm in her resolve 'not to rush into things', determined to savour these early days of her God-sent maternity. After six years of childless marriage, Audrey was in no hurry to abandon her dreamchild.

24

*'I'm no Laurence Olivier, no virtuoso talent.
I'm basically rather inhibited. I find it
difficult to do things in front of people.
What my directors have had in common is
that they've made me feel secure, made me
feel loved.'*

AUDREY DASHED OUT of the Women's House of Detention in Greenwich Village, New York, to the accompaniment of the Sixth Avenue traffic din and the sing-song chant of the inmates within. 'If I had the Wings of an Angel,' the girls wailed as they peered out of the barred windows of the austere prison at Tenth Street and Sixth Avenue and watched the movie star fall into the arms of her leading man, George Peppard. The two of them then leaped into a waiting taxi and sped – to freedom – west on Christopher Street. The scene was repeated again and again – eleven takes to be exact – and hundreds of Villagers flocked behind police barricades to get a glimpse of Audrey, who looked right at home in that area of New York City in her grey, turtleneck blouse and dark, skinny pants.

Next day, Fifth Avenue sightseers, attracted by the crowds of policemen in front of Tiffany's, obviously expected to see a jewel robbery in progress or, at the very least, a glimpse of visiting Soviet premier, Nikita Khruschev. But the cause of the commotion proved to be the sight of a remarkably thin girl in a precarious hairdo and a stark Givenchy evening gown who strolled to the showcase window, peered appreciatively at the jewellery and proceeded to take a sip from a container of delicatessen coffee and a healthy munch from a Danish pastry delicately balanced in her long, black-satin glove.

The girl on the town was Audrey, but her breakfast at Tiffany's was strictly for the benefit of the Technicolor camera concealed inside the window of the staid old jewellery store.

Audrey, it transpired, had no affection for the Danish pastry, preferring ice cream at Schrafft's, and even less enthusiasm for the gaping sightseers – she and the rest of the cast seldom worked before crowds of less than 5000 as supposedly-blasé New Yorkers gathered to see Audrey and Peppard, and sometimes Patricia Neal, Buddy Ebsen, Martin Balsam and Mickey Rooney, do their bit for the camera. Her maternity leave was over.

With Sean left behind at Burgenstock with the Baroness and the nanny, Audrey had arrived in New York in October to start work on Blake Edwards' two-million-dollar-plus movie adaptation for Paramount of Truman Capote's novel, *Breakfast at Tiffany's*. Mel tagged along. This was to be a landmark for Audrey, for while in the Fifties she had established a sense of aristocractic innocence, of fawn-like vulnerability, of pixie-ish charm blended with a vixenish soul, it became clear towards that decade's end that, at thirty-plus, she would soon be too old to play such ingenuous parts. Wisely, Audrey began to search for new areas in which to express her cinematic personality. What she needed, she and Mel reasoned, was a vehicle which would provide the proper transition into more mature, sophisticated roles without ever turning her back on her old appealing, charismatic screen image. Luckily, she happened on Holly Golightly.

Audrey's Holly Golightly, to offer a word of the period, was 'kookie'. The part, in fact, proved to be quite a departure for Audrey, whose roles up to then had certainly not embraced 'kookiness'. 'I'm a wacky, dizzy girl who takes nothing seriously,' is how she explained it. In the script Holly's agent and friend provides a more apt description of her: 'She's a phoney, all right,' he insisted, 'but a *real* phoney!'

At first, Audrey did not think she was right for the role. She had believed all the publicity that claimed Capote had written the story with Marilyn Monroe in mind, and so she had hesitated to read George Axelrod's script; she thought she lacked the right sense of comedy. Even having read the script, she remained unconvinced of her suitability. The part called for an extrovert, and she was an introvert. It called for the kind of sophistication that she found difficult; she did not think she possessed sufficient technique to put it across. But everyone, Mel, Kurt Frings, Blake Edwards, the Baroness, pressed her to do it. So she did; and she suffered through it all. She lost weight. Very often while doing the part she was convinced that she was not doing the best possible job.

Her decision to do it illustrated a continuous conflict. On the one hand, she was tempted to play it safe – as do most Hollywood stars – and portray a part in which she had scored big successes. At the same time, she wanted to try something new. That conflict made her extremely nervous right from day one. Her anxiousness, reflected between takes in a series of stubbed-out cigarettes, soon infected the rest of the company, who required ten takes after as many rehearsals to complete the first difficult dialogue scene inside the venerable jewellery establishment, and culminated with a yelp of rage from the cameraman, Franz Planer, the distraught recipient of an alleged 220-volt shock.

Of course, in the guise of Holly Golightly, Audrey had cause for concern. She was playing one of the most memorable characters of then-recent American literature, an amoral teenager from the Texas backwoods who had been blessed with a fashion model's figure, an income from a notorious racketeer in payment for her weekly visits to Sing Sing, and an inclination to boast about her lovers ('I've only had eleven,' she conservatively brags). There was one consolation. Anthony Perkins excepted, Audrey's leading men (Bogart, Holden, Fonda, Astaire, Cooper, Finch, Lancaster) had been notable for being considerably older than their leading lady. Now, with Peppard, a mere eight months her senior, the film's 'love interest' was imbued with a more plausible quality. They were physically well-suited.

Peppard played a not-very-struggling young writer who moved into the same New York brown-stone apartment house as Holly and discovered, via the fire-escape, a new love. But Audrey had never worked with anyone quite like this graduate of the Lee Strasberg school, sometimes known as 'method' acting. Then a relative newcomer, with only a handful of screen credits to his name, he was none the less regarded in Hollywood as a young tyro with the impact of a James Dean or an unfledged Clark Gable, a serious technician with a sense of humour. But Audrey found working with this method actor a very strange and unnerving experience. He was kind to her, but she was disturbed by his need to *analyse* everything.

Working alongside such a technician gave Audrey an inferiority complex. Compared to Peppard, she had very little

189

experience on which to fall back. She had no technique to help her to do things for which she was patently unsuited. She had to operate entirely on instinct. 'I started as a ballet dancer, and it's often hard for me to believe I'm an actress,' she would tell people.

William Wyler described her yearning to succeed in the acting department as 'the right kind of ambition', and referred to her 'sincere and honest drive to get ahead without stepping on anyone's toes in the process.' Whenever she was engaged on a picture, her work always came first, to the exclusion of her social life. One merry Italian family, who gave a party in Audrey's honour during the filming of *War and Peace*, were surprised when the Ferrers left before the party really got going. 'I have a difficult day tomorrow,' Audrey explained – and left the startled hostess to pacify her other guests.

'Her acting is so *simple*, although a lot of people can't see how good it is,' explained her *Nun's Story* friend, Rosalie Crutchley. 'There's nothing overdone. She's a most un-obvious actress.'

Tiffany colleague Patricia Neal called her 'first-rate both as an actress and as a person', and it was her person, or persona, that inspired so sensationally the most successful and highly rewarded composer of film music in our time. 'It's unique for a composer to really be inspired by a person, a face or a personality,' said Henry Mancini. 'But Audrey certainly inspires me. Normally, I have to see a completed film before I'll compose the music, but with *Tiffany* I knew what to write for Audrey just by reading the script. Then, when I met Audrey the first time, I knew the song would be something very, very special. I knew the exact quality of her voice and that she could sing "Moon River" beautifully. To this day, no one has done it with more feeling or understanding.'

'Moon River' was written to explain that Audrey/Holly was really a yearning country girl; it becomes an anachronism, therefore, to have it sung by a male singer, although Danny Williams's version later became a top-of-the-hit-parade best-seller. It was Audrey's rendition of the song, in fact, which first convinced many critics that they were dealing with no ordinary talent. The cigarette-girl extra in the British quickie had reached the Olympian heights and become a Hollywood superstar; most agreed that it would have been hard to think of any other actress who could have suggested as convincingly as Audrey did the desperate frailty beneath Holly's smart façade.

190

One critic noted that she roared through the film as if it was not coffee she had for breakfast but a gallon of high-octane fuel. Another observed that Audrey's delicious performance made us forget that a girl who had to subsist on cottage cheese between dinner dates could not afford a Givenchy wardrobe. But while, in America, the *Newark Evening News* found her a 'daffy delight' and the *Motion Picture Herald* commended her for playing the role 'with dash, winsome appeal, vibrant excitement, all at the same time', the British critic Penelope Gilliatt complained that the film expressed little more than Audrey's 'vivacity and sweetness', and the London *Times* despaired that the picture's general effect was uneven and that Audrey herself could not 'bring off the impossible'.

Most acknowledged, however, that this new cinematic persona was a treat, reflected in the fact that Audrey was again nominated for an Academy Award, although the Oscar finally went to Sophia Loren for her performance in *Two Women*; the film's only Oscar, in fact, went to Henry Mancini for his song, 'Moon River'. But the annual film critics' poll conducted by the American *Film Daily* trade magazine named her Actress of the Year, and in Italy the judges for the prestigious David of Donatello awards proclaimed her the best non-Italian actress seen in Italy that year.

While working on the film, a newspaper interviewer in Hollywood asked about her ambitions and what role she would most like to play. 'That's easy to answer,' she told him. 'I'd do anything to play Eliza Doolittle in *My Fair Lady*.' Maybe somebody, somewhere, would take note. In the meantime, she could but wish.

Sean and his nanny flew to Hollywood to spend Christmas with his parents. Since separated from Audrey, he had grown into a big, strong baby with an almost insatiable appetite and 'an extremely powerful voice'. That Christmas, her first with 'my two men together', was the happiest she could remember. On 8 January, at a testimonial dinner in Hollywood by the Friars Club for Gary Cooper, whose mortal illness was then not generally suspected, Audrey read a lovely poem called 'What is a Gary Cooper?' The actor rose to his feet in acceptance of the cheers of his filmland friends and said, 'The only achievement I am proud of is the friends I have made in this community . . . and if you asked me if I'm the luckiest guy in the world, all I can say is "yup".' Four months later, Coop was dead.

The Ferrers then embarked on their travels again, first to Paris, where Mel directed and acted in a film, then to the Ivory Coast for a month of location work, on to the French Alps and Yugoslavia and then back briefly to Beverly Hills, where they rented a lavish hillside villa. Audrey continued to turn down several more movies, including *A Taste of Honey*, *In the Cool of the Day* and *Hawaii*, roles which subsequently went to Rita Tushingham, Jane Fonda and Julie Andrews, because to have accepted them would have meant being away from Mel and Sean. (The film she *really* wanted to do, as did Elizabeth Taylor and Jean Simmons, went to Leslie Caron – *The L-Shaped Room*, about a young woman, unmarried but pregnant, who finds an uncertain happiness in a seedy London lodging house.) She described their life together as 'a whole series of four monthses: six months here, three months somewhere else, four months somewhere else, constantly renting houses and packing, shipping'.

Her public may have regarded the reality of Audrey Hepburn as waltzing through a swan-studded lake in white tulle with Fred Astaire in *Funny Face* and asking for $50 for the powder room in *Breakfast at Tiffany's*, but for the woman concerned that was 'an interlude'. Real life was when the cameras stopped, and she packed up the dog, baby and nanny and dashed to the chalet at Burgenstock, and there took out her wedding china and snatched at family life. 'We've worked hard at working it out, and we're together most of the time,' she explained.

Sharing their life from time to time was near-neighbour Sophia Loren, who fussed over Sean as if he was her own. Like Audrey not long before, she was still childless in her marriage to Italian producer Carlo Ponti but longed (so far without success) to embark on motherhood. So, many a night, as the sun set behind the hilltop pines and Audrey prepared one of their shared favourite pasta meals, Sean would be coaxed to sleep by the statuesque sex goddess.

That summer, in an annual poll conducted by America's Caricaturists' Society to find the world's ten most beautiful women, Sean's Italian 'baby-minder' headed the list, followed by Brigitte Bardot, Princess Grace of Monaco, Jackie Kennedy and, placed fifth, Audrey. In the same list, which included Kim Novak and Doris Day, was Warren Beatty's kid sister, Shirley MacLaine, who teamed up with Audrey that year in William Wyler's *The Children's Hour*. If *Breakfast at Tiffany's* heralded a significant new off-beat side to Audrey's screen image, the departure was as nothing compared with her role in this new venture, based on Lillian Hellman's famous play. The subject of this tragic drama, called *The Loudest Whisper* in Britain, was latent lesbianism, first brought into the open by a series of lies by a wilful, neurotic twelve-year-old child, who accuses Audrey and MacLaine, the two headmistresses of the girls' school which she is attending, of having an 'unnatural' attraction for each other.

Audrey Hepburn as an alleged lesbian was about as improbable a piece of casting at that time as contemplating Jayne Mansfield as the Virgin Mary. Taking into account the tremendous pains she took to maintain a 'respectable' screen image, her decision to take on this new challenge bordered on the staggering.

William Wyler had first filmed the play in 1936 under the title of *These Three*. For his latest version, he paid $300,000 for the screen rights, considered casting Katharine Hepburn and (God forbid) Doris Day as the headmistresses, and then thought that Audrey and MacLaine (who had recently received two Academy Award nominations) would be more charismatic. James Garner, having just finished four years of playing *Maverick* on television, was chosen as the town doctor whose engagement to Audrey would go up the flue of doubt.

The Hollywood director had been trying for twelve months to get away from his own creation, *Ben Hur*, the biggest thing since movies began. *The Children's Hour*, a modest black-and-white job, only one and three quarter hours long, and costing peanuts (a mere one million pounds' worth), was Wyler's method of redressing the balance. At first he contemplated changing the title to *Infamous*, 'so people won't think it's a Walt Disney', but then common sense prevailed. 'It's going to be a clean picture with a highly moral story,' he promised. 'The reason I chose Audrey is that she is so clean and wholesome. I don't want bosoms in this.'

In fact *The Children's Hour* became the first film to receive a Production Code Administration seal since the PCA rules, created in the early Thirties by the Motion Picture Producers and Distributors of America, under Will H. Hays, were relaxed to permit the portrayal of sexual aberrations on the screen provided 'references are treated with care, discretion and restraint.' The ruling had previously been that sex perversion,

193

of which lesbianism was deemed a part, or any inference to it, was forbidden. Nevertheless, while the dialogue did not include a single mention of lesbians or lesbianism, there were plenty of signposts along the way.

But none of this concerned or deterred Audrey, who breathed nothing but enthusiasm for her role. For her part, however, Shirley MacLaine could not at first fathom Audrey's restrained, unshowy personality, misinterpreting class as aloofness. Billy Wilder had already enunciated it: 'Audrey has that rare class, something which Garbo also has. It's a personal style, a kind of breeding that positively radiates from the screen.'

Frank Sinatra's Rat Pack labelled Audrey 'the Princess', and Sinatra himself at this time very much wanted to work with her. 'It's still an unfulfilled ambition of mine,' he said. 'She's the kind of girl you know Mother would love, the kind they built musicals around.'

The best-selling American novelist, Judith Krantz, elaborated Sinatra's 'princess' analogy many years later. 'She's so elegantly constructed and perfectly dressed that she makes all other women look gross,' pointed out the author of *Princess Daisy*. 'Yet she has escaped malice and envy because she's the quintessential waif. Under all the immaculate, cultivated style we sense someone who's incredibly fragile, someone who, for reasons we don't know, seems to need *us*. In Audrey Hepburn we have the image of a princess orphan, just as in Streisand we once had the image of a princess urchin.'

The 'princess orphan', for the moment, had Shirley MacLaine confused. Audrey's reserve was not to her taste, and neither was Mel's pomposity. 'I had plenty of qualms when I met Audrey for the first rehearsal for *The Children's Hour*,' recalled MacLaine. 'It took me quite a while to thaw her out – about three hours. From then on, it was one big kick. Audrey and I had a running gag all through the picture. She was supposed to be teaching me how to dress, and I was supposed to be teaching her how to cuss. Neither of us succeeded.'

Whatever else Audrey did or did not do, she certainly did not cuss. Her personal code – she was always remarkably concerned about the impression she made – was so highly developed that its impact affected everyone with whom she came into contact. Her sole presence made any coarse remarks out of the question. 'From the moment she walks on the set,

194

the mere thought of swearing is made redundant,' said a film publicist. 'She commands *that* sort of respect automatically, without ever asking for it.'

'Because of her flawless manners, her innate good taste and inbred goodness,' admitted Van Johnson, 'it would be unthinkable to utter four-letter words in front of her.' Added Billy Wilder: 'You find yourself putting your talk through a mental sieve, even though you know Audrey's no prude.'

But not everyone observed, or was influenced by, the Hepburn 'code' – her future co-star, Rex Harrison, for instance. A colleague observed: 'From time to time, Rex could behave pretty badly on the set and swear a lot. That used to upset Audrey.' Her personal code even extended into her screen roles. The only occasion on film when a profanity passed from her lips, in fact, came in *Two for the Road*, when she twice accused Albert Finney of being a bastard. Its impact was all the greater because it was completely at odds with the 'decent' Audrey Hepburn image.

What sustained the two actresses' friendship throughout the filming of *The Children's Hour*, was their shared sense of fun, even though MacLaine's outrageous hilarity was quite unlike anything which Audrey could muster. Audrey enjoyed listening to MacLaine's jokes, but found herself incapable of reciprocating in kind. 'I'm a giggler,' she offered by way of apology.

Her humour was impish and quite often unexpected. Irene Worth talked of 'her laugh, her sense of fun and her glorious, uncorrupted character;' and *Nun's Story* co-worker Lionel Jeffries, who met Audrey again when he was at Warners in Hollywood to make *Camelot*, found himself using words like 'waggish' to describe one surprising aspect of her nature. 'I was *totally* disguised in a four-and-a-half-hours make-up as the King,' Jeffries remembered, 'and was getting a breath of air outside the sound-stage. A car passed and a voice called, "Hello, Lionel!" It was Audrey. I was both delighted and baffled that she'd seen through a ton of rubber and plastic. To this day I've always believed it was a set-up.'

As for the film itself, *The Children's Hour* was heavily slammed by the critics, who called it 'lugubrious', 'sensational' and 'turgid'. The general consensus was that it had a dated air which not even the winsome sadness of Audrey nor the burning sincerity of MacLaine could enliven. One critic, nostrils issuing fire and brimstone, fumed: 'Instead of being wowed by an off-beat combination, we get a pair of off-hand performances in a sentimental slob of a film.'

But no one ever accused Audrey of being 'off-hand' in her appearance, and, as the year ended, the New York Couture Group, which had already announced its list of the world's twelve best-dressed women in 1961, went one step further and elevated Audrey to its Best-Dressed Hall of Fame. This was a permanent non-competitive status to which only women who had been listed annually for more than three consecutive years were eligible. Unlike what many thought about her last film, Audrey was no slob.

25

*'Why do people keep on saying that Mel
makes all my decisions, decides what I am
going to play and with whom and where?'*

THE FIRST HALF of the new year would be as restful for Audrey as the second half of the old one had been hectic. She reduced herself to skin and bone working with Wyler, and now she was determined to make steady progress in a big weight-gaining campaign organised by Mel; in the first month alone she added three pounds, which even Audrey had to admit was 'little short of miraculous'. She was aiming at an even six pounds gain by July, in readiness for her next film commitment in Paris.

During this period of 'battery recharging', Audrey told Mel that there was no doubt in her mind that, if necessary, she would willingly give up her career to devote the rest of her life to her family. For the time being, though, she would continue with her career; the marital/career ratio was properly balanced and working according to plan. She could travel all over the world with Mel, Sean and Famous, secure in the knowledge that she had a home to return to in Burgenstock. There was a time when they would be in Rome, London, Paris, New York or Hollywood and she would collect knick-knacks for a future home and put them in storage. There was nothing in storage any more. Everything was in their Alpine chalet.

The hilltop perch was almost deserted between September and June, so Audrey now spent the time doing what she loved doing most: being a mother and housewife. They got up at seven or eight in the morning, and Audrey cooked and took care of Sean; sometimes a cook would help out, but mostly

Audrey did it. Mel played tennis and did a lot of reading, and two or three times a week they would go down to Lucerne to market and make the rounds of the shops. They walked many miles, ate early and went to bed by ten o'clock. People accepted them as they were and there were no 'star' problems, though they would occasionally be irritated by some wild Italian photographers hanging around outside the gate. To the staid local people, she was 'Frau Ferrer'.

As she rested, she agreed 'in principal' to play the title-role in a screen version of *Peter Pan*, in which Peter Sellers would portray Captain Hook and Hayley Mills would be Wendy. But legal wrangles with London's Great Ormond Street Hospital for Sick Children, who owned the rights to J. M. Barrie's famous play, would prevent the venture ever getting off the ground – and more than twenty years later, Mel would still be working on the development of *Peter Pan* as a motion picture. Briefly, at this time, too, Alfred Hitchcock toyed with the idea of having Audrey for his next chiller, but then felt that his new young discovery was ready for the role; and thus Tippi Hedren's screen career was launched with *The Birds*.

Soon after leaving for Paris, in July, the unoccupied chalet was burgled. Among the items stolen were pieces of underwear and Audrey's Oscar statuette for *Roman Holiday*. When the culprit, a twenty-two-year-old science student named Jean-Claude Thouroude, later gave himself up, along with the stolen property, he told the police that he had committed the crime in the hope of meeting Audrey Hepburn. He was madly in love with her, collected her photographs, and possessed six letters from her secretary. He had taken a job in Switzerland, near Audrey's chalet, in the hope that he would see her. Finding that Audrey had left for Paris, he used the opportunity to rob her home, envisaging that he would then eventually meet his idol in court. He failed again. The magistrate ruled that 'love is not a crime', and released him on a suspended six months' jail sentence and a £22 fine.

These 'non-crimes of passion' were becoming a common occurrence in Audrey's life. The previous year, in Australia, a thief broke into Paramount Pictures' fireproof vault in Sydney and, ignoring the hundreds of other films stored there, got away with the only films starring Audrey, which included *War and Peace, Funny Face, Sabrina* and *Roman Holiday*. 'The only use the thief could have for the films would be to screen them for his own benefit,' concluded an aggrieved Paramount executive. 'It looks as though whoever stole the films had a wild crush on Audrey Hepburn.'

When officials at the Studios de Boulogne in Paris were told that Audrey would like dressing-room number 55 during the filming of her next picture, *Paris When It Sizzles*, they promptly moved some French VIPs around and made it available. They did not know, however, that this was the number of the dressing room Audrey had for *Breakfast at Tiffany's* in Hollywood and for her Oscar-winning *Roman Holiday* in the Italian capital. Her success in these two films had convinced her that 55 was her lucky number.

Luck, though, played little part in one rather more vital realm of Audrey's life. On the surface, despite Mel's strong-willed, domineering ways, her marriage seemed to be blissfully untroubled. In public, the couple always presented a picture of cheerful compatibility. Was this how people behaved when they had marital problems? How wrong the gossips were being proved to be.

In private, for all that, things were somewhat different, and the situation came to a head soon after Audrey arrived in the French capital to work on *Paris When It Sizzles*, an incredibly juvenile comedy that fizzled and frizzled rather than sizzled, and which reunited her with an old friend, William Holden. Based by *Breakfast at Tiffany's* writer George Axelrod on the screenplay by Julien Duvivier and Henry Jeanson for the 1954 French-made *Holiday for Henrietta* (which starred Hildegard Neff and Michel Auclair), it told of top Hollywood screenwriter Holden who hired bright young secretary Audrey to act out fantasies in his movie in order to help him finish his script. The problem was that it confused itself, and everyone else, by being a film within a film. It was uniformly panned. Cameos by Mel, Marlene Dietrich, Tony Curtis, Noël Coward (as a Roman emperor surrounded, improbably, by a clutch of starlets), and others, did not help.

Although many scenes were filmed by director Richard Quine in the parks, cafés and streets of Paris, the bulk of the picture was made inside the studio, which became Audrey's second home. Her first home, for the moment, was not with Mel – he was away in Madrid working on exteriors for *Fall of the Roman Empire* – a state of affairs which precipitated their first major crisis. Because they could not be together, it was not long before there were misunderstandings.

Audrey was convinced that she had to do something drastic, particularly as Mel was not flying back at weekends as had always been his custom when their filming commitments coincided. She decided to remedy the situation by using the oldest and most effective of women's wiles. By making him jealous. He would then waste no time in lavishing her once again with his affections.

Holden gallantly agreed to help his co-star in her ruse. The only thing was, he was not trying to be gallant: his heart still beat with fervour where Audrey was concerned. Meeting her again brought back all the old passions. He was almost beside himself with an inner conflict. 'In all the relationships I've had with leading ladies,' he said later, 'I found that the less involved I was with them the better. Oh listen, I have people I absolutely adored – two women, three – I just think the world of, and if they had ever been willing to change their way of life and say "I'll go with you"' – and Audrey made it plain she would not – 'it would have been fine. But we never stepped over the boundaries. So after all these years we have the same kind of respect for each other that we had in the beginning. I'll tell you, it's worth a lot more to me than a piece of ass.'

In Audrey's plan to arouse the emotion of heartburn and doubt in Mel, she sought Holden's company often and, as she anticipated, they soon excited the curiosity of the gossip-mongers. When the affair began to look serious, friends made it their business to inform Mel how Audrey was spending her time. Mel took the news calmly, saying that he did not wish to make himself look ridiculous by showing jealousy. Audrey was dismayed, but not disheartened, and when she and Holden returned to America to dub the film she carried on the association but to little avail.

Mel continued to appear unmoved. Deciding that even more drastic measures were needed, Audrey asked for a divorce – and this time her husband's reaction was prompt. Within seven days he arrived in New York to talk things over and patch up their differences. For the time being, all was well again. There was also no more talk of the vivacious Duchess of Quintanilla, in whose company Mel spent so much of his time while in Madrid.

Golden boy Holden, having played his part, faded discreetly out of the picture. Before disappearing from the scene entirely, he considered with amazement Audrey's discipline and drive. In all his years in movies, he had seen nothing like it. 'If that girl ever disappoints herself,' he reflected, 'if she ever seriously lets herself down, there is going to be the greatest wrist-slashing and gas-jetting ever seen!'

Hardly had Audrey made arrangements to vacate the old Bourbon château on the road to Fontainebleu, where she and Sean had been living during the summer, than she found herself extending the lease for another period of four months. A new Paris-based film came up unexpectedly. *Charade*, with Cary Grant as her latest leading man, had been one of those quick and effective deals when everything seemed to fall into place for Audrey. She had known Grant for years, and they had always hoped that one day they might make a picture together, but somehow they were always in the wrong place at the wrong time to make it possible. Stanley Donen, the diminutive producer-director who had last worked with Audrey on *Funny Face*, was not only Grant's favourite moviemaker but also a good friend and an on-and-off partner. When the veteran English-born star of *To Catch a Thief* and *The Pride and the Passion* was visiting his mother in Bristol, Donen appeared on the doorstep and presented him with the script for *Charade*.

'It's delightful,' enthused Grant. 'If only Audrey would play the girl, Reggie. . . .'

Donen left immediately for Paris to show the script to Audrey.

'It's delightful,' she said eagerly. 'The role of Peter, the mystery man, would fit Cary Grant to a tee. I wonder . . .?'

'Don't wonder,' Donen interjected. 'It's in the bag.'

Charade, which cost three million dollars and grossed many times that sum, was an improbable Hitchcockian comedy-thriller with the excitement overtones of James Bond. It showed Audrey at her most charming and wide-eyed and Grant at his most suavely appealing, falling in love against lushly romantic backgrounds in the Alps and around Paris, even though death was just around the corner for one or both of them if James Coburn, Ned Glass and George Kennedy, the ruthless criminals with whom they were involved, did not get what they were after – a quarter of a million dollars belonging to the US Government. Walter Matthau, as a bonus, was a tiredly amusing fellow at the American Embassy, and Peter Stone's screenplay was literate, witty and chock-a-block with deadpan cracks like 'Any morning now you can wake up dead.'

For Audrey, making the film at the Studios de Boulogne was a sad–happy affair. She could not forget that she had made *Love*

201

in the Afternoon at the same complex, on the southern fringe of the Bois de Boulogne, just six years earlier with the late Gary Cooper. What especially upset her was that the furniture used in her film with Coop was again being used in *Charade*. 'I don't like to think of it,' Audrey said. 'It's sad. We loved him so.'

Audrey, now on her way into the economic stratosphere of big-earning actors, had negotiated (thanks to agent Kurt Frings) a deal which gave her a participation in the profits of *Charade*. The last woman to be in on a percentage as co-star of a Cary Grant film was Doris Day, whose percentage earnings alone from *That Touch of Mink* topped more than a million dollars in the first twelve months of its release. Audrey, too, would earn a tidy sum; even without access to the profits, her fee was now a million dollars.

Frings, a large, red-faced man with a thick German accent and the body of a prize fighter, which he once was, moved well and dressed with initials-embroidered-on-shirt-cuffs style. He had a reputation for being a great women's agent. When Elizabeth Taylor saw the kind of fees he was negotiating for Audrey, she wasted no time in becoming his client; neither did such disparate actresses as Lucille Ball and Brigitte Bardot, Maria Schell and Olivia de Havilland – though such male top-liners as Cary Grant, Joel McCrea and Edward G. Robinson were not excluded from his books.

A funny, energetic, explosive man, he became the toughest, most powerful agent in the business. He was a partner with Eddie Fisher in the Swiss corporation called MCL Films (formed by Elizabeth Taylor for her children, Michael, Christopher and Liza), which owned thirty-five per cent of the 1963 spectacle, *Cleopatra*, and, because of the exorbitant fees he negotiated for Audrey and other movie superstars, he found himself dubbed one of the men who killed Hollywood. 'How can they say that?' he would ask in his deceptively cute accent. 'Hollywood is still here.' And then: 'I always try to get the most for my clients. It is my job to guide them, boost them, protect them. They are the people I work for, not the studios.'

Audrey certainly thrived under his aegis, and, indeed, like many other women, found him more than mildly attractive. He delivered the goods. The fees were agreeable, and she worked alongside only the best directors and leading men. 'He was good for her,' noted David Niven, 'because she was always doing good things.' That about summed it up.

Good things, however, sometimes come in awkward packages. Her leading man was once again, well – mature. Cary Grant was fifty-eight when filming got under way, fifty-nine when it was finished, and sixty when *Charade* was finally released – to Audrey's thirty-four. 'My great problem is finding suitable co-stars,' Grant was forced to admit. 'The public obviously won't accept me romancing girls if they're *too* young. That's why, in *Charade*, I muted the love interest with Audrey a little. And really I don't think I can be seen romancing a girl any younger than she is.'

But screenwriter Peter Stone got round the obvious age disparity by facing it boldly and actually capitalising on it. Thus, when Audrey grew romantic, Grant uttered: 'At my age who wants to hear the word "serious"?' In fact, because of the chasm of twenty-six years that divided the world's two most popular box-office stars, and to avoid any accusations of bad taste (as happened, of course, when she played opposite Fred Astaire and Gary Cooper), Audrey this time did all the chasing – and Grant repeatedly reminded her that he was old enough to be her father.

Off the set, nevertheless, there were what Grant himself described as 'ridiculous rumours' linking his name romantically with Audrey. He refused, he said, to discuss the 'wild stories' that were written about him in the fan magazines, which, he pointed out, had in previous years placed him into close relationships with Sophia Loren, Marlene Dietrich and Ingrid Bergman. So that was that.

Yet he and Audrey were close workmates. All Audrey's leading men, with the exception of Bogart, were charmed by her. Grant was merely the latest to fall under her spell. 'All I want is another movie with Audrey Hepburn,' he said, almost with tears in his eyes, on the last day of filming. 'Working with Cary is so easy,' Audrey responded. 'He does all the acting – you just react. It's that simple.' When she had said goodbye to the studio and flown from Paris into the sunset, Grant told a visitor, 'That girl mothered our entire company. The day she left we were bereft. We had to stick around for our fight scenes without her, and we were absolutely lost.'

Audrey spent the rest of 1962, and the first half of the following year, either resting at Burgenstock with Sean or accompanying Mel to his various film locations. In May 1963 she even turned up at that staid and solid aristocrat of New York hotels, the Waldorf-Astoria, to sing 'Happy Birthday, dear Jack' at President Kennedy's forty-sixth birthday party. But having made *Paris When It Sizzles* and *Charade* back-to-back, with but a single day separating the completion of the first picture and the commencement of the second, Audrey found herself completely run down, physically as well as mentally. Even so, she was asked to embark immediately on another film without a break.

But Mel insisted she had a rest. As he told a newsman, 'I must say she looked tired. I don't usually put my foot down about her work, because I know she loves it – but this time I had to. Working with Bill Holden and Cary was a wonderful experience, but those two haven't been at the top for so long for nothing. With their experience they work at a hell of a pace. It's not always easy for an actress to keep up with them.'

The Swiss air would do her good.

26

*'I'm happy for Julie Andrews, but sad and
disappointed for myself – but that's the way
the members of the Academy of Motion
Picture Arts and Sciences voted.'*

THE TELEPHONE RANG in the little chalet in
Burgenstock. Audrey answered it, not even suspecting what
the call could be about. It was her agent, Kurt Frings, and he
was advising her to sit down. *'My Fair Lady,'* he said, trying to
sound very casual, 'is yours.'

Audrey gave out a yell that almost echoed across the lake in
Lucerne. She ran out of the room, eager to find someone with
whom to share her magnificent news. Mel was away in Cannes
at the Film Festival, but the Baroness was upstairs, taking a
shower. She banged on the bathroom door and screamed
something unintelligible about the movie she was to star in and
the Baroness came running out, soaking wet, wrapped in a
towel, thinking the house was on fire. Audrey dashed back
immediately to the telephone, practically in tears, to call Mel.
He said he would catch the next plane home. They then celebrated, Mel in Cannes and Audrey in Burgenstock, he over
champagne with his colleagues, and she (having never liked
the old bubbly) over a glass of beer with the Baroness.

A short while later, the Ferrers invited the Fishers – singer
Eddie Fisher and screen goddess Elizabeth Taylor – to dinner
at their house in Rome. The crooner, of course, had always
adored Audrey, from the moment she first flashed across his
consciousness in *Ondine*, but now he desperately wanted his
superstar wife to befriend Audrey because, he said, 'Elizabeth
didn't have many women friends'. Audrey was not quite herself
that night. She was still floating on Cloud Nine from the heady

realisation that the role of Eliza Doolittle in the cinema version of the musical *My Fair Lady* really was hers. Her guests also seemed to share her exhilaration.

Later that evening, however, when the Fishers were in bed and had just turned off the light, Taylor uttered right out of the blue, 'Get me *My Fair Lady*.'

Her husband was stunned. 'Elizabeth,' he said, 'Audrey has the part. You saw how excited she was about it.'

'Get me *My Fair Lady*,' Taylor repeated in a tone of voice Fisher had never heard before.

'You know I can't do that,' he protested.

'Get me *My Fair Lady*,' she said for the third time.

Eddie Fisher refused to argue with his wife. He had always catered to her whims, but this latest request was going too far. Eliza Doolittle was *that* sort of role: one of the most coveted female screen roles in a decade – a role worth fighting for, worth arguing and bitching for. Many people within the industry, and certainly many movie-goers, were at first openly antagonistic towards Audrey because Julie Andrews, who created the part with great success on Broadway and in London, had not been pegged for the screen role. The industry expressed its indignation at the Academy Awards, when Audrey's performance was not even given an Oscar nomination. Yet *My Fair Lady* swept the board that year, receiving Oscars in every possible category save best actress – this went, ironically, to Julie Andrews for her screen début role in *Mary Poppins*. Justice, in Hollywood's eyes, had been accorded to a 'wronged' but deserving actress.

The original stage musical of 1956 was based on George Bernard Shaw's renowned play, *Pygmalion* – or, more correctly, based on Shaw's *screenplay* for the British film version of 1938, starring Wendy Hiller as Eliza and Leslie Howard as Higgins – with book, lyrics and score by Alan Jay Lerner and Frederick Loewe, who had previously collaborated on such successes as *Brigadoon* and *Paint Your Wagon* and who had yet to pool their resources on *Camelot* and *Gigi*. In London and New York, Rex Harrison was brilliant as Henry Higgins, the arrogant professor of phonetics who sets out, after a wager with his good friend Colonel Pickering, to teach a shrill and unkempt cockney flower girl, a squashed cabbage leaf named Eliza Doolittle, to speak her 'native language . . . the language of Shakespeare and Milton and the Bible' and thus pass her off as a duchess at an Embassy Ball. He succeeds, but in the process falls hopelessly in love with his protégée. Shaw's wit and wisdom remained very much alive and well in the musical version, giving this light (but hardly lightweight) show a sly undercurrent of social satire on the English class system.

Jack L. Warner, production chief of Warner Bros studios, was bowled over by what he saw when he attended the world première of *My Fair Lady*, and began negotiating immediately for the screen rights. The discussions would continue for five years, but would eventually bring Lerner and Loewe a cool five and a half million dollars – the most expensive screen rights in the history of movies. Audrey herself was again paid one million dollars, while the total budget for the film soared to seventeen million dollars, the most elaborate and costly production ever undertaken by Warner Bros since the studio was born four decades earlier.

Within a month of its Broadway opening, it was being rumoured that in the proposed screen version Henry Higgins would be played by Laurence Olivier to Audrey's Eliza. Shirley Jones was also mentioned, as were Richard Burton and John Gielgud. Warner made it plain from the outset that, although Julie Andrews and Rex Harrison had been undeniably wonderful in their original stage roles, their names were simply not big enough for his multi-million-dollar movie. For the part of the professor he favoured either Rock Hudson or Cary Grant, both of whom wisely turned the film chief down, Grant going so far as to inform Warner that he would not even go to see the film if anyone but Harrison played the role. Warner bowed to Grant's superior judgement, and Sexy Rexy's portrayal as Higgins brought him his first (and only) Oscar. (Julie Andrews and Rex Harrison, it is worth recalling, were actually the *fourth* choices for their roles in the stage version, earlier candidates having been Mary Martin – who declined the role – Deanna Durbin and Dolores Gray, and Noël Coward, Michael Redgrave and George Sanders.)

Audrey, however, was always Jack Warner's (not to mention Kurt Frings's) first choice for Eliza, a role which by now had acquired the same kudos as Scarlett O'Hara, Anna Karenina and Cleopatra. (Did Audrey ever turn to Mel in bed and demand, 'Get me *Cleopatra*'?) Every agent in Hollywood believed he had just the actress to play Eliza; the problem was, not every agent had Audrey Hepburn. Frings did not have initials on his cuffs for nothing.

'There was nothing mysterious or complicated about my decision to cast Audrey,' said Warner. 'With all her charm and ability, Julie Andrews was just a Broadway name, known primarily to those who saw the musical. But in thousands of cities and towns throughout the United States and abroad, you can say "Audrey Hepburn" and people instantly know you're talking about a beautiful and talented star. In my business, I have to know who brings people and their money to a theatre box-office. I knew Audrey Hepburn had never made a financial flop, and I also knew that she had given exhibitors a big money shot in the arm with *The Nun's Story*. For that picture, we gave her a guarantee of a quarter of a million dollars against ten per cent of the gross, and she came out with nearly one and a half million dollars – in other words, the film grossed fourteen million, and that was remarkable.'

Warner, a frustrated vaudevillian who ran the studio with a firm and frugal hand, was nobody's fool. The principal casting, meanwhile, was completed by Stanley Holloway repeating his original role as Eliza's anti-social dustman father, Alfred Doolittle, and Wilfrid Hyde-White replacing Robert Coote as the urbane anchor man, Colonel Pickering, with the marvellous Mona Washbourne as the Higgins housekeeper, Gladys Cooper as Higgins's *svelte*, sardonic mama, Theodore Bikel as the language expert who tries to prove Eliza a fraud at the ball, and Jeremy Brett as the aristocrat who falls in love with her. The stalwart George Cukor, who was a genius in directing women and understanding the feminine mind, and who was one of the favourite moviemakers of Garbo and the *other* Hepburn, was the inspired director. Audrey could not have been happier.

She had been studying singing for several months, and learning how to acquire a Cockney accent, when, in May of 1963, she arrived in Hollywood for pre-production work on the film. She wanted to play it honest and do her own singing. This was very important to her.

Audrey and Mel rented a large Bel-Air villa, all white and cool in the Spanish style, replete with swimming pool and tennis court, and brought along Sean and his plump, cosy Italian nanny, Gina. Two smiling girls served tea and home-made apricot jam roll when Cukor, Lerner and the film's designer, Cecil Beaton, arrived for a formal call. 'Are you going to use my voice for the songs at all?' she suddenly asked with candour.

Cukor explained that it was quite possible that, like Leslie Caron in *Gigi*, some of her singing would be interpolated from another voice. 'I'll understand if you do,' she said, 'but in any case I'll work hard on my voice, have as many lessons as you like. It's all part of the business, to learn to sing and dance.'

In the event, the studio chose to ignore Audrey's impressive vocal achievements, as exemplified in *Funny Face*, and allowed her to provide only two per cent of Eliza's singing voice, the remaining ninety-eight per cent being dubbed by songstress Marni Nixon – who did most of the singing for Deborah Kerr in *The King and I* and all of the singing for Natalie Wood in *West Side Story*. There the matter might have rested; but a row blew up following reports that Audrey had actually sung 'almost half' of the role. Miss Nixon's husband issued a statement calling the reports 'unfair and inaccurate'. 'The whole thing is a great bore to me,' Cukor replied in retaliation. 'Marni did it prettily, then we had to re-do it to get in some of Audrey's expressions and interpretations. But it is mischievous and unattractive to make a Federal case out of it.'

The well-publicised incident shook Hollywood to its *papier-mâché* foundations, and it was widely thought to be one of the main reaons why Audrey was not nominated for an Academy Award that year, a tribute which had been universally expected. Years later Audrey would become annoyed when someone brought up the fact that she did not actually sing in *My Fair Lady*. 'You could tell it wasn't me, couldn't you?' she would fish. 'Next time, I'll do my own singing.' But there would not be a next time.

Between early June and the first day of shooting on 13 August ('This is one time when we can't afford to be superstitious,' Warner intoned), Audrey spent up to twelve hours a day on rehearsals. Dancing rehearsals under Hermes Pan. Singing lessons under Susan Seton. Cockney lessons under Professor Peter Ladefoged, a phoneticist at the University of California, Los Angeles ('an American who probably knows London like I know Peking,' quipped Audrey). Work under musical director André Previn. And endless fittings, make-up tests, and pre-shooting recordings: although they did not end up in the film, her own interpretations of Eliza's songs *were* recorded by Audrey, recordings which still exist in the Burbank vaults.

Cukor was determined to film the story in continuity and

therefore carry Audrey logically from the Cockney flower girl of the London gutters, 'a girl so deliciously low, so horribly dirty', to the Embassy Ball where she emerges as London's most enchanting lady. 'It will cost us more this way,' said the director, 'but I feel it's essential to Audrey.'

Audrey claimed it was the most difficult characterisation she had ever undertaken. 'In some ways,' she said, 'Eliza is the first real character I've attempted on the screen. In other roles there has also been at least a little bit of me; in this one there's none.' She had to arrive at the studio each day far earlier than even the extras to allow the make-up people to go to work on turning her into the 'deliciously dirty' flower girl. Dirt was pushed behind her finger-nails and ears, her face was dirtied-up, and even her hair was matted with soot and vaseline to look sufficiently tatty for the cameras. Her one concession to non-realism – known at the time only to a few fellow actors and the technical crew – was to cover herself from head to toe with fragrant perfume before the wardrobe and make-up 'despots' went to town on her.

A singing voice one day invited Cecil Beaton to 'Come on in and see my secrets.' It was Audrey in the make-up department. 'Now, you see, I have no eyes!' she said, grinning profusely. Beaton was amazed by what he saw. 'Without the usual mascara and shadow,' he noted, 'Audrey's eyes are like those in a Flemish painting and are even more appealing – young and sad. Yet it was extraordinary to see that it is simply by painting her eyes she has become a beauty in the modern sense.'

During filming, a visitor to the studio remarked that Audrey had the most beautiful eyes in the world. Overhearing the compliment, the actress replied: 'Oh no, the most beautiful eye make-up perhaps – but all the credit belongs to Alberto.' The Italian make-up expert Alberto de Rossi, whose clients also included Ava Gardner and Elizabeth Taylor, had begun his association with Audrey on *Roman Holiday* and had been with her ever since. He was the man responsible for the distinctive 'Audrey Hepburn look'.

A couple of days after Beaton had photographed Audrey in some of the dresses worn in the film by women extras, she handed the designer a bunch of roses with a note attached: 'Dearest C. B.: Ever since I can remember I have always so badly wanted to be beautiful. Looking at those photographs last night I saw that, for a short time at least, I am – all because

210

of you. Audrey.' This was no 'Isn't she modest?' ploy. She was acutely conscious that she was plank-thin, that her eyes were huge, that her eyebrows flew away into the air, that her nose was too big and her teeth too crooked. 'I'm so ugly,' she told a lady reporter, 'that I've never become used to myself; it's still a complex with me.'

She certainly never regarded herself as glamorous. 'Elizabeth Taylor, all violet eyes, is glamorous,' she would reason. 'Rita Hayworth, Ava Gardner . . . they have a *beautiful* kind of beauty. My face is more personality than beauty.' Elizabeth Taylor, it should be noted, once told a *Ladies' Home Journal* interviewer, 'I have never considered myself a beauty.' Well, then, who *did* she consider was beautiful? Replied Taylor, 'Ava Gardner, Audrey Hepburn. . . .' No doubt Ava Gardner's list of beauties excluded herself but included 'Audrey Hepburn, Elizabeth Taylor. . . .'

With expressive eyes set in a small face under a casual fringe of hair, Audrey looked at times like a Persian kitten suffering from milk deficiency. Paramount's make-up genius, Wally Westmore, explained that when Audrey's face was transmuted through the movie camera, she seemed to be all eyes and intensity. 'With Audrey, the trick is to use a very light over-all base,' Westmore disclosed. 'Light make-up reflects light, thus making her face look filled out and healthier.'

Jack Cardiff, ace director-of-photography on *The African Queen*, *The Prince and the Showgirl* and *Death on the Nile*, believed there were 'faults' that were even more fundamental than milk deficiency. 'Her problem is the jaw-line,' he said. 'It doesn't photograph well. You must concentrate on those great big brown eyes.' He added: 'Audrey has made a symbol of her eyebrows, emphasised to make them thick and black. I filmed her in *War and Peace* and they didn't seem right for the period. I asked her to soften the bold effects that characterised her success. She agreed. But she has steel determination and delicacy that girl.'

No one could doubt, however, that Audrey's appearance succeeded because it embodied the spirit of the day. Seen at the full, the outline of her face was always perhaps too square; yet she intuitively tilted her head with a restless and perky asymmetry. She was like a portrait by Modigliani where the various distortions are not only interesting in themselves but make a completely satisfying composite. 'She actually turns all

211

her disparate facial faults to her *advantage*, and that's all that counts,' said English make-up expert Barbara Daly, among whose clients number the Princess of Wales. 'Most of all, her personality comes through her face.'

There was no lack of vigour in her rejection of the softly pretty. She wore no powder, so that her white skin dazzled with a bright sheen. Using a stick of greasepaint with a deft stroke, she drew heavy bars of black upon her naturally full brows; and almost in Fratellini fashion, liberally smudged both upper and lower eyelids with black. To complete the clown boldness, she enlarged her mouth even at the ends, thus making her smile expand to an enormous slice from the Moor's watermelon. In its acceptance of such an uncompromisingly stark appearance, the general public had radically forsaken the prettily romantic or pseudo-mysterious heroines of only two decades earlier.

The beauty consultants on *My Fair Lady* observed that Audrey's face was wide and her head flat; by building the *coiffures* wider they made her head look flatter. But while she was willing to be as ugly as anyone wished in the early sequences, to the extent of going without make-up, she insisted that when the time came for the 'transformed' Eliza, she should be allowed to be beautiful. They obliged.

During the film's four-and-a-half-month shooting schedule, Audrey had only one inviolable rule, which became known as 'Hepburn's law'. Nobody was allowed to enter her 'eyeline' range, the point or points at which she was looking while in her characterisation. Cukor set up a series of black baffles to screen the immediate action from all but the minimum essential crew. Everybody on the set swore that never before had they seen an actress work with the drive, the fervour and dedication that Audrey exhibited. It was as though she had to prove that the studio was right in passing up Julie Andrews and giving her the role. She knew, too, that there was a fantastic seventeen million dollars riding on her talents, and, come what may, she was going to give them their money's worth.

From the very beginning, from that day in May when Cukor, Lerner and Beaton called round to see her at her Bel-Air villa, she was determined that *My Fair Lady* was going to be the big one. 'This picture is one we must all remember,' she announced to the visiting trio. 'Wonderful talents, everyone right, everyone happy. It's the high spot, let's enjoy it!' Cukor soon found that Audrey intended to do just that. 'She's no emotional stuffed shirt,' he was forced to admit. 'She even goes in for high jinks once in a while. During one scene, for instance, the assistant director had to keep Audrey wet all the time. One day she surprised everyone by grabbing the hose away from him and letting him have it, but good!'

During the morning of 22 November, immediately before the lunch break, Audrey had just filmed the song 'Wouldn't it be Loverly?' when a studio workman came on the set with some awful news: President Kennedy had been assassinated in Dallas, Texas, while driving in a motorcade. Audrey, everybody, was stunned. She was in tears upon hearing the news . . . only six months ago she had sung her birthday greetings at his party; and now *this*. Nevertheless, she insisted that something ought to be said to the crew about the tragedy. Since Cukor deemed himself incapable of doing it, she borrowed a loud-hailer from one of the electricians and made the announcement herself: 'The President of the United States is dead. Shall we have two minutes of silence to pray or do whatever you feel is appropriate?' At the end of the two minutes she ended her brief statement by saying, 'May he rest in peace. God have mercy on our souls.' She had tears in her eyes, but it was done with great dignity. A short while later, however, she broke down and filming was suspended for the rest of the day.

While the film was in production, Mel had worked at Warners on *Sex and the Single Girl*, and shortly after *My Fair Lady* was released he announced that he would direct Audrey in a five-million-dollar spectacle that would be titled *Isabella – Queen of Spain*. But rumours were then circulating that all was not well with their marriage, the resulting undercurrents of which were detected by some members of the company. 'Her marriage certainly wasn't very safe at that time,' affirmed Mona Washbourne, the English character actress who played Higgins's housekeeper. 'I didn't like Mel very much on those few occasions when he visited the studio. He was always rather condescending and patronizing towards me, probably because I played a small part and he thought that was a bit infra dig. I think he was wildly jealous of Audrey – though I'm unable to back that up; it's only my feeling. Anyway, I didn't think he was half good enough for her. But I admired Audrey enormously: she was never late, she always knew her lines and worked really hard. She was also a great giggler.'

213

During filming Audrey lost eight pounds, which was twice as much as she usually lost from the strain of movie production. Cukor and Warner were greatly disturbed about her health, especially during the last month of filming, and it was therefore an exhausted Audrey Hepburn who left for Burgenstock when filming finished just before Christmas. Eventually, by embarking on an eating spree ('I even wanted to put jam on my meat'), she regained the lost weight. She was in no hurry to resume work, so she placed all the scripts sent by Kurt Frings into a chest in her study and refused to even steal a glance at the titles. Among the movie properties, in fact, were *The Genius*, to be directed by Otto Preminger; a title-role starrer in an Anglo-Egyptian project, *Nefertiti*; an invitation to co-star as Brigitte Bardot's sister in a Franco–West German production of Michel Legrand's film operetta, *The Umbrellas of Cherbourg* (roles which subsequently went to Catherine Deneuve and Anne Vernon); an offer to appear in George Stevens' ultimately elephantine folly, *The Greatest Story Ever Told*; and the tantalizing proposition that would have cast her as the star-cross'd lover in *Romeo and Juliet* (director Franco Zeffirelli later chose newcomer Olivia Hussey.)

In due course, Audrey embarked on an extensive tour that took in ten major premières of *My Fair Lady*; it included four separate trips to America – Chicago, San Francisco, Los Angeles and a big splashy opening in Washington. General Sir Michael West, chief of the British Military Mission in Washington, danced with a pretty girl at a party at the British Embassy afterwards. 'You're a most attractive lass,' said the diplomat. 'What's your name?' The star of the film he had just seen replied graciously, 'Audrey Hepburn.'

There were a couple of premières in France, at one of which President de Gaulle attended a charity reception. And then there was Rome, Madrid, Brussels, London. 'It was easier working in the picture than promoting it,' said Audrey, who always hated these publicity-drumming shindigs. Following the London opening, Princess Margaret and Lord Snowdon joined the cast of the film for an impromptu party at Cecil Beaton's palatial home in Pelham Place, South Kensington; the Royal couple drove up discreetly in their black Morris 1100 and mingled with the guests, who included Vivien Leigh and Rachel Roberts, as well as Audrey and Mel.

If there had been disappointment among the devotees of the

original stage version of *My Fair Lady* when it was decided to pass over Julie Andrews, they were mollified when they saw Audrey in her place. Almost to a man (and woman), Audrey's performance was hailed as a triumph, while the film itself was described by American critics as one of the best of its kind ever produced and having some of the best tunes: 'I Could Have Danced All Night', 'With a Little Bit of Luck', 'Wouldn't it be Loverly', 'Show Me', 'Get Me to the Church on Time', just for starters. Most agreed she was a shade better and more at home as the 'lady' than the 'guttersnipe', but the overall impression was of a first-rate and winning Eliza.

Members of the Academy who chose the nominees for the year's Oscars, of course, thought differently. But on the day after Audrey had learned that she had not been nominated, she received a telegram from Katharine Hepburn. It read: 'Don't worry about not being nominated. Some day you'll get another one for a part that doesn't rate.'

Some saw poetic justice in Julie Andrews being nominated for, and ultimately winning, the best actress Oscar for her performance in *Mary Poppins*, but a major Hollywood row broke out over the Academy's decision to snub Audrey that year. 'Outrageous' was the word at Warners, freely translated, when it was learned that Audrey's name was not among the five nominees. Warner took it as a personal affront against the stature, validity and integrity of his studio, and a few weeks before the ceremony in Santa Monica, when Audrey received the Hollywood Foreign Press Award, he could not, or pretended he could not, remember her name.

There were other factors working against her nomination. Her songs had been dubbed by Marni Nixon, she had fired her press agent, and she had remained aloof during the normal-for-Hollywood campaigning for a nomination. In the event, pro-Hepburn members of the Academy began a unique campaign to win her the Oscar – even without a nomination. They were so shocked by her omission from the thirty-seventh annual Oscar derby that they decided to write-in her name on the ballot papers. But it did not work. *My Fair Lady* won twelve Oscar nominations in all, tying with *Becket*, while *Mary Poppins* led the field with thirteen.

Bob Hope was the master of ceremonies of the two-hour Oscar show, which had a special appearance by Judy Garland who sang a Cole Porter medley. Because the previous year's

215

best actress, Patricia Neal, was convalescing from a series of strokes, Audrey was chosen to make the best-actor announcement. Even though the Academy's snub cut Audrey deeply, she behaved like the gallant lady, holding her head high and never once showing the tremendous disappointment she was really feeling inside. And she found herself, paradoxically, handing the award to her co-star, Rex Harrison, for his performance as Henry Higgins.

Her joy when she announced that Harrison had won was unfeigned, and when he reached the lectern she kissed him several times. He patted her back, and the mutuality of their affection was the evening's pleasantest, and least staged, event. He seemed to be pleased more by Audrey's pleasure in his victory than by the victory itself, and he murmured that the Oscar should be split in half so he could share it with her. (*My Fair Lady* was also named the year's best film, because it claimed several other Oscars, including best director, best colour art direction, best costume design, best colour cinematography, best adaptation of a musical score, and best sound.) After she had returned to her table, she turned to her old admirer, Eddie Fisher, and, with tears in her eyes, said, 'Are you *still* my number one fan?'

At the end of the ceremony, having read a telegram from Patricia Neal, Bob Hope looked straight into the television camera and expressed what many people at the presentation were feeling: 'We're all pulling for Pat Neal who couldn't be here tonight.' As Audrey had taken Patricia Neal's place, it was assumed that *she* would make the announcement that Hope subsequently made; but, due to the excitement of the evening in general, and the awkward position in which she found herself in particular, the announcement completely escaped her mind. And, by the omission, she unwittingly caused a worldwide headline-making rumpus: 'Oscar show protest – Pat Neal's husband accuses Audrey' screamed one newspaper, 'Audrey accused of snub to star' wailed another.

Miss Neal and her author husband, Roald Dahl, had been watching the Oscar telecast at their Hollywood home and were extremely upset when Audrey failed to mention the sick actress whose place at the ceremony she had taken. 'Pat knew exactly what was going on, although she could not speak,' said Dahl. 'Hepburn graciously made the presentation and said a few words, but, rather less graciously, failed to mention the fact

216

that she was there as a substitute for a very sick woman. Pat made gurgly noises of fury and I myself, when the reporters called me immediately after the show to ask what Pat thought of it, told them exactly what we felt. The newspapers caught up with Hepburn on her way back to Paris, at Kennedy Airport. She phoned me to apologise and I told her to bugger off.'

But Patricia Neal, who had known Audrey for some considerable time, and who had worked with her in *Breakfast at Tiffany's*, wrote to me many years later (at the time when she and Dahl had just separated) to give me *her* side of the story. She concluded her letter with the statement, 'The incident at the Academy Awards occurred under enormous pressure and has long since been forgotten, certainly by me. I hope Audrey remains my friend, as I am hers.'

Audrey remained the reluctant superstar, and she was never more reluctant than when her press agent, Henry Rogers, asked her to do interviews and photo sessions for magazine features. Rogers constantly found himself performing a balancing act between appeasing Mel's insatiable desire for Audrey to receive a blaze of publicity on the one hand, and succumbing to Audrey's reluctance to give interviews or pose for photographs on the other.

Gradually, her American publicist – who was the best in the business – began to realise that he was being stretched to the limits of diplomacy and that it could not continue. What would prove to be the beginning of the end of his professional relationship with the Ferrers came one Sunday afternoon in their Swiss chalet where Audrey, Mel and Rogers had been spending a number of hours talking about Audrey's career.

Mel had a favourite axe to grind: he had always resented the fact that Audrey had given Hubert de Givenchy her name and likeness to launch his first venture into the perfume business. Magazines all over the world, among them *Vogue*, *Harper's Bazaar* and *Town and Country*, were carrying a magnificent full-page portrait of Audrey, indicating with pride that the fragrance – L'Interdit – had been created exclusively for her. The crux of Mel's grievance was that Givenchy had built a million-dollar empire using Audrey – without compensating her.

Givenchy's brother, Claude, handled the financial side of the business and, prior to his arrival at the Ferrer home, Rogers had stopped off in Paris at Mel's request to discuss with Claude the proposition that Audrey should be compensated financially for the use of her endorsement.

217

'For Christ's sake, Henry, she doesn't even get a discount on the clothes he designs for her,' Mel had said to him. 'As for the perfume, wouldn't you think he would send her gallons of it – as a gift? She buys it herself – retail!'

So there was Rogers, telling Audrey and Mel about his meeting in Paris – as it happened, the Givenchys *were* amenable to working out some reasonable form of compensation – when Audrey looked disapprovingly at the publicist and then at her husband.

'Neither of you seems to understand,' she began, a well of hurt in her dark eyes, 'I don't want anything from Hubert. I don't need his money. He is my friend. If I've helped him build his perfume business, then that's exactly what one friend should do for another. If someone else offered me one million dollars to endorse a perfume, I wouldn't do it . . . but Hubert is my friend. I don't want anything. Yes, I even want to walk into a drugstore and buy the perfume at the retail price.'

An uneasy tension began to engulf the room – and then the doorbell rang.

'That must be Favre Le Bret,' said Mel. 'He said he would be dropping by about now. Henry, you're going to talk to him alone as we agreed. Right?'

As director of the Cannes Film Festival, Le Bret had been almost solely responsible for making the festival the most successful of its kind in the world. He was a dynamic, aggressive man, and Audrey, Mel and Rogers had enjoyed an amicable relationship with him for many years. The purpose of his visit that particular afternoon was to try and persuade Audrey to attend the opening-night celebration of that year's festival. Mel had asked Rogers what he thought about it, and Rogers declared his immediate opposition to the idea: she did not need or care about such publicity. Mel was insistent, but Rogers remained adamant in his resolve that she should not attend the opening, unless . . . 'I'll agree,' he had finally said, 'if I can figure out a good reason for her to attend.'

And he did come up with a good reason:

'The Cannes Film Festival should make a slight change in its usual format. During your opening ceremonies every year you should give a special tribute to one person, an actor, an actress, a producer, or a director, who has made an outstanding contribution to the art of international motion pictures. This year it could be Audrey, who is certainly worthy of receiving the first award. Next year you could select Cary Grant or Sophia Loren or Alfred Hitchcock.'

That night Rogers caught a plane from Geneva to London, where he had a number of business meetings arranged. At 8 a.m. the next day, Audrey rang Rogers in his London hotel room to tell him she did not require his services any more.

'Henry, it's Audrey,' a voice sobbed at the other end. 'I'm sorry to call you so early. I've been up all night. I haven't slept, I'm so unhappy.'

'What's wrong?' Rogers asked, suddenly worried for her. 'Is something wrong with Sean?'

'No, Henry, it's you. You know how much I care about you – how much I value your friendship. I'm crying because I have decided that I don't want you to represent me anymore. I won't hire anyone else. I just can't stand any more of this. I just don't like what is happening to me, and my life and my friends.'

Rogers, the most tactful, diplomatic and courteous of publicists could not understand what Audrey was talking about. He asked her.

'First you embarrassed me with Hubert. You and Mel made such a thing about his taking advantage of me, and I told you last night – I don't care. He's my friend. And last night, after you left, it was terrible. I was embarrassed. I was ashamed. I started to cry and ran out of the room. Favre Le Bret told me you had tried to blackmail him, that you told him the only way I would go to the Cannes Film Festival would be if he gave me some kind of phoney, trumped-up award. Henry, I don't want you to work for me anymore. Will you still be my friend?'

Not surprisingly, Audrey did not attend the film festival. She and Rogers did, however, remain good friends, and he would later entertain her at his own home. But since that fateful day in Switzerland, he has never again spoken to Favre Le Bret, the man he supposedly tried to blackmail. 'Blackmail indeed!' Rogers fumes today. 'I had given him an idea that would have made the Cannes Film Festival increasingly important every year, and he had turned it against me.'

By dispensing with the services of a man like Henry Rogers, Audrey lost much more than a good publicist: she lost an Oscar nomination for *My Fair Lady* – and she began to lose her husband, for Mel was directly responsible for Rogers' approaches to Le Bret and the Givenchys. Their marriage, certainly, would never be quite the same again, despite the merry front they put on for the world.

219

However, the mood of apparent mutual compatibility continued – indeed, appeared to be strengthened – when they bought a picturesque old Vaudois farmhouse at Tolochenaz-sur-Morges, above Lake Geneva, ten minutes from Lausanne. They wanted to move closer to a good non-German language school for Sean. He had always travelled with his parents, but now that he was of school age, this was no longer practical. The Burgenstock chalet, however, was kept on for sentimental reasons. At Tolochenaz, Sean would live in French-speaking surroundings and therefore learn the language properly.

To this day, Tolochenaz is a rather sleepy village with no particular landmarks, a somewhat unpretentious, low-income community on a high plateau next to the Geneva-Lausanne motorway and yet off the beaten track. There is only one street, Route de Biere, where the Ferrer house still stands, protected by a tall stone wall bordering the street itself, and its grounds surrounded by a fence. There were then two shops, a hardware store and a greengrocer. Less than five hundred people lived there, mostly farmers tending their orchards and vineyards, and three cattle farmers.

Sean's school was not fifty metres away from the Ferrers' spacious eighteenth-century farmhouse which Audrey had christened 'La Paisible' (The Peaceful). Because of the foreign labour force brought in to help the Swiss on their farms and in the factories, his schoolmates were Spanish and Italian as well as Swiss. Italian was the first language he ever spoke, since Gina, his Italian nanny, could speak Italian only. He also understood English, though Audrey did not force it on him, out of respect for Gina and out of regard for the French-speaking world they now embraced. At home, he would hear any of four languages being spoken; like his parents, he was a natural linguist, and would in time add fluent Spanish to his linguistic accomplishments.

'La Paisible' had lots of rooms and a large attic ('so we can expand'), and Audrey put loose covers on all the chairs and sofas so that Sean could bring his friends in and not worry about where they put their feet. 'A house isn't a home,' she maintained, 'if a child and a dog can't go into the main room.' For Mel and Audrey it was also a zone of neutrality, the place where they could work out a connubial truce.

27

'I love Albie, I really do.'
'I've had to cope with rumours all my life.'

HOW, IT WAS reasoned, could the film formula fail? The combination would be explosive.

You took Audrey Hepburn, and you teamed her with a tall, lean Irish ruffian with an infinitely suggestive air and astonishing smoky-blue eyes by the name of Peter O'Toole. You added Oscar-winning director William Wyler, working with Audrey for the third time, and you gave the sophisticated comedy a do-it-yourself title like *How to Steal a Million*. Audrey was again in Paris, but this time with a leading man renowned for much more than his portrayals of Lord Jim and Lawrence of Arabia. O'Toole was 'the wild one of acting', 'leader of the angry young men's clan', 'fiery' and 'a rebel' whose Irish blood could boil in some pretty outrageous off-stage antics. He liked his booze, not to mention a pretty leg. But Audrey would tame him.

As O'Toole enjoyed explaining it: 'We were filming . . . there is a story of Edmund Kean, the nineteenth-century English actor whose closest friend was a man called Cooke, and they were playing, respectively, Richard III and the Duke of Buckingham in Shakespeare's *Richard III*. Kean tottered on to the stage, thoroughly polluted with liquid light, started his soliloquy and the audience began to call and bawl "You're drunk!", "He's drunk!", etc. Kean glared at them and said, "If you think I am drunk, wait till you see the Duke of Buckingham"; and, waiting at the side of the stage, was indeed the Duke of Buckingham on his hands and knees . . . we were filming an exterior in Paris and the weather turned round and became very, very cold indeed. Audrey had to walk across the street, get into a waiting car and drive off, but the poor child had turned bright blue with cold. The light was going and the shot was needed. I pulled Audrey into the caravan and gave her a shot of brandy. She went all roses and cream, bounced out of the caravan, radiated towards the motor car, hopped into it and drove off, taking with her five great big lamps, the trimmers of which had flung themselves on the cobbles out of the way. And from then on she was my Duke of Buckingham.'

Wyler's new comedy, his first in that genre since *Roman Holiday*, derived from that time-honoured school of fiction which had it that crime can be made a lark. The end product received mixed reviews, the American critics being much more favourably disposed to it than their British counterparts. The setting was intriguingly bizarre: the thriving world of art forgery in France. An art museum in Paris is robbed of a piece of sculpture ('Venus', by Cellini), ostensibly worth a fortune. The sculpture is a forgery, though the motive of the thieves – Audrey and O'Toole – was honourable.

Audrey's secret apprehension about being teamed opposite the cinema's new 'wild man' was as nothing compared with O'Toole's own misgivings about working with the actress with the classy, regal image. He was convinced that this lady would not take kindly to his merry, extrovert, rumbustious nature. The real test came very early in the shoot, in a funny 'caper' scene where Audrey and O'Toole find themselves at close quarters in a broom cupboard in the museum housing the Cellini forgery they wish to steal. If they fail to pull it off, her father (played by Hugh Griffith), who paints and sells his own versions of famous masterpieces, will be exposed as a fraud.

The two stars spent a total of eleven days in that cupboard, and a lot of those days in a dustbin within it. 'Neither of us was Herculean or Junoesque; nevertheless, it was a tight fit,' said O'Toole. 'We were pretty close and we talked a lot and I found I liked her a great deal.'

They had overcome their first mutual hurdle, but there would be others of a less apprehensive, lighter nature. O'Toole had recently been occupied on *What's New, Pussycat?* with one of the film business's great gigglers, Peter Sellers; but the arch goon was a model of decorum compared with Audrey. Although they both worked extremely well together, countless 'takes' were ruined when one or both of them burst into laughter at the wrong moment. She recalled having the same 'problem' with Gary Cooper.

In one scene, after Audrey had just spoiled O'Toole's third take by exploding with laughter, he begged her to leave the set. Audrey, sitting demurely on the sidelines, said – with mock indignation – that she was not even looking. 'Yes, but I could just *hear* your expression,' O'Toole protested. Wyler stared at them both severely, but with a giveaway smirk around the mouth. 'They react on each other like laughing gas,' said the director in despair, 'and the trouble is they're in almost every scene together.'

Audrey explained, in self-defence, that O'Toole was marvellous at imitations, that he would do something hilarious just before they did a scene, and that she would then have to hold her giggles until her stomach hurt. 'You must learn to *control* it,' the Irishman admonished. She managed to comply for a short while, but it was too good to last. On the tenth take she gave way and started to shake silently. 'Audrey 'Epburn, shut up giggling. That's ho'fficial!' roared O'Toole.

It was Wyler, of course, who first detected in Audrey the embryonic potential of a new Hollywood dreamgirl. Had he not seen something in her screen-test for *Roman Holiday*, she might still be drifting around today, not well enough known even to be forgotten. Wyler – the brutally tough director who always, on his own admission, resisted the temptation of being Mr Nice Guy; Wyler – the man who once sacked George C. Scott for not being on the set on time. 'He's got three gold-plated Oscars and acts like a tin-plated god,' said one disenchanted actor.

But with Audrey something seemed to come over the man. In her presence he became gentle, kind, considerate, and sent fresh flowers to her dressing-room every day. Inside the velvet glove was a velvet hand. Wyler came along and liberated her. He uninhibited her. He gave her confidence where before there was only a sort of numbed fear. He taught her what it was all about, showed her the way, and turned her loose.

It worked both ways, though, as Peter O'Toole observed: 'I saw from Willy, when Audrey was working, a sense of professional and personal admiration.' Audrey was Wyler's girl, and he didn't care who knew it. He had turned her loose but, like the homing-pigeon, she kept returning to base. 'We're in such close communication we hardly have to talk,' the pigeon would muse. 'I *know* when he feels it's wrong.'

During the shooting of *How to Steal a Million*, Audrey lived alone in Paris while Mel remained at Tolochenaz with Sean. To those who suspected that the Ferrers' marriage was on a slippery slope, Mel's absence from the Boulogne Studios could only mean one thing. Audrey did, however, fly back to Switzerland at weekends to be with her family, though it did little to allay the whispers of a marriage rift. 'Two years ago there were all these rumous, and in another two years they will probably crop up again.' She never uttered more prophetic words. 'If they haven't seen us around together for a while they spread the rumour that we're about to split up. It's all nonsense, of course.'

In reality, as time would bear out, it was no such thing. Their marriage was already under considerable strain . . . but neither Audrey nor Mel was going to offer so much as a crumb of scandal to the gossip columns. Unlike so many of their contemporaries, the Ferrers did not go in for public airing of their marital washing: as far as pronouncements to the media were concerned, they believed at all times in a strictly 'all's well' approach.

As their marriage began to come apart at the seams, so, coincidentally, they started to show an avid interest in real estate. First 'La Paisible' took their fancy; so they bought the property. Now, as their relationship floundered even more, they decided that what they really needed was a place in the sun; and so, as soon as Audrey finished work on her film in Paris, the Ferrers flew to Spain to oversee the building of their new villa near Marbella, overlooking the Mediterranean on the Costa Brava. It was almost as if they believed that, by moving to a new environment, the change would serve as a conjugal elixir.

Just before Christmas, Audrey discovered that she was expecting another child. She was elated and, momentarily, all thoughts of a fractured marriage receded into a now-murky background. She started to plan, with much enthusiasm, the décor and furnishings for the nursery, and prepared long lists of boys' and girls' names: she quietly prayed it would be a sister for Sean. But it was not to be. Early in January she was rushed to a Lausanne clinic, and there lost her expected baby. She was heart-broken; where there had previously been hope there was now only despair. In an attempt to alleviate her sorrow she telephoned Paris and ordered a ready-to-wear outfit from Givenchy, plus four plastic coats and two skinny knit dresses from Emanuelle Khan, and some two-toned coats from ex-model Victoire.

It was poor consolation. And it was Sean – tall, strapping Sean, now nearing six – who brought most comfort to his mother in this moment of need. Because he *was* so tall, he tended to refer to Audrey as 'a little girlie'. Sometimes, when he really wanted to be very grown-up, he told his friends that she was not really his mother at all. 'She's Mr Ferrer's little girlie, and my little sister,' he would announce.

While she convalesced at 'La Paisible', Kurt Frings continued to shower her with scripts. There was one property in which he was particularly interested: MGM's projected film musical based on James Hilton's novel, *Goodbye, Mr Chips*, which served as the basis for a straight dramatic film in 1939 starring Robert Donat and Greer Garson. The studio was offering one million against ten per cent of the picture's gross; only a handful of stars could demand and get deals that cut them in on a picture's gross rather than its net, among them Elizabeth Taylor and Cary Grant. Unfortunately, she was already committed to make another film that year, and she was no longer keen to do movies back-to-back. The roles finally went to Petula Clark and Audrey's old mate, Peter O'Toole.

Her new film, *Two for the Road*, would take her back not only to France but also to director Stanley Donen. It would be the third picture on which they had collaborated. *How to Steal a Million*, despite the 'formula', had not been the wonderful runaway hit everybody had anticipated, and it was in this light that Mel intimated to Audrey that she should perhaps consider changing pace – or, at the very least, consider changing her appearance. What he meant was that she should do a drastic re-think on her *image*.

She was more than happy to oblige, as it happened, because the man who would be helping to effect her transformation was O'Toole's old drama-school classmate, Albert Finney. The son of a Lancashire bookie, Finney was the tough, talented English cinema star of *Tom Jones* and *Saturday Night and Sunday Morning*, the dynamic personification of rebellious youth in *Billy Liar* on the London stage, and the rage of Broadway following his huge success in John Osborne's *Luther*. He had already been branded his generation's genius; but, like Audrey, he abhorred the cult of the personality: 'It's deadly,' he said.

225

The film which would compel the world to sit up and take stock of the 'new' Audrey Hepburn – a sexier, earthier Audrey Hepburn – was a comedy of modern moods, manners and morals in marriage by Oscar-winning screenwriter Frederic Raphael. Set in sunny, blue-sky locations ranging from the French Riviera northward to Paris and beyond, it covered twelve years in the lives of a couple whose marriage was heading for the rocks – just as her own twelve-year-old marriage seemed to be.

Raphael and Donen went to see Audrey at Tolochenaz to discuss the film and to allay certain fears she had concerning its treatment. 'She had been highly sceptical of the idea of *Two for the Road*, since she had just been badly "burned" (her term, I think) by a film which *sounded* as if it had a similar *donnée*,' said Raphael. 'However, once she had read the script, she became a totally committed and honourable member of the cast, without conceit or self-importance. By "honourable" I mean that having agreed to do the film, she did not ask for changes or betray the idea to which she had agreed. The absurdity of thinking that film actresses are inferior to those who appear on the stage was never more plainly revealed than by Audrey.'

Mel, meanwhile, continued to work on his plan to endow his wife with a new, dynamic, hotted-up image. The script called for Audrey to have her first really sizzling love scene with Finney in which she wears nothing. But *nothing*. 'It's inconceivable that it could have been submitted to me ten years ago, even five,' said Audrey, somewhat stating the obvious. But then Mel insisted that the part would be good for her . . . and good for his master-plan.

He and Donen had already decided that, in pursuance of Audrey's new-look personality, her darling Givenchy would not, on this occasion, be providing her wardrobe. One of her closest friends demurred, 'The beautiful simplification of her life was gone when Givenchy wasn't to dress her.' Another friend saw Mel as the villain of the piece: 'He was trying to tear away some of the cocoon which had been wrapped around her for too long.'

Yet what everybody had forgotten, or perhaps deliberately chose to ignore, was that Audrey actually felt *safer* while maintaining the status quo, felt *happier* enclosed within her protective screen-image wrapping. 'Hubert,' she said simply, 'makes me feel so sure of myself.' And so . . . for the first time in her career she found herself being decked out in ready-to-wear clothes from Paris boutiques, something which may have given French *prêt-à-porter* one of its first shots in the arm.

The transformation continued: she was talked into changing her hairstyles and the shape of her eyebrows. 'Audrey's eyebrows are twice as thin now as when she made her first film,' explained make-up aide Alberto de Rossi. 'Then they were immense – but you never noticed how I brought them down, film by film. I've given her completely new eyes for this film.'

There was also another crucial factor concerning her change, and it was probably the most important turnabout of all. Previously, she was rarely one for horseplay, for fooling around on the set between takes. But, presto! – this new woman actually enjoyed being one of the gang, actually enjoyed being on an equal par with co-workers Eleanor Bron, William Daniels, Claude Dauphin and Nadia Gray. Instead of retiring to her dressing-room, she delighted in a give-and-take with her screen husband, Albert Finney: they laughed, talked and joked together; some called it a kind of child's game of flirtation, some called it something else. It was completely open.

Novelist and screenwriter Irwin Shaw, who was on the set and who, as a fellow Swiss-resident, had known Audrey for a dozen years, would later report: 'She and Albie had this wonderful thing together, like a pair of kids with a perfect understanding and a shorthand of jokes and references that closed out everybody else. It was like a brother-sister in their teens. Very attractive and very appealing.' His face registered a recollection of mirth: 'When Mel was there it was funny. Audrey and Albie got rather formal and a little awkward, as if now they had to behave like grown-ups.'

Peter O'Toole started the trend. As her leading man, he was actually *younger* than Audrey – three years younger. Now there was Finney: at thirty, he was seven years her junior. All this was such a novelty for Audrey, whose leading men were usually cocking an eye to their State pension, that she literally flipped. Explained Donen: 'The Audrey I saw during the making of this film I didn't even know. She overwhelmed me. She was so free, so happy. I never saw her like that. So young!' He thought for a moment. 'I guess it was Albie.'

Audrey had no doubts about it. 'I love Albie,' she said with candour. 'Oh, I really do. He's so terribly, terribly funny. He

227

makes me laugh like no one else can. And you can talk to him, really *talk*. He's serious, too, completely so about acting, and that's wonderful. Albie's just plain wonderful, that's all there is to it.'

Was she now beginning to compare her husband with much younger men, with men of her own age group and temperament? It would have been amazing if she had not. Finney was young, wacky, sportive, frolicsome, prankish, impulsive, reckless, riotous, playful, absurd, funny . . . all the things Mel was not. He excited her. She spent her off-hours visiting local bistros with him, or with her old admirer, William Holden, then estranged from his wife, Brenda Marshall, and even occasionally with Mel.

As the company watched this transformed woman, cast in her new film as a disenchanted wife who indulges in a brief and slightly pathetic adulterous affair with a Frenchman, they could not help but reflect on the parallel that existed between the liberated nature of her screen role and the amazing 'opening up' of her real-life persona. Never before on the screen had she succumbed to temptation of the flesh, never before had she uttered a blue line or been detected in a lusty, compromising situation. This was a challenge.

She was extremely nervous, though, about the first bedroom scene with Finney. Elaborate precautions were taken before the scene was shot. The production unit took over the whole of the Hôtel du Golf on the Riviera coast at Beauvallon, near St Tropez, and the set was rigorously closed to any but the official cameramen and production assistants. Off the set, Audrey and Finney romped and swam together on the near-deserted beach 'to get that right relaxed feeling into the whole business', as one production assistant put it. He added, 'Audrey was very strung up when it began. We all knew she realised this was a tremendous break from everything that had gone before in her career. But in the end it worked. It was a great professional effort – and she triumphed.' This was a proud woman; and also, at last, a liberated one.

During location shooting, however, actress Judy Cornwell (in one of her earliest screen roles, along with Jacqueline Bisset) observed two very different perspectives to Audrey's character: 'My first impression was of a very thin and sad-faced woman. But talking to her, I was immediately at ease in the obvious presence of an ex-dancer; I was also a dancer and there is a

228

"shorthand" spoken which one only gets if you've been in the chorus. We got on very well. On the set, though, it was a very different Audrey, a tremendously composed woman who knew every flicker of her own facial muscles. This was Hollywood training and something I had never seen before. Her movements were contained, her concentration as acute as a yoga expert. No matter how many times we did a scene, each time an eyebrow was raised it was subject to a strict discipline.'

As writer Frederic Raphael discovered for himself, 'Audrey's capacity to give a number of variant readings to the dialogue, even of unimportant phrases, from which you could select the most suitable, was remarkable. She monitored herself, as a speaker of lines, with singular accuracy. She always knew what was right and she could then repeat that reading as often as required. Yet there was never anything wooden or actressy about her performance, either as a speaker or when acting. She combined naturalism with a sort of stylised reticence to a rare degree.'

He reflected. 'Only once did she query the script seriously, and that was when, towards the end of shooting, I decided that the final scene was not right and that it needed clarification. I therefore rewrote it so that it said exactly what it was meant to say. Audrey received the new pages with polite dismay and said that she preferred the first version. I disagreed: the dialogue was muddled, I thought, and if you read it carefully it said the opposite of what was intended. Would I at least read it through with her? We took both versions into her caravan. No one could have been more chastely seduced than I was by her entirely fair reading of both scenes: she was right and I was happy to say so.'

One further incident threw some additional light on the changed, tougher Audrey Hepburn. She was on the set one day, waiting for Jackie Bisset, who was having trouble getting her hair right. 'I'm ready, so why are we waiting?' Audrey called out, proffering a half-smile.

'It was light-hearted enough,' said Judy Cornwell, 'but there was *authority* in that statement which made everyone hurry Jackie up.'

While Frederic Raphael received an Academy Award nomination for his literary efforts, the film itself split the critics straight down the middle, some finding it perceptive and refreshing where others bemoaned that it was laboured and confusing. 'As for Audrey,' cooed one distinguished reviewer, 'she remains a screen phenomenon.' Raphael was not going to argue with that. 'I am somewhat biased,' he murmured, 'but I don't think I have ever seen a performance more manifestly worthy of the Oscar, if that matters, than Audrey's in *Two for the Road*.' But that was show business; perhaps next time.

At the moment, Finney and Audrey had become a column item, and friends were hinting that the rise and fall of the Ferrers' marriage was caused, partly at least, by the fact that Mel treated his superstar wife like a child. She herself was convulsed with guilt over leaving Sean in Switzerland during the filming, but close observers were suggesting that she was perhaps enjoying herself more than the script called for. Mel tried to put on a brave face, but the end was in sight. 'It was no secret that Audrey's marriage with Mel was not a happy one,' said her former press agent, Henry Rogers. 'It seemed to me that she loved him more than he loved her, and it was frustrating for her not to have her love returned in kind. She had confided these feelings to me and a number of other intimate friends many times. She never complained but I always saw the sadness in her eyes.'

Audrey's old admirer, Eddie Fisher, who had lost his own wife, Elizabeth Taylor, to Richard Burton two years earlier, felt a certain sympathy for Mel. He could even equate with the man's 'dilemma'. 'Mel and I were the husbands of two of Hollywood's biggest stars, which can be a problem in itself,' he declared openly. 'But I sensed that Mel's relationship with Audrey was difficult not because she was demanding and unpredictable, like Elizabeth. Just the reverse: Audrey was always so gracious and perfect in every way that Mel must have found that almost impossible to live up to.'

None the less, in concert with Mel, Audrey was able to sustain the largely successful pretence – certainly as far as the world at large was concerned – that her marital problems were really nothing more than so much scurrilous gossip. When the going got hot, as in January 1967, she invited the press to her temporary Hollywood home for an English-style 'high tea' – complete with silver urn, crescent-shaped cucumber sandwiches, and the cutest little pink-and-white *petits fours*. No liquor was served, causing may thirsties of the fourth estate to set their tea cups clattering from withdrawal symptoms.

The Hollywood press had not seen anything like it since

silent-screen star Vilma Banky married matinée idol Rod La Rocque half a century earlier. Audrey, dressed in an orange angora wool mini-shift ending four inches above her knees, and with no jewellery except her simple gold wedding band, smiled warmly while, for two hours, the banks of radio, television, magazine and newspaper reporters fired questions at her from all directions. Yes, she was happy to be back in Hollywood after three years; yes, it was just like being home again on the Warner lot; yes, she approved of the short skirts; yes, her hair was quite, quite short; and – the *raison d'être* for the whole public-relations spree – yes, her husband was producing her next film, *Wait Until Dark*. Did this not prove, if nothing else, that they were still in love?

It was once again a million dollars up front for Audrey, in this film adaptation of Frederick Knott's long-running Broadway suspense-drama, about a commercial photographer who unwittingly smuggles a drug-filled doll into New York. His blind wife, here played by Audrey (Lee Remick on the stage), alone in her flat, is terrorised by murderous crooks. Efrem Zimbalist Jr was cast as her husband, with Alan Arkin (Rod Steiger was originally ear-marked for the role), Richard Crenna and Jack Weston as her tormentors. It contained one of the most terrifying incidents ever depicted on the screen; yes, she was thrilled to be back in Hollywood.

Her impressive tea party had also finally scotched the Finney rumours.

28

'These rumours about us breaking up are all nonsense.'

THE FERRERS registered at the Beverly Hills Hotel, where they secured one of the establishment's most luxurious super-deluxe bungalows. Along for the ride, too, came their cook from Switzerland, as well as Audrey's personal maid. Naturally, they enjoyed a limousine with uniformed chauffeur always standing by. Mel even arranged to have an entire tea garden constructed at the side of the studio set; and there, at exactly four o'clock every afternoon, *Wait Until Dark* temporarily ceased production and the silver tea service, the tiny watercress sandwiches and dainty cakes appeared. When it came to his leading lady nothing, it appeared, was too much trouble for the producer. There was a picture to make, with England's James Bond director, Terence Young, taking the helm in his first American movie; Audrey called him 'The Toff'.

And so the charade continued. Their marriage was now all but over, but the chief protagonists in this real-life drama refused to let on. 'It was only later we heard that Audrey was having a very difficult time in her marriage to Mel,' noted co-star Richard Crenna. 'At the time, though, we weren't aware that anything was wrong.'

Behind the scenes, nevertheless, all was not what it might have seemed. But Audrey maintained her public 'no-fuss' posture; she hand-painted with her own pink nail-varnish the names of every member of the crew on individual tea cups ('so that when we had tea in the afternoon, we all had a proper cup, not a paper cup'); she laughed, joked, teased and giggled on

232

the set until Terence Young threatened to evict her, along with co-giggler Crenna; and overall she won Crenna's admiration for being 'a supreme professional'.

He quoted one particular instance: 'She was playing a very difficult scene – I was already dead – where Alan Arkin was waving a flame under her nose . . . and for some reason it wasn't working for Alan, and it was a scene where Audrey had to be hysterical. Again and again they tried to get a take, and again and again it wasn't working, for whatever reason, for Alan. He was either blowing the lines or blowing the action, yet at no point did Audrey visibly show or articulate her impatience to him as an actor, because she sensed that he was trying. It was almost an entire day that this went on, during which she was required to scream and holla; very emotional stuff. That, to me, showed what true professionalism was. I'll always remember that vividly. I would have jumped up and down on Arkin's head.'

At a time when her personal life was in ruins, portraying an hysterical blind girl for the camera provided a vital catharsis for Audrey, an emotional release which was far more purgative than any psychological 'remedy' dispensed by the average Hollywood headshrink. It also happened to be the most difficult dramatic role of her career, and in her research for the part she visited a clinic for the blind in Lausanne and spent several days at the Lighthouse Institute for the Blind in New York City, undergoing blindfold training along with real-life trainees. She wore contact lenses to help her simulate blindness.

Along the way, she lost more than a stone in weight, which the Hollywood gossips blamed on her marriage breakdown. But Terence Young thought otherwise: 'The part was probably one of the most rigorous roles Audrey has ever played. She worked herself so hard that you could see the pounds rolling off her each day.'

The film was generally well received as a masterly suspense-thriller that out-Hitchcocked Alfred Hitchcock, and one reviewer, mentioning Audrey's performance alongside the character-creations of Bette Davis, Joan Crawford and Greta Garbo, was convinced that 'Audrey Hepburn will take her rightful place with the greatest actresses of all time.' It was no secret, indeed, that for her gruelling, sensitive performance in the film, Audrey polled the second-highest number of votes for the best-actress Oscar, and only Katharine Hepburn (*Guess*

Who's Coming to Dinner?) could wrest the Academy Award from her.

In July, Audrey's doctor confirmed that, at thirty-eight, she was expecting another child. If the timing was somewhat incongruous, at least the pregnancy served the purpose of cheering-up an otherwise disconsolate actress. But, according to the Dutch newspaper *De Telegraaf*, she had nobody with whom to share the confinement, since Mel had been living alone at their Marbella villa 'for several weeks'. Also, according to the London correspondent of another newspaper, the Johannesburg *Sunday Times*, the Baroness had confirmed that a divorce was pending. Audrey suffered a miscarriage soon after.

On 1 September, the bubble finally burst. The atmosphere in the screening room at Warner Bros' studio was tense. It was an uncomfortably hot night, but the room was filled to the last seat. The entire press corps was there for the screening of Audrey's newest film. Yet it was not *Wait Until Dark* which had turned the press out in such unusual numbers. It was the announcement which had been made earlier that day by the couple's respective lawyers: 'Audrey Hepburn, thirty-eight, and Mel Ferrer, fifty, have separated after thirteen years of marriage. Ferrer is in Paris and Miss Hepburn is at their home in Switzerland with their son, Sean, seven.' The news came as a shock to all but those who knew the couple intimately, and to the latter the only surprise was that the break-up had not happened sooner.

What went wrong?

There were those who said the marriage was doomed from the start, that it was no more than an optimistic fusion of two irreconcilable opposites. 'Although she loved acting,' said publicist friend Henry Rogers, 'she wanted to work less and spend more time in private with Mel and Sean. She was filled with love. Mel was filled with ambition, for his wife and for himself.' Those closest to the couple held the belief, additionally, that the changes which Mel masterminded for his wife's new screen image, first in *Two for the Road*, then in *Wait Until Dark*, turned Audrey into two women – both of them Audrey; both of them different – and that two women broke up her marriage. Until Mel sought to change her, Audrey had been one very definite personality.

For almost a year, Mel engrossed himself as producer in *Wait*

Until Dark, which had been conceived originally as a 'starrer' stage property for the Ferrers. Right from the start, there were problems with the film, with countless script changes from day to day. They both faced the situation under constant strain, Mel bearing the burden of the production problems, Audrey the intense strain of playing the tortured heroine. Some years earlier Audrey had decided that, for her height, seven-stone-twelve was her ideal weight, and that was how she stayed; nobody could get her to eat a single extra calorie that would make her go above that 'norm'. But during the strain of living with Mel *and* their new film, she was not able to maintain even seven-stone-twelve. At the time of the separation announcement, her weight had reportedly dropped to six-stone-twelve, which was certainly a danger level. One wit observed that she resembled 'an emaciated grasshopper'.

As the weeks of filming went by, everyone connected with the picture felt the tension – or, rather, *a* tension. And yet the combined exasperation of both producer and star did not become evident on the set itself in front of the fifty or sixty people engaged in the film's completion . . . but it was obviously more than evident in the privacy of their home. 'Audrey was a very strong-willed lady, and I think she did what she wanted to do,' Richard Crenna would later argue in Mel's defence. 'True, Mel came on with a very *strong* attitude, but that was in himself: he was the producer, he was acting the producer. But I don't think he manipulated Audrey in the sense that John Derek manipulated his women. I don't think that would be possible with Audrey, I really don't. If Mel *was* manipulating her, then I give her less credit than I did at the time.'

None the less, visitors to the set, as the picture was shooting, noticed a new mood in Audrey. A sense of restlessness pervaded her personality. But, in the end, the film role was too exacting, the movie too shocking, and the toll it took on her already weakened constitution was severe. It had also been rumoured – a rumour that was neither confirmed nor denied – that Audrey had blown her top because the exquisite Catherine Deneuve had been chosen to play the lead opposite Omar Sharif in Terence Young's big-screen version of *Mayerling*, a project in which Mel at one point had a share. The woman's role in that tragic love story was so right for Audrey that she had already played it in Anatole Litvak's disastrous TV version.

Now, as they talked about divorce, *Mayerling* was already before the cameras.

But this was no ordinary separation, just as their marriage had been no ordinary relationship. In fact, it gave the distinct impression of being the cosiest separation of all time. The day the parting was announced, the couple flew to meet each other for a spell of tender togetherness. They arrived separately at 'La Paisible' in Tolochenaz, and emerged from the villa only to stroll together across the lawns and in the garden. They lounged together in the sun in a chaise-longue on the terrace; and, in a moment of affection, as Audrey gathered roses, Mel ran after her and then they walked together, his arm around her shoulders. It was like some bizarre film script. In fact, the situation could have been lifted straight out of *Two for the Road*. Divorce, indeed, seemed the least likely event that day in Tolochenaz. It was certainly the last thing in the world Audrey wanted.

Many years later she explained to a friend exactly how she felt. 'When my marriage to Mel broke up, it was terrible; more than that, it was a keen disappointment,' said Audrey. 'I thought a marriage between two good, loving people had to last until one of them died. I can't tell you how disillusioned I was. I'd tried and tried. I knew how difficult it had to be, to be married to a world celebrity, recognised everywhere, usually first-billed on the screen and in real life. Believe me, I put my career second. Finally, when it was clear it was ending, I still couldn't let go.' Thus, the rendezvous at Tolochenaz-sur-Morges.

Audrey already knew the failure-rate of Mel's previous marriages, she had seen the marriages of their Hollywood friends end in disaster, and she could not forget that even her own mother had not found happiness in love. And now it was happening to her. She could not believe it. For a woman who believed that love was made in Heaven, and made to last, what was happening to her life was more than she could bear.

She went into temporary self-imposed exile at 'La Paisible', rarely venturing further than the local village. In Audrey's heart there was no question about it – it was *her* failure. When she surveyed the ruins of her life, all she could feel was *personal* defeat. In all that would be written about the breakdown of her relationship with Mel, not a single word would be uttered from her mouth suggesting that Mel was to blame for what happened to their marriage. It was *her* catastrophe, *her* downfall, *her* loss – never Mel's.

Within four months of the separation announcement, however, a new man had entered Audrey's life – Prince Alfonso de Bourbon-Dampierre, one of the pretenders to the Spanish throne. According to the French weekly newspaper *France Dimanche*, theirs was 'a long-standing friendship'. They saw each other frequently. The couple spent one evening, for instance, dancing cheek to cheek in a Madrid nightclub, The Box, where, over supper, they held hands across the table and gazed into each other's eyes, apparently oblivious of the crowd around them. They also welcomed in the New Year together in Madrid after Audrey flew in specially from Geneva. 'They were obviously completely happy in each other's company,' said *France Dimanche*. And why not?

But Mel, hearing of the friendship, grew more and more depressed. He wanted her back. 'I'm still very much in love with her,' he said. 'I prize her more than anything else. I can only hope she'll change her mind about me.'

His behaviour, alas, did not encourage Audrey to contemplate such a thing. He first learned about his estranged wife's displeasure with him when, at the end of August, he arrived at New York's Kennedy Airport to meet Sean. Discovering to his dismay that his son was not among the passengers who disembarked from the Geneva plane, Mel enquired at the airline office – where he found a letter from Audrey. It told him that Sean was not coming.

Audrey, it seemed, had chosen this tactic to persuade Mel to renounce – at least till the divorce – the rollicking life he had been leading since their separation a year earlier. Since his return to Hollywood to direct films, Mel had been living like a bachelor playboy. This behaviour Audrey viewed with complete dismay. She had decided, according to friends, that the climate in which Mel was conducting his life was not a healthy one for their son. This decision followed an agreement at the time of their separation that Sean should spend some time with his father during the school holidays. Anticipating Sean's visit, Mel had leased a luxurious villa in Hollywood, with extensive grounds and a swimming pool, at a rent of $2000 a month. But after receiving a message from Audrey to say he was not coming there was nothing left for him but to return to Hollywood and his magnificent but lonely mansion. A short while later, however, it was arranged that Sean would spend one week with his father during his six weeks' holiday. Audrey relented at the last moment because Mel promised her that he would lead an exemplary life while Sean was with him.

They were divorced three months later, on 21 November 1968. Their marriage had endured fourteen years and two months, although they had been living apart for more than a year when the decree finally came through. The grounds for the divorce were not declared publicly, though privately it was said to be one of 'incompatibility'. Audrey was devastated. 'I have a feeling that when the divorce with Mel came it was very upsetting for her,' reflected her old friend, David Niven. A decade later, indeed, she would admit that she still shuddered when hearing the word 'divorce'. 'It's horrible,' she would confess. 'It's bad enough to hear what friends have said about you, but when you read things that people speculate about you in print. . . .' And the speculations were legion.

Mel subsequently walked briefly aloof and alone. But two months after the divorce he had found something to smile about in London, in the shape of twenty-nine-year-old mother-of-three, Tessa Kennedy – a beautiful heiress and interior decorator who had once figured in a much-publicised runaway romance with Dominic Elwes.

Their friendship lasted but a year – until, in fact, Mel met a Belgian woman of Russian origin, Elisabeth ('Lisa') Soukhotine, who edited children's books. They met in a London nightclub and married in London in February 1971 – his fifth marriage, her first. Sean was in attendance and surveyed the Caxton Hall ceremony with a bemused smile. Lisa and Mel are still together, sharing an apartment just outside Lausanne. Today, too, he still produces films, still appears in front of the cameras. Among his latest roles has been the smooth-talking lawyer friend of matriarch Jane Wyman in America's long-running TV soap-opera series, *Falcon Crest*. Life goes on.

But there is scant friendship left between Svengali and Trilby. On one occasion not so long ago they came face to face in Rome's fashionable Orsini Restaurant. Audrey cut Mel stone dead.

PART FIVE

The eternal phoenix:
Roman interlude and Dutch courage

29

*'Let me put it simply. I have absolutely no
desire to work. And it's not worth going to a
psychotherapist to find out why.'*

RARELY HAD AUDREY endured such fragile feelings, such unveiled insecurity.

When the awful trauma of the separation and eventual
divorce sailplaned to its most crippling peak, she found herself,
as always when under prolonged stress, on the verge of a nervous breakdown. Tolochenaz was her haven. Occasionally, she
would venture out into the world for a brief liaison with Prince
Alfonso de Bourbon-Dampierre, or with the Spanish bull-
fighter Antonio Ordoñez; but, in general, she remained
firmly secluded in her beloved old farmhouse perched above
Lake Geneva. It was, in every sense, 'The Peaceful'.

In the course of time, however, her friends feared that the
Swiss retreat was perhaps *too* peaceful, *too* remote, *too* rarified,
permitting Audrey rather more opportunity for introspection
than was good for her. The moment eventually came when, for
her own state of mind, she should be dragged out of her luxurious shell. The solution was to be found in Rome. Audrey had
been returning to the Eternal City so frequently since her esca-
pades with Gregory Peck, all those pre-megastar years ago,
that she had long since come to regard it as her second home.

There, over the years, she had slowly established a small
coterie of like-minded friends, comprising influential, local jet-
setters – the Agnellis, the Princess Pignatelli and other assorted
members of the aristocracy – with more money and time on
their hands than they knew what to do with. Some three or
four years before her break with Mel it had already become cus-

tomary for her to stay in Italy with Lollo and Lorean Gaetani Lovatelli, at whose magnificent palace at Piazza Lovatelli, with his formal gardens and antique statuary, the actress found both privacy and organised fun.

The Countess Lovatelli – sister of the Countess Afdera Franchetti (the ex-Mrs Henry Fonda), herself a Roman of the La Dolce Vita generation – was generally regarded to be very much 'in' with both the liberated, go-go aristocracy of Rome and the cream of the artistic world; and it was at one of Lollo's regular soirées that Audrey was introduced to the Princess Olympia Torlonia and her French industrialist husband, Paul Annik Weiller. Before the evening was out, Audrey had accepted an invitation of the Weillers to cruise the Greek islands, in June, aboard a chartered yacht.

Also on board was the handsome, young Dr Andrea Mario Dotti (pronounced 'Doh-tee'), a wealthy Italian jet-setter and psychiatric assistant to Professor Giancarlo Reda, head of the Psychiatric Faculty at the University of Rome. There, Dr Dotti taught and did research in psychopharmacology (the use of drugs in the treatment of nervous and mental disturbances), and was head of a psychiatric clinic dealing exclusively with women patients. The energetic, outgoing doctor was nine years Audrey's junior . . . and, before the Mediterranean cruise was over, they had fallen in love. At that time, after years of self-discipline and the perfected art of hiding her unhappy life with Mel, the evidence of her private sufferings were etched on Audrey's face and body. 'It was a great sense of timing to get those two together,' said a friend belonging to the Gaetani Lovatelli circle. As an anti-depression expert, he was the perfect man for Audrey, who was still in the depths of despair over her divorce.

The doctor exuded proverbial Latin charm and, although a hardworking scientist, he had already acquired a well-earned reputation for being a hardplaying playboy. Some likened him to a younger version of TV's Dr Kildare. His fun-packed, women-adorned night-life was every bit as important to this handsome man-about-town as his day-time work at the clinic: each perfectly complemented the other; women, professionally and privately, were a lifetime's occupation. Born in Naples on 18 March 1938, to the Count and Countess Domenico Dotti, he was a man in pursuit of life's little pleasures – though he certainly did not do his daytime work for money, since his take-home pay from the university would not have been enough to pay, for instance, Audrey's cleaning bill. He was immensely rich from his family, and so he could have easily chosen a less demanding job.

For Andrea, meeting Audrey on that romantic yacht cruise was love at first sight. But for Audrey, who by nature was extremely cautious both in her private and professional life, it was a slow, gradual awakening of affection. By the end of the cruise, the passionate young Roman had won her heart. How could she ever forget the moment she felt *love*? 'My God, are you aware when a brick has fallen on your head?' she would exclaim. She thought for a moment. 'It just happened out of the blue. He was such an enthusiastic, cheerful person, which I found very attractive. And obviously, as I got to know him, I found he was also a thinking, very deep-feeling person.'

During the voyage, Andrea had reminded Audrey that they had previously met when he was a child and he had watched her shooting on location in Rome for *Roman Holiday*; but she had barely noticed the fourteen-year-old boy in the crowd who approached her after the director had said 'Cut!' and earnestly shook her hand. 'I know I should, and it broke my heart to have to admit to Andrea that I honestly couldn't remember meeting him,' she said later.

But now she was in love, and happy again. She never believed it could happen, not to her: real, true love. She had almost given up. She loved Andrea much more than she would admit to him. In part, she was afraid of their nine-year age difference, that it might be a major handicap to a new relationship, let alone to a possible marriage. They talked about it a great deal. 'I had lived longer than Andrea, but it didn't mean I was more mature,' Audrey found herself reasoning. 'Intellectually, he was older than I. His work had matured him beyond his years. Also, we were very close emotionally. So we met somewhere between thirty and thirty-nine! Even so, I always knew that there was that physical difference in time and, in the beginning, I wondered if some day it would make a difference. . . .'

Andrea was a gentle-spoken man with an unhurried manner, and he was a good listener. Also, despite being Audrey's junior by nine years, he was a man of maturity and great stability. There was additionally the fact that they both had fatherless childhoods: Andrea was quite young when his

243

parents divorced. His mother, the countess, remarried and reverted to plain Signora Paola Roberti Bandini; Andrea, in turn, became the stepson of Vero Roberti, London correspondent of a Milan newspaper. The doctor's brother, Gianpiero Dotti, was an influential Rome banker. There was money in the family.

Due to Andrea's teaching and research work at the university, the couple continued to see each other only at weekends – sometimes in Switzerland, sometimes in Rome. Six months after their first meeting on the Mediterranean, they spent Christmas together in Rome, and it was then that Andrea gave Audrey a ruby engagement ring. Almost immediately, in the first week of January, the banns were published outside the little village post office at Tolochenaz.

The volatile Signora Paola was ecstatic. 'For years and years, Andrea has spoken of getting married and having a handful of children, but he just never was able to make up his mind. He continued to study and study and think about a career, talk about marriage, and then study again. But when he returned from the cruise with Audrey he was deeply in love. I must say that Audrey will be an ideal daughter-in-law. She is such a delicious person, a dream. The age difference doesn't matter. She has become so much the perfect woman for all the family that, for us, she doesn't have any age.'

When they first discussed marriage, Audrey had two fears. She asked him, 'Will the fact that I'm an actress in any way hurt your career in medicine?' She said it would bring him publicity and all kinds of things he should not have as a serious doctor. 'That was the big reason for not marrying him, more than the age difference,' said Audrey. 'But there *was* also that. I was physically nine years older than he was.'

Andrea assured her that he did not intend to let marriage to a movie star make him a celebrity. 'I will continue my career,' he explained quietly, 'and after a while all this interest in us will die down. I'm not a public figure and won't become one.' It was wishful thinking. He told his friends, 'I never think of Audrey as an actress but as a human being. Once anyone meets her, they think she's a very nice woman and they forget she's a star.'

And so, in the shadow of the snow-capped Swiss mountains, on a slightly overcast day on 18 January 1969 – seventeen months after separating from Mel, two months after the divorce – the actress and the doctor were married at a simple, private ceremony in the town hall of Morges by the local regist-rar, Madame Denise Rattaz. Audrey was now officially Coun-tess Dotti – but she would never use the title; she became sim-ply Signora Dotti. Witnesses for the bride were Mrs Doris Bryn-ner (then-wife of actor Yul) and Mrs Germaine Lefebvre, better known as *Pink Panther* actress Capucine; the groom's witnesses were the Italian painter Renato Guttoso and cruise-loving Paul Weiller. Among the forty guests were Sean who, in two years, would also be attending the remarriage of his father. It was a confusing time for the gangling boy who was approaching his ninth birthday.

Audrey, wearing a pink jersey ensemble from Givenchy, her head protected from the drizzle by a matching foulard, was captured in one picture biting her lip – a teenage gesture some critics found too cute for a woman just four months short of her fortieth birthday. The point was, she did not *feel* forty. 'I felt twelve years old or maybe twenty, I don't know,' she said in retrospect. 'I remember only feeling happy, deliciously happy, and Andrea holding my hand.'

They spent part of their honeymoon searching Rome for an attic flat with a terrace, and, while they were looking, they lived in the three-storey villa in Rome's old quarter which belonged to Andrea's mother. Eventually, close by – some 500 metres down the street, by Ponte Vittorio – they found a delight-ful penthouse apartment which, four centuries earlier, had been the private home of the mistress of a famous cardinal. The rooms, which overlooked the Tiber, were large and high-ceilinged and adorned with a mixture of modern and antique furniture, as well as expensive paintings, lots of books and even more treasured old mementoes. As she surveyed her new home, she almost cooed with contentment.

Audrey also revelled in the knowledge that Sean adored Andrea: he was not so much a stepfather as a good friend. 'Sean's already got a father, and a very good father, whom he loves very much,' the doctor was careful to point out. He loved Sean because the youngster was not only intelligent and mature for his age, but also because the boy was a part of the woman he loved.

Marrying a Latin might well have brought an enormous change to a non-Italian wife, for customs and lifestyle were totally different in Italy; and she was, after all, a divorcee. But if

Audrey's life changed, and it did, it was not because she married an Italian but because she married a psychiatrist. A new Audrey emerged, a woman buoyant and outrightly careless. Her phone number was listed in the Rome telephone directory; she shopped around Via Frattina or Via Condotti; she lunched with lady friends at the popular Trattoria Bolognese at Piazza del Popolo, and, every once in a while, on a sleepy afternoon, a passerby might bump into her and Andrea holding hands like young lovers in a small cinema in the centre of town.

They mixed with architects, painters, and writers; except for one or two close friends, they totally ignored the movie crowd. Givenchy was pushed into the background; instead, she wore fun boutique stuff: mini-minis. She went dancing with Andrea and held on to him in a way that the 'old' Audrey would never have done. Andrea, she liked telling people, was 'a cuddler'. What she found appealing about him, too, was his 'kindness and goodness . . . and, you know, he's not *ashamed* of it; that's what attracted me most in the beginning.'

Peering from an opened window at the distant view of Rome across the Tiber, Audrey tried to put into words some other facets of her husband's personality. 'He has a great sense of humour. He's a very, very good person. He's very warm, very affectionate with me and Sean. . . .' The words just poured out. 'He's also quite brilliant at his work; and he's dedicated, but not competitive, which is very nice. He doesn't care about being rich or making lots of money. He's had various chances to go that way, but turned them down. He loves to teach, and to cure people . . . and he also loves to turn it all off when he comes home. He laughs and jokes with us. We go out to a movie or a nightclub. We see friends. It's a way for him to let off steam after being involved all day with people's emotional disturbances. I think if he didn't do it, he'd go out of his mind.'

Marriage, observed Audrey, should be only one thing: two people decide they love each other so much that they want to stay together. Whether or not they signed a piece of paper, it was still a marriage, with a sacred contract of trust and respect. So, if in some way she failed to fulfil what he needed in a woman – emotionally, physically, sexually, or whatever it was – and if he needed somebody else, then she could not stick around. She was not the kind to stay and make scenes.

246

Meanwhile, there was a new life to lead. In May, four months after the wedding, Audrey was pregnant – an important event for Audrey, doubly so for Andrea in this, his first marriage; he was one hundred per cent Italian, and Italian men are known to be intensely conscious of their masculinity. There was also the question of his mother. Signora Bandini had been telling everybody that Andrea wanted 'lots and lots of children', but Audrey, who was now forty – and who would be nearing forty-one when the baby came along – knew that 'lots and lots of children' were going to be a veritable impossibility. Yet she was not entirely ignorant as to the crucial place of children in an Italian home. The fact that she already had a son from her marriage to Mel did not necessarily make her a mother in Italian eyes. So aware of these circumstances was Audrey that she even placed Sean in an Italian school, believing he would be better accepted if more 'Italianised'.

Audrey spent the first two months of her pregnancy by letting life go by pretty much as before, often playing a rough-and-tumble ball game with Sean at Rome's fashionable Gambrino Beach Club. But by August the news of the forthcoming happy event had spread like wild-fire among the Hepburn–Dotti fraternity. The Dottis, in the meantime, took off briefly for the Isle of Giglio, a tiny spot in the Mediterranean where cars and telephones were still a rarity and where privacy was not a pipe-dream but a reality.

For the last six months of her confinement, Audrey spent most of her time in bed or on a couch. Her personal obstetrician had warned her that, with her long history of miscarriages, she must take things absolutely easy or tragedy would strike again. Towards the latter part of the pregnancy, she retreated to her bed at 'La Paisible'. It was during this delicate, tranquil period of convalescence that Audrey began to receive early indications of what marriage to a Latin playboy could actually mean. Andrea had very liberated ideas about the role of a husband, and it was only a matter of time before he was back on the Rome nightclub circuit – always with a beautiful young woman, but rarely with his wife in tow. One of his favourite pastimes, too, was playing backgammon, which bored Audrey to distraction.

And so, while Audrey was laid up in Switzerland awaiting the imminent arrival, the tall, fair-haired Dr Dotti resumed the merry nightlife that had always been such an integral part of

247

his social behaviour. He was seen on the town with, among others, Daniela, the beautiful fashion model and star of *Fumetti*, the Italian photographic comic book that once gave Sophia Loren her start in show business. Andrea had apparently known her for many years. At that time a sophisticated twenty, she boasted an action-packed past: four years earlier, while the Beatles were appearing in Milan's Palazzo dello Sport, Daniela arrived with her mother at the Hotel del Duomo for a Beatles press conference and demanded that they listened to her.

Inevitably, the news of Andrea's nocturnal flings began to filter back to Audrey's bedside in Switzerland. Although she tried to understand her husband's motives, his nightlifing with beautiful young women – often women half Audrey's age – did not entirely boost her confidence at such an emotionally vulnerable period. She wept inwardly, though outwardly she maintained a cheerful, dignified countenance.

'Baby for Audrey Hepburn at 40' . . . 'Another baby for Audrey' . . . 'Son for Audrey Hepburn' . . . 'To Audrey – a brother for Sean'. These were very different newspaper headlines, and this time nobody was complaining. For, on Saturday night, 8 February 1970, at the Cantonal Hospital in Lausanne, Audrey gave birth to a baby boy by Caesarian section. He weighed seven pounds and eight ounces. Swiss gynaecologist, Professor Willy Merz, had decided to operate to avoid unnecessary delay and suffering to Audrey.

'I'm overjoyed about the baby and especially that he and his mother are in such perfect shape,' said a jubilant Andrea, who was at the hospital for the birth. 'It's great to have another man in the family! We're calling him Luca. The name has always been in the Dotti family.'

The Dottis returned to Rome, where Audrey put every ounce of nervous energy into being the perfect mother – and the perfect doctor's wife. In that capacity, she often joined Andrea for dinner at the hospital when he had to work late, while her travelling now was limited mostly to medical conventions. Audrey believed that when you were in love, you became madly interested in anything your husband did, and Andrea's work was especially involving. He dealt with people, not with their bones or stomachs but rather with their minds and emotional disturbances, which mattered a great deal to this particular wife.

248

Visiting hours at Lucerne's Municipal Maternity Clinic: Mel arrives
to say hello to his new son, Sean — Audrey's 'Gift of God' — who
was born on 17 January 1960
(Rex Features)

Studio publicity photograph, showing Audrey, James Garner and Shirley MacLaine, for *The Children's Hour* (1961) *(United Artists)*

Audrey administering through-the-shirt first aid to co-star Cary Grant in *Charade* (1963) *(Universal)*

'La Paisible', Audrey's eighteenth-century Vaudois farmhouse at Tolochenaz-sur-Morges, above Lake Geneva *(Rex Features)*

Audrey and Mel at play. *Above:* Riding at Santa Barbara, California *(Pictorial Press)*
Below: On holiday in the South of France *(Rex Features)*

In Hollywood with co-star Rex Harrison to discuss with Jack L. Warner,
head of Warner Bros Studios, the new film musical, *My Fair Lady*
(Keystone)

All set for Ascot...in one of Cecil Beaton's
award-winning costumes, in *My Fair Lady* (1964)
(Warner Bros/CBS)

The Spanish-style Bel-Air villa rented by Audrey and Mel during the
Hollywood filming of *My Fair Lady*
(Pictorial Press)

Togetherness…*(above left)* with *Two for the Road* co-star Albert
Finney in the French Riviera *(Rex Features)*, and *(above right)* with
How to Steal a Million co-star Peter O'Toole in a broom cupboard
(Twentieth Century-Fox)

New York's Mayor John Lindsay welcomes
Audrey to the city for location shooting for
Wait Until Dark (1967) *(Warner Bros/Seven Arts)*

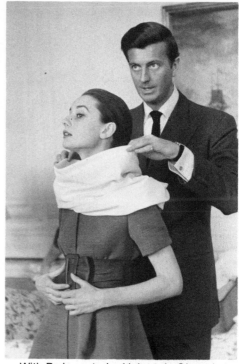

With Paris couturier Hubert de Givenchy,
whose clothes promoted Audrey into the
'best-dressed' lists *(Pictorial Press)*

Audrey marries Rome psychiatrist Dr Andrea
Dotti, on 18 January 1969, at the town hall of
Morges, in Switzerland
(Rex Features)

'Baby for Audrey Hepburn at Forty' blared the
newspaper headlines. Luca, Audrey's son by
Andrea, was born on 8 February 1970
(Rex Features)

Audrey, Sean and Andrea attend a puppet theatre in Rome
(Keystone)

With co-star James Mason in a pensive moment
from *Bloodline* (1979)
(Paramount)

As maid-turned-abbess in her
'come-back' film, *Robin and Marian*
(1976) *(Columbia)*

Attending the Lifetime Achievement Award
ceremony for Fred Astaire (in 1981)
with son Sean *(Rex Features)*

With Peter Bogdanovich, who directed Audrey
in the film comedy, *They All Laughed* (1981)
(Keystone)

Audrey arrives at a Hollywood gala with Dutch
actor-producer, Robert Wolders, about whom
she says: 'Yes, it's true love. Rob is my man...'
(Rex Features)

For the first time as a married woman she was not just merely happy, she was sublimely happy. She could be what she had always wanted to be: herself. She was simply Signora Dotti, housewife. There were no extraneous distractions associated with being a world-famous film star, with being somebody else. The spontaneous, thoughtful woman who was always there, hidden beneath all the fuzzy habiliments of superstardom, now emerged in her full glory. A friend who was out of sorts would receive a basket of spring flowers, created by Audrey, with a note: 'Cheer up, old chum . . . it'll be better soon . . . Love, Audrey.' Another friend would awake from a hospital operation to find Audrey by his bedside, attending to his needs. Yet another buddy would find Audrey on his doorstep one morning, there to give a helping hand with moving house.

'People may find such things trivial, but they are not trivial to me,' she insisted. 'All this is part and parcel of a normal, healthy existence I never really experienced before. I'm functioning as a woman should function and I don't think I'm robbing anybody of anything . . . but by working as a busy film actress I think I *would* be robbing my family, you know, my husband and children, of the attention they should get. Otherwise there is no point in having wives and mothers. The truth of the matter is, I've always thought this way, but I didn't do anything about it. Now I have.'

She was relaxed, for the first time that she could remember. She was freer than she had ever felt before, unshackled from film contracts and learning lines and from being the Movie Star. She was free to do as she pleased.

Audrey was never more convinced that the lifestyle she had chosen was the right one than after she had met Italy's most respected leading man, Marcello Mastroianni, for the first time. They talked most of the night. 'I was thrilled,' recalled Audrey, 'because I'd been dying to meet him for years. He's a very warm and generous person and I understand him.' He was a kindred spirit. Mastroianni replied: 'She proves what I've always said. Being a woman, all woman, means much more than playing it as an actress.'

Acting, certainly, no longer commanded her interest. 'Now Mia Farrow will get my parts,' she declared flatly. To her friends she had confided, 'If I could have a part in a film to be made on the street in front of my house, and I could come home for lunch, I might accept it. I don't want to be tossed around the world any more or be a prisoner in a movie studio when Andrea comes home.'

She also delighted in telling people that she 'kept house' in Rome. 'It's sad,' she reflected, 'if people think that's a dull world. But "keeping house" is in a very real sense just that. You have to be there to contribute. You can't just buy an apartment and furnish it and walk away. It's the flowers you choose, the music you play, the smile you have waiting. I want it to be gay and cheerful, a haven in this troubled world. I don't want my husband and children to come home and find a rattled woman. Our era is already rattled enough, no?'

Her province as a pasta-eating Mamma seemed to be light-years away from the days when she made all those glamorous Hepburn films. It was as if, to Signora Dotti, they never were. To the outside world, however, her stardom remained undiminished. Scripts continued to pour in, while the *paparazzi* pursued her in the streets as zealously as ever, usually when she was out walking with Sean and Luca.

This was her life now. As the years rolled by, her routine barely wavered. She got up early to see Andrea off to the university at 7.30, and on the way home again she did some shopping. She cleaned the apartment, she cooked, and she met Andrea later to walk him home from work. They rarely went to parties, but they had many friends and so they were always entertaining or being entertained. Sometimes they went out for quiet dinners to intimate restaurants. She told people that she felt very saturated – but in the good sense, not in boredom. Living, she said, was like tearing through a museum. Not until later did you really start absorbing what you saw, thinking about it, looking it up in a book and remembering – because you could not take it all in at once.

After a few years of Rome life, Audrey was drawn back more and more to her old farmhouse in the Swiss mountains. 'La Paisible', at Tolochenaz – where the Baroness now lived – had been her spiritual home from the moment she first caught sight of the property silhouetted against the skyline one bright autumn day in 1964. 'Because you go back, you search for what made you happy when you were smaller,' she said in one moment of nostalgia. 'We are all grown-up children, really. Our lives are made up of childhood and adulthood, all together. So one should go back and search for what was loved and found to be real. I would rather that my children one day went back to the country, on weekends or when they want to relax, to search for a blade of grass, than for more sophisticated things which are terribly unreal and disappointing.

'So we consider the house in Switzerland our real home, even more than our apartment in Rome, because it has a garden and trees. Besides, there is something about society and life in the city that oppresses me, a procedure of obliteration. The air is polluted, the backfire of cars is reminiscent of guns, and the noise is so bad you can't hear properly. We love the Swiss privacy, and Andrea says it's the only place where he can really write. In one afternoon and evening, he can write more than in days in Rome. He loves working there.'

Andrea's reputation as a playboy, nevertheless, made few concessions to the fact that he was a married man with a young family. If, back in Rome, Audrey did not feel up to nightclubbing until three or four in the morning, then he simply went alone – though more often than not he was accompanied by young, very pretty women. All Audrey would say about their differences was, 'Andrea's an extrovert. I'm an introvert. He needs people and parties, while I love being by myself, love being outdoors, love taking a long walk with my dogs and looking at trees, flowers, the sky.' Yet, despite all her press statements to the contrary, those close to Audrey were well aware that she was far from happy with the lifestyle that her husband was pursuing.

Said one old friend, David Niven, 'When Audrey married Dotti and was swept off to Rome she was, I think, determined to be a very good wife to this very socially minded Roman. She was indeed looked upon as a wonderful wife to him and, the longer it went on, many people felt she was much too good for him and that he took incredible advantage of her and that she gamely played the wife of the social Roman and really let her career just stand still, on purpose, to help him.'

She admitted it. 'Nobody forced me to stop working. It's what I wanted. My home gives me more happiness and pleasure than anything else. It would be terribly sad, wouldn't it, to look back on your life in films and not to have known your children? For me there's nothing more pleasant or exciting or lovely or rewarding than seeing my children grow up . . . and they only grow up once, remember.'

Yet this did not discourage Kurt Frings from continuing to

forward scripts to Rome and Tolochenaz for her due consideration. Perhaps one day . . .? Audrey rejected one film proposal, *The Survivors*, based on Anne Edwards' harrowing novel about a girl who survives the mass murder of her family by psychopaths, simply on the grounds that she felt she was 'too old' for the part. But there were other, more obviously suitable roles on offer, among them the Czarina of Russia in *Nicholas and Alexandra* (a part which eventually went to Janet Suzman), a sophisticated housewife in a sophisticated comedy called *Further Adventures in the Erogenous Zone*, Richard Burton's leading lady in Terence Young's *Jackpot*, and a co-starrer with Liz Taylor in *Father's Day* – about two women who divorce their husbands and set up an odd-couple home together.

She told one interviewer during this period, 'I'm afraid I may have nothing to express in a movie since I'm very fulfilled at home.' But it was for reasons other than domestic bliss that she turned down a major role in Luchino Visconti's *Conversation Piece*, a film with an oedipal theme. She considered it to be 'dirty and immoral', and she did not want to have her name linked to the character of a 'corrupt mother'. The part subsequently went to Silvana Mangano.

Her old soulmate, director Willy Wyler, wanted her to play the forty-ish New York divorcee who is pursued by a twenty-ish suitor in the comedy, *Forty Carats*. The film company could not accede to her request that it be filmed in Rome; and so Liv Ullmann was finally miscast as the divorcee – and Milton Katselas, *not* Wyler, directed.

The American director, screenwriter and author, Garson Kanin, next offered to give away, free, the valuable screen rights to his latest best-selling novel, *A Thousand Summers*, about a lifelong illicit romance between a country pharmacist and a diplomat's wife, if the taker would guarantee to lure Audrey back from retirement for the leading feminine role. Such enthusiastic male-lead contenders as George C. Scott, Jack Nicholson, Dustin Hoffman and Jack Lemmon were among those hoping Audrey would say 'Yes'. She did not, and the book has yet to be filmed.

Audrey's only appearances in front of the camera during this period were as unexpected as they were novel. Early in 1971 she was persuaded by producer Alexander Cohen and director Clark Jones to make her 'comeback' in *A World of Love*. The film was made, in fact, to swell the funds of UNICEF, the United

252

Nations' charity which benefited poor and needy children, and different scenes were played by various actors representing a country or state. Audrey represented her adopted country, Italy. (Richard Burton represented Britain; Barbra Streisand, California; and Harry Belafonte, Florida – to name just three.)

Her services, naturally, were offered free – which was certainly not the case with her next film assignment a few months later when she made four one-minute TV commercials for a Tokyo wig manufacturer. The location, which was one of the reasons she accepted the job, was an idyllic piece of countryside just outside Rome. There was also the fact that, for two short days' work, she received a handsome £30,000.

But Audrey's response to all motion-picture offers was always the same. In any language.

'Nessuno!'
'Nein!'
'Non!'
'No!'

30

*'Andrea is very Italian. He's gregarious, and
after working very hard he loves to go out.'*

*F*IESTA-INFESTED Pamplona, that early summer
of 1975, was a man's town, with more macho in the air than left-
over bull-dung in the streets. Fortified by Charles III in the
fourteenth century, when it was the capital of the kingdom of
the Navarre, it was now sadly worn out, a crumbling, dusty
Spanish throwback whose life-pulse raced only in July, during
the Feast of St Firmin, when the daily running of the bulls mes-
sed up the nondescript streets. And so this old Basque strong-
hold was the last place on earth where you might have expected to find romance – legendary or real.

A young waiter blushed with pleasure at Audrey's gentle
smile as, in her cool, quiet suite near the porticoed Plaza del
Castillo, in a town described with such enchantment by Ernest
Hemingway in *The Sun Also Rises*, she ordered sandwiches and
beer. Beer? She had been told it would keep her weight up,
which, God only knows, was not very much.

She was wearing jeans and a blue pullover, her dark chest-
nut hair put in a cap of flattering ringlets by Sergio of Rome.
This pale, blue, cool, anemone-like creature, this perennially
fragile and slimly beautiful wood-nymph, had finally emerged
from the contentment of her Roman marriage and motherhood
to make her first film in eight years. Thus it was, in her hotel
suite that parched July day, that she contemplated the prize
bait that had lured her back to movies: to star as Maid Marian to
Sean Connery's Robin Hood in a darkly romantic new screen
treatment of the legendary bandit of Sherwood Forest. Filming

on *Robin and Marian*, an elegy for vanished ideals, was now over – it had been a lightning six-week shoot under Dick Lester's whizz-bang direction – and Audrey was talking for the first time about her re-emergence from the shadows.

Signora Dotti, Rome housewife, was once again Audrey Hepburn, superstar. The limelight was on, and all around, her. Oh, no, it was not 'a comeback'. How could it be, she asked, when she had never really left? Well, eight years was a mighty long honeymoon. She stressed, nevertheless, that she had had no intention of staying away so long. It just sort of happened, mainly because she felt her family needed her, and she them, more than she needed to make movies. But now her eldest son, Sean, aged fifteen and a strapping six-foot-three, was almost a man, and Luca, a sturdy five-year-old, was out of swaddling clothes. The timing was right, that was all.

What also helped to change her mind was an imaginative screenplay by James Goldman, the American playwright who wrote *The Lion in Winter*, plus the opportunity to work with swashbuckling director Richard Lester (fresh from *Royal Flash* and *The Four Musketeers*) and with the first and best James Bond, Sean Connery, whom Audrey had met at a party a few months earlier.

'It would be interesting to know why Marian appealed to Audrey,' Goldman reflected when the film was in the can. 'You know, in her former roles, she always played the innocent woman who had been swept up by circumstances rather than her own choices. As Marian, she seduces herself. It is Marian who chooses to go back to Robin after all these years, to give up her religious vows and return to the uncertainty and the brawling. Marian is a strong woman with a determined will and yet impulsively emotional – it's not what one expects of Audrey's image.'

For once, Audrey was determined to fight against her image. This time, it was *her* choice – not her agent's, not her husband's, not the Baroness's. There was also the added attraction that the enterprise boasted arguably the best supporting cast of British actors ever assembled for a film – Robert Shaw (straight from *Jaws*) as the Sheriff of Nottingham, Nicol Williamson as Little John, Denholm Elliott as Will Scarlett, Ian Holm as King John, Ronnie Barker as Friar Tuck, Kenneth Haigh as Sir Ranulf de Pudsey, and Richard Harris as Richard the Lionheart. All that, and Audrey wanted to test her mettle.

255

The outcome on celluloid of this five-million-dollar saga, which was both melancholic and magnificent, was a far cry from the rumbustious doings of Douglas Fairbanks, Errol Flynn and Co in previous tales of Sherwood Forest. Robin and Marian are now middle-aged – Robin, gnarled, bearded and disillusioned, is thoroughly browned-off with the hare-brained schemes of not-so-good King John; Marian, piqued at her lover's long absence on Crusade duty, has taken up good works and been promoted to abbess of a priory. 'Everything I had been offered before then was too kinky, too violent or too young,' she declared. 'I had been playing *ingénues* since the early Fifties, and I thought it would be wonderful to play somebody of my own age in something romantic and lovely.'

Another reason for choosing this particular film stemmed from the reaction she got from Sean and Luca when they heard she was considering it: 'They both begged me to do the film. They were so thrilled at the idea of meeting big stars like Sean Connery and Richard Harris and Robert Shaw!' And so she arrived in Pamplona with a retinue comprising her personal hairdresser, her make-up woman, and Luca's briskly efficient nanny, Yolanda; Luca was on holiday from his school and, before the film was completed, had learned to ride a horse and use a bow and arrow.

Starting a new picture had always frightened Audrey, due to an inherently introverted nature; it had always been hard for her to do things in front of people. 'It's not like riding a bicycle,' she reasoned. 'It doesn't just come back.' She told a newsman, 'I knew I could do it, but I had to prove it. It was a marvellous experience.'

But much had changed, during her eight-year 'sabbatical', in the way that films were made. Even the film-makers were different. Accustomed to the deference and more leisurely tempo of old-style Hollywood film-makers, she was unprepared for the whirlwind thirty-six-day shooting schedule. Lester's frenetic pace permitted few concessions to star status. Even the canvas chair, that basic symbol of stardom, was not provided. Audrey was compelled to use an aluminium chair from her trailer. 'I don't think she felt very secure on the film,' observed continuity girl Ann Skinner, 'nor did she get much reassurance. It must have been nerve-racking for her, anyway, after being away from films for so long. I mean, I can't remember anyone spending any time with her, taking care of her.'

Lester refused to slacken speed for retakes that Audrey wanted. Once he insisted on shooting a key scene between Marian and Little John even though Audrey was suffering from a sore throat and had lost her voice. Aiming, too, for greater realism, Lester kept cutting down on the love story between Robin and Marian, and Audrey found herself in a perpetual war of words with Lester in her attempt to retain some of the best romantic lines with Connery. But her greatest anxiety was not knowing how she looked on the screen after her long absence, because she did not see daily rushes on location.

While Lester would later confide that 'she was a delightful professional who took her return after an eight-year absence in her stride', a studio executive noted at the time, with his own brand of diplomacy, 'Audrey could get along with Hitler, but Lester is not in her scrapbook of unforgettable characters'. But there was something else wrong with the film, something much more fundamental than a mere clash of temperaments, and that was the suitability (or otherwise) of the leading lady for the part of Marian. Another senior executive on the film later stated, quite categorically, 'Audrey was totally miscast. She was playing a role which Billie Whitelaw would have been right for: an earthy person who had been tilling the ground for years with her own hands, and living in poverty in a nunnery. Audrey just wasn't that person. In fact, Sean wasn't right either; Richard Harris would have been a better Robin, because it's a very romantic part, and Sean is a very down-to-earth person.'

Much of the film was shot in a fourteenth-century Spanish castle with prefab crenellations. The mountains and forests around Pamplona, filmed to look like the medieval East Midlands, were enduring the worst heatwave in twenty years. Birds dropped out of the sky with sunstroke. It took a heavy toll on the cast, Ronnie Barker suffering from dizziness, Audrey and others going down with assorted stomach complaints. Denholm Elliott was among those who had contracted 'Spanish tummy' and, as he sprinted to the toilet (a large oak tree) in the woods for the eighteenth time one morning, Audrey emerged from her caravan. 'Are you all right?' she enquired. The English actor's reply was sort of up-market barrack-room. 'Stay there,' she instructed, 'I've got just the thing for you.' She subsequently presented him with a bottle of pills. 'They may not be the real answer,' she told him, 'but

257

they're a damn good *cork.* . . .' She had been using them all that week.

Everybody loved her. 'A joy to work with,' said Ronnie Barker. 'A lovely, graceful, well-mannered professional – believe me, that's something to write home about,' added Kenneth Haigh. And yet many saw her on the set, and privately, as an enigma. Colleagues noted that she worked hard, concentrated harder, but that she was quiet and reclusive, happiest in her own company; always, there was a sadness in her eyes. 'In the evenings,' explained Ann Skinner, 'she rarely had supper in the hotel dining-room, preferring to have it in the privacy of her room. Sean Connery, on the other hand, would come down every night, go in the bar, and share in the jollity with every member of the crew. But Audrey kept herself very much to herself.'

Robin and Marian was not a financial success, and most critics felt that the film's dual theme of frivolity and tragedy went hand in hand without ever coming to grips or amounting to much. Connery was generally admired: and *Time* magazine summed up the sentiments of most reviewers to Audrey's performance: 'The moment she appears on screen is startling, not for her thorough, gentle command, not even for her beauty, which seems heightened, renewed. It is rather that we are reminded of how long it has been since an actress has so beguiled us and captured our imagination. Hepburn is unique and, now, almost alone.'

While the film was being made in Spain, however, some observers could not help speculating that it had been the failure of Audrey's marriage to Mel Ferrer that had precipitated her retirement from movies, and that it was now the probable breakdown of her offbeat marriage to Andrea that had brought about her return to the medium. In some respects that was probably true. All sorts of subtle pressures were constantly plaguing her, this second time around. She needed to demonstrate to her strong-willed husband that she was still her own woman, that she was capable of being more than just a good wife and mother. She needed to prove that she could still hold the spotlight. She needed to prove, above all, that she was still attractive to men after six years of being just plain Signora Dotti.

Andrea, besides, was still adding to his reputation as a playboy. Although Audrey returned to Rome at weekends, during location shooting for *Robin and Marian*, that still left the good doctor with several free evenings to kill during the week. 'It's his way of relaxing,' Audrey would explain considerately. 'I wouldn't expect him to stay home in front of the TV every time I go away.'

But another, more sinister aspect of the Eternal City occupied Audrey's mind on her return to the Dotti apartment by Ponte Vittorio – the fear of kidnapping. This seemingly incurable sickness of the 1970s struck primarily at the very rich, because the very rich had the money to pay. Less than a fortnight after unpacking she learned that Sean and Luca were being followed in the streets of Rome. And then the mysterious telephone calls began to come – part of a softening-up process calculated to bring the parents to instant submissiveness when the snatch was made.

Yet it never happened, and that was due entirely to a prompt, desperate decision on the part of Audrey and Andrea. Early one morning, while most of Rome was still asleep, a car drew up at their home and a small group was driven at speed to Leonardo da Vinci Airport. Before the sun was reflecting on the prospective kidnappers' dark glasses, Sean and Luca were safely installed at the family's old farmhouse above Lake Geneva.

'La Paisible' became their secret hide-out, and they were subsequently educated, out of harm's way, at the exclusive lakeside academy of Le Rosey, where the roll-call included names like Niven, Lollobrigida, Von Thyssen and Niarchos. By all accounts, Sean flourished there. 'One of my two daughters, along with every other girl in the school, was madly in love with Sean at one time or other,' said David Niven. 'He was a most spectacular young man, and Audrey was a sensational mother.'

Hardly had the memory of her sons' would-be kidnappers receded into a painful subconscious, than Andrea next fell victim to their violent ways. He had just left his clinic at Via Ettore Ximenes, in the quiet Rome suburb of Parioli, when, in a busy street – and in broad daylight – he was set upon by four gunmen, wearing balaclavas, and dragged towards a blue Mercedes getaway car, which had its engine running. Fortunately, they had forgotten their customary chloroform and, despite a nasty knock on the head with a pistol butt, Andrea was able to create enough commotion by screaming to catch the attention of two policemen guarding the nearby Egyptian Embassy, and the assailants fled in their car, leaving the exhausted professor lying half on the pavement and half on the road. Andrea's head later required seven stitches.

So life for Audrey, as always, was not without problems. The world had changed, and now she shuttled back and forth between Andrea and his work in Rome and the children in Switzerland. In March 1976 she flew in a snowstorm from Lausanne to Hollywood to appear on television in the American Film Institute's tribute to William Wyler. She read the director a poem. That evening, America enjoyed its first glimpse of the mature Audrey Hepburn, in a bright red Givenchy dress, little changed, still reed-thin, still smiling; and, for a short time, Hollywood went mad, touched by her presence, her magic.

Next came the New York première of *Robin and Marian*, with a terrified Audrey on stage at Radio City Music Hall before 6000 fans – many chanting, 'We love you, Audrey.' She was genuinely moved. Later, the photographers blinded her, somebody stuck a fountain-pen in her eye, and an eager autograph hound spilled ink all over her clothes. Next morning she sat down for breakfast at the St Regis with 200 members of the international press. She was also due to appear on the *Today* show but then cancelled because after eight years away in Rome she was not familiar with Barbara Walters and did not want to discuss her personal life with a stranger on television.

For the New York jaunt, she brought an escort. Not a boyfriend, but a bodyguard – a sharp-eyed heavy who went everywhere with her on her rounds of parties and interviews. If friends or fans looked like ignoring him, he would pull out a lapel badge and pin it on his trendy suit. Although Audrey was following the example of thousands of well-heeled Americans, unnerved by the kidnappings of such victims as young Paul Getty and Patty Hearst, this was not the first time she had employed the services of a bodyguard.

After a week's rest in Rome, Audrey returned with Luca for the second *Robin and Marian* opening in Hollywood. 'Welcome back,' said the legendary Jack Valenti, president of the Motion Picture Association of America, in his address from the stage. 'You've been away too long.' Audrey, her dark eyes sparkling, rose to her feet to receive the ensuing applause. The audience went wild, and, as Audrey stood there, proffering waves all around the auditorium, she somehow became a sort of Ruritanian monarch acknowledging the warm approbation of her adoring subjects.

The next night she was at the Academy Awards to present the Oscar for the year's best film – *One Flew Over the Cuckoo's Nest*. Andrea escorted her to the ceremonies at the giant Santa Monica Civic Centre and, although on camera she was all serene elegance, it was a different picture backstage: she was so nervous that she lost her handbag and, after the telecast, she refused to go to the pressroom. It was all too much for her. Now she knew why the tranquillity of 'La Paisible' meant so much to her.

On her return to Tolochenaz, Audrey surveyed the latest batch of scripts that had poured in for her attention. Richard Attenborough approached her for his mammoth production of *A Bridge Too Far*, which sought to recreate the disastrous Allied parachute push into the Netherlands in September 1944, during which an attempt was made to capture a critical bridge at Arnhem. It would have been inspired casting, but the scenario was just too close to Audrey's past for comfort. Liv Ullmann got the favourite role. Miss Ullmann, in fact, was now becoming the second choice for many roles first offered (and later turned down by) Audrey. First it was *Forty Carats*, then *A Bridge Too Far*, and next it was Frederic Raphael's made-for-television film, *Richard's Things*, a sensitive romantic tragedy with overtones of female homosexuality.

Another project would have featured Audrey as the mother of Tatum O'Neal. Called *Six Weeks*, the proposed film was a tear-jerker of the variety known as a 'six-hankie special' and concerned an eleven-year-old girl dying of leukaemia while her mother had an affair with a Washington politician. The film actually appealed to Audrey, but it was then abandoned in mysterious circumstances. A further film which appealed to her at that time was *The Turning Point*, director Herbert Ross's posh person's soap opera, set in the world of ballet, in which Anne Bancroft plays the ageing star of the American Ballet Theatre. The film had already been cast when Audrey heard about it, but the Bancroft part continued to fascinate her: 'I wanted to work with the director and it was about dancing, of course, my background; but there was no way. . . .' For once, an 'Audrey Hepburn script' had got away.

Unlike, say, Jane Fonda or Karen Black, Audrey was in no

hurry to do one project after another. She now told people that she was no longer primarily an actress, that nowadays making films had become more like a hobby. Certainly, she had no economic need to work, for she had been receiving a cool million dollars plus profits for each of her last seven films. She was a multi-millionairess in her own right and she would never go hungry. Having been a Swiss resident since 1955, she was protected by a tax umbrella. This meant that she had kept most of what she had earned. Unlike other superstars who owned castles in Marino, yachts in Monte Carlo Harbour, villas in Fregene, the coastal resort near Rome, her principal luxury – apart from the small chalet at Burgenstock – was her four-hundred-year-old farmhouse at Tolochenaz. She did not even own a canoe on nearby Lake Geneva.

Audrey had always had a reputation for being very tight and never spending a penny she did not have to. All her life she had hoarded her earnings. Her obsession with security was a legacy of her turbulent youth, when she witnessed the plunder of her family's fortunes by the Nazis. She invested her earnings in such a way that she could not touch them except in cases of extreme emergency . . . 'then if I should ever get sick and can no longer work, I won't have to worry about money; and I know that my mother will always be taken care of.'

Her Dutch frugality, however, worked both ways. Film actress Barbara Rush, an old friend, referred to it as 'Audrey's sense of honour'. When under contract to Paramount in Hollywood, Audrey was given an expense account. 'She itemized every single dime she spent and sent the balance of the money to the studio,' explained Miss Rush, whose husband (Warren Cowan) was then Audrey's press agent. 'In all the history of Paramount, no star had ever done that.'

Early in 1978, Audrey flew to London for the British Academy Awards, during which she presented her old friend Fred Zinnemann with the Academy's highest award, the annual Fellowship; at the dinner later, she was the real star of the evening as she signed autographs for the phalanx of waitresses who surrounded her. 'It was a lovely idea, whoever thought of it, to bring Audrey over for the occasion,' said the deeply moved director of *The Nun's Story*.

Back in Switzerland she considered a proposition from NBC Television to star with Efrem Zimbalist Jr and Timothy Hutton in a lavish mini-series called *The Best Place to Be*; when she dec-

lined, *From Here to Eternity* star Donna Reed came out of retirement to play the role – that of a protected widow forced to discover what life is all about. Audrey, at forty-nine, felt a little
uncomfortable at some of the parallels in the plot to her own
life. 'I'm not dying to film,' she subsequently confided. 'The
older you get, the more you have to resign yourself to either
not working or taking inconsequential or frightening parts.
Fortunately, I've been able to avoid that trauma by dedicating
myself to my family. I may not always be offered work, but I'll
always have a family.'

Yet even that sentiment could no longer be regarded as an
absolute certainty . . . not, at least, as far as her marriage to
Andrea was concerned. One possible strain on their marriage
was her husband's reluctance to give up his psychiatric clinic or
his teaching at Rome University to join Audrey, Sean and Luca
in Switzerland. The constant strain imposed on the actress and
the doctor by living two different lives, in two different countries, certainly did not help their relationship. On top of everything else, and no matter how open-minded she appeared to be
in her public statements on the subject, she could no longer
ignore, privately, Andrea's passion for nightlifing with pretty
women companions.

One Rome photographer, Tony Menicucci – a member of
Rome's famed *paparazzi*, who had hunted and haunted Andrea
and his dates since 1970 – maintained that in seven years he
had succeeded only once in snapping Audrey out on the town
with another man, whereas he had shot Andrea with dozens of
women. Menicucci said that in his circles Audrey was regarded
as a 'saint', while her husband was a 'son of a bitch'. Only
when Audrey was in town, explained the photographer, did
Andrea turn into an 'angel'; but when he was with other
women, such as the actress Dalila di Lazzaro, he was a different man – a 'devil', no less. He became as 'wild as a hyena',
and would run away quickly to his parked car where he would
promptly try to hide the woman.

Publicly, Audrey continued to claim that she never became
irritated with Andrea when he was gossiped about because 'if
he wasn't married to me they wouldn't gossip about him' –
which made it sound as though *she* was somehow to blame for
his seeming indiscretions. But to friends, she would quietly
point out, 'People love to cut you down, don't they?' There
would be an edge to her voice. 'They're always interested in

263

any breath of scandal they think they can find. But what they're trying to dig out is true for anybody, any woman, any marriage. Every one has its rough moments. Ours is no different.'

She admitted that it was impossible to ignore all those photographs of Andrea in the newspapers, which turned the most innocent evenings into lovers' trysts. 'It's not pleasant for either of us when these pictures appear, of course it's not,' she emphasised. 'We have words, just like any couple, but we have to cope with it and ignore it as best we can.' A mutual friend of the couple, in Rome, commented: 'Of course the *paparazzi* hound Andrea, and that is unfortunate. But it is also unfortunate that they are able to snap those awful pictures with him trying to cover his face while some little blonde simpers up at him.'

The nearest Audrey got to admitting that life with Andrea was not wholly ecstatic was when she declared, 'My marriage is *basically* happy.' After a moment's reflection: 'I can't measure it in percentages, because you can never do that with a relationship.' Her marriage was falling apart all around her, but not a word about marital discord would escape her lips. She was forever the diplomat's granddaughter.

31

*'What I always wanted, what I still want, is
to create a warm and loving atmosphere for
those I care about – my family and my friends.'*

THE HECK WITH ART. Audrey worked for love.

In November she was in Munich for location shooting for the
movie version of Sidney Sheldon's best-seller, *Bloodline*. It was
the script for this twelve-million-dollar mish-mash which
Audrey had chosen, from all the dozens that had winged their
way to Tolochenaz and Rome, as the last-ditch gambit that
would persuade Andrea, once and for all, to mend his playboy
ways. Audrey had threatened to go to work if he did not stop
seeing other women. He thought she was joking. A fortnight
before work started on *Bloodline*, a considerably chastened husband told Audrey he would reform. Audrey agreed to take him
back, an arrangement that would last for at least another
month or two.

She was venturing forth into movies for only the second time
during an eleven-year retreat into domesticity. But now, having made the first move in this new strategy to rebuild her marriage, her endeavours were not much helped by the Rome
scandal sheets, or by the studio chauffeur who took to fetching
reporters at the airport with the commentary, 'Oh, yes, Miss
Hepburn – we all know she have troubles with the husband.'

Throughout the entire ten-week shooting schedule, the
film's publicist had his work cut out trying to steer reporters
towards co-stars Ben Gazzara, James Mason and Omar Sharif,
trying to drum up copy on Irene Papas, Romy Schneider or
Michelle Phillips – trying to arouse interest in *anyone* but the
movie's main luminary, whose role claimed eighty-five per

265

cent of camera time and one hundred per cent of press curiosity. As had always been the case throughout her film career, Audrey had had it written into her contract: no production interviews. This, in turn, made the world's media even more crazy for Hepburniana.

When Audrey is first seen in *Bloodline*, she is cleaning a dinosaur. The shot is symbolic of her task in the film, about a thirty-ish heiress who takes over a family pharmaceutical business and becomes the target for a psychopathic mass-murderer. At an age approaching fifty, she was still as leggy as Veruschka, still as chic as a Parisienne model, still a marvel, not because she did not look her age, but because her spirit defied it. She could still look hurtfully at the camera and make your fist rise in reflex to ward off any harm that might come her way. And she could still use her tremulous voice as an instrument of torture: one whimper was like the scratch of a long red fingernail across an open heart. As a victim, she was ideal – an *haute couture* Mia Farrow. Yet her victimisation extended beyond the bounds of the film, the sloppiest, most luridly absurd international soap opera since *The Other Side of Midnight*, also based on a Sheldon story.

As soon as Sheldon heard that Audrey had been suggested for the part of the super-chic heiress Elizabeth Roffe – dressed by Givenchy – he became 'terribly excited'. Audrey's agent, Kurt Frings, had called him and said, 'Audrey wants to know how you feel about her playing the part. She loves the book, but thinks she could be too old.'

'Tell her I think she'd be perfect,' an elated Sheldon responded. 'If necessary, I'll rewrite the story for the paperback edition.' In the book, the heiress was twenty-three. 'It only needs ten pages changing to make her a thirty-five-year-old.'

The first hurdle was overcome; but *Bloodline*, like all Sheldon stories, was not without its sex scenes. The romantic elements in the ensuing film, in fact, were sublimated to the violence, murders and pornographic snuff murders that had been added gratuitously for hype's sake. The reasons for her accepting this tacky script over the many other (patently better) ones she had turned down remains obstinately unclear. Officially, her friendship with the Youngs (director Terence Young, cameraman Freddie Young) and ease of working conditions were the deciding factors; plus the fact that here she was also in the world of a West German tax shelter international-starrer.

Most of the movie's millions went to show-business agents and travel agents: locations in New York, Copenhagen, Rome, Munich, London, Paris, Sardinia, and Zürich. Her role was originally offered to Jacqueline Bisset, best known for making the most out of a wet T-shirt in *The Deep*, who demanded one and a half million dollars. Audrey settled for her usual million, plus a profits' percentage; but she insisted money was not the primary motivation – and, of course, with thoughts of Andrea back home in Rome, it was not.

The only encouraging thing about Audrey's part in the film remained the fact that, at first, the project did not interest her. Momentarily, her innate good taste prevailed. Explained Terence Young: 'Audrey said no. Emphatically. She wasn't going to make any more movies, thank you. I spent two weeks persuading her to accept the principle that she might make another movie. The next step was persuading her to read the script. Then persuading her that it was a good script. Then persuading her that she wouldn't wreck Luca's life by working again. She's a very good mother.'

Luca, rapidly approaching his tenth birthday, was now firmly settled in Rome's Lycée Français. This enabled Audrey to organise her life more easily these days with the help of friends and a nanny. 'I'll only make a film if I can slot it in with family commitments,' she was still telling people. 'I don't think you can just go off and leave a child for two months. I waited until they showed me a schedule before I said "Yes". There were four weeks in Munich, but I didn't feel panic-stricken because I was only an hour away on the plane.'

Sean, now in his nineteenth year and studying modern literature at university in Switzerland, 'comes and stays whenever he can'. He would follow her into the movie business eventually, she said, but not as an actor: 'I'm not going to pull strings, but I won't be embarrassed to ask somebody if they need a nice, tall, strong, energetic, multi-lingual boy to help on a movie.' She would be true to her word.

On the set, she still suffered the same old nervous fears of the unknown: 'Am I going to be able to do it? You don't gain more confidence, you gain a certain philosophy.' It did not much help matters that she was left regally alone by respectful cast and crew members. There was no small talk, only the utmost deference. Had she not brought along her wealthy Italian socialite friend, Arabella Ungaro, she would have felt completely lost on many a European location. 'It can be very lonely in a crowd,' she told one member of the crew. 'Why is everybody so worshipful?' The answer was that for many members of the unit, who were not even born when Audrey made *Roman Holiday*, she had acquired the patina of a legend, on a par with Garbo, an image considerably heightened by Audrey's similar love of privacy. Hepburn, however, unlike Garbo, did not want to *be* alone – just *left* alone.

What she most liked about New York, in fact, while filming *Bloodline* there, was that she could stand in a doorway on a busy Manhattan street during the lunchtime rush-hour, while munching a hamburger, and nobody took any notice of her. 'My privacy has always been precious to me, and in New York it's almost guaranteed,' said Audrey. 'I can take long walks, as I understand Greta Garbo does, and no one interferes with my thoughts and tranquillity. Come to think of it, the other day I was on Fifth Avenue and I wasn't certain, but I saw a woman who could very well have been Garbo; I was a bit tempted to go up to her, but then I thought, "My God, practise what you preach! If it is her, you'll be intruding – just the thing you don't like yourself."'

Because the public had shown such complete indifference to her last film, *Robin and Marian*, Audrey agreed that, with *Bloodline*, she would embark on a week-long, post-production publicity binge: no television and a dozen hand-picked print journalists from around the world. She vetoed anyone who had once inflicted wounds, but even so, it became a trying experience. 'They walked in and said, "Is you marriage falling apart?"' she related, still shaken. '"Is it true you had a nervous breakdown?" I mean, in the first place, I haven't. But to start in on a person cold like that. One person told me that if he didn't ask me about my marriage, his editor wasn't interested in the story. It's indiscreet, to say the least, no?'

Publicity or not, the film was a critical disaster. A typical comment (from the *Sunday Express*) was: 'It is a ghastly film, hackneyed, humourless, grubby and, worst sin of all under Terence Young's direction, so disjointed as to be a pain to follow.' Audrey was devastated by the bad reviews. Although, as always in a Hepburn film, the critics had nothing but adoration for her own particular contribution, she was none the less convinced that some vital spark in her personality had abandoned her and that, subsequently, the overall quality of any film in which she appeared became somehow affected by it. She began to wonder, too, whether her former talent for picking potential movie winners was perhaps now a thing of the past. Producers, of course, never doubted the pulling power of Audrey's name over a film's title, as the continual flow of scripts being pushed through her letterbox affirmed; but that did not comfort the actress to whom they were addressed. Her inner confidence, what there was of it, had been shaken.

A long, get-away-from-it-all holiday was in order. In the event, she managed to kill two birds with one stone. When filming was finished, Audrey put into operation the next phase of her marriage-reclamation plan. She and Andrea embarked on a 'second honeymoon' in Hawaii and places east. But within a few weeks it was obvious to both that they had grown so far apart, and their lifestyles and temperaments were fired by two such conflicting sets of principles, that the gulf between them was insurmountable. They talked of divorce.

Audrey partly drowned her sorrows by flying to Los Angeles to meet Peter Bogdanovich, once hailed as Hollywood's wonder-boy after making films like *The Last Picture Show*, *What's Up Doc?* and *Paper Moon*. They discussed the film they would make together in the spring, a romantic comedy called *They All Laughed*, with screenplay and direction by Bogdanovich.

While in Los Angeles, in January 1980, she also pulled a few strings. Sean had left his university in Switzerland and had just worked as assistant director on the Korean war epic, *Inchon*, in which Laurence Olivier impersonated General MacArthur; and now he was job-hunting. Coincidentally, he was given a job working as assistant to the production staff on *They All Laughed*. Who said nepotism?

In *They All Laughed*, Audrey played a European tycoon's lonely wife who goes to New York City for a short interlude of romance and escape. It was a role not unlike her very first in an American film, *Roman Holiday*. 'All the things I could say about Audrey could also be said of this character,' said Bogdanovich, who created the role specially for his leading lady. 'She's witty and fragile and strong. What I think is interesting is bringing an actor and character together so you don't know where one leaves off and the other begins.' The role he had written for her, in fact, was closer to Audrey's current life than he could possibly have envisaged.

A few years earlier Audrey had made two revealing pronouncements. She said, 'We all want to be loved, don't we?
Everyone looks for a way of finding love. It's a constant search
for affection in every walk of life. I need it. I want to give it and
I need to receive it.' Exactly six months later she confessed to
Curtis Bill Pepper, 'I think I'd never worry about age if I knew I
could go on being loved and having the possibility of love.
Because if I'm old and my husband doesn't want me, or my
children think me ugly and do not want me – that would be a
tragedy. So it isn't age or even death that one fears, as much as
loneliness and the lack of affection.'

Two men dominated her life at that time, two men to whom
she was as inexorably drawn as the night-flying moth to the
lighted window. One was her director, Peter Bogdanovich; the
other was her leading man, Ben Gazzara, with whom she was
happily reunited after the fiasco of *Bloodline*. On reflection,
perhaps, two obvious focal-points for an actress, since one provided the motivation and the other the means by which she
could accomplish her dramatic ends; but for Audrey, at this
point of emotional insecurity, the strength and stability of each
man was positively life-giving. Without them, she would possibly have gone under.

Gazzara, the son of an immigrant Sicilian labourer, resembled a slightly older, more 'lived-in' version of Andrea: whereas
Andrea grew up with a silver spoon in his mouth, Gazzara
grew up with a copper-plated fist on New York's tough Lower
East Side. Audrey had first met him when they were in their
twenties, but their paths had not re-crossed until a Sidney Sheldon thriller commanded their services. Seeing him after all
those years, she was drawn to conclude: 'Now I think he's
becoming far better looking.'

There was a caged, coiled-spring air about him that made
most people tread with extra caution in his presence; but that
was a quality which attracted Audrey. She, the gentlest, most
sensitive of souls, had all her life been drawn to men with
strength of character and strong wills – men who, on the surface at least, seemed to be quite incompatible with her own particular anything-for-a-quiet-life personality. Audrey had a compulsion to be emotionally dominated. It made for impossible
relationships.

Soon after working with Sean in Korea on *Inchon*, in which
he played a marine major in the thick of the Inchon landings,

Gazzara and his former-actress wife, Janice Rule, parted after eighteen years of marriage. When he started work on *They All Laughed*, therefore, he was at the nadir of his life; Audrey, herself at a critically low ebb, was drawn by a mutual emotional heartache to the man whose resonant voice reputedly sent shivers down the spines of women the world over.

It was not long before the gossip-columns were clocking-up great mileage with stories of the on-screen lovers carrying on their romance off the screen. Gazzara's subsequent divorce from his wife, said their friends, 'was because of Audrey', although Gazzara had already disclosed that his drinking, raging and night-long gambling sessions had 'almost destroyed my marriage' long before Audrey came on the scene.

Although the stars played down their romance – 'We're close friends. We see each other professionally,' said Gazzara – crew members disclosed they could not help but see it. The relationship, however, was inclined to be rather one-sided. Although Audrey was reputedly 'hot and heavy' with Gazzara, Gazzara did not reciprocate in kind. At one point he was so alarmed by the intensity of their affair, that he went to the extraordinary length of importing his estranged wife, Janice, to the New York film set to cool matters down.

Gazzara, plainly, had great respect for Audrey, but no amorous feelings. 'I'd work with her anytime, anywhere, anyhow,' he told inside sources. 'She's a beautiful, sexy, talented woman – much more than the public gives her credit for.' But their affair was at an end. A year later he had eyes only for thirty-three-year-old German photographer Elke Krivat.

Audrey subsequently switched her affections to the younger (by nine years) Peter Bogdanovich, who had recently directed Gazzara in the loquacious black comedy, *Saint Jack*. A former film critic and an unabashed sentimentalist, Bogdanovich was the archetypal strong-willed male to which Audrey was irresistibly drawn. He was autocratic and arrogant, opinionated and outspoken. Barbra Streisand described him as 'a horny bastard but brilliant'. He admitted all that. He was a gentleman not lacking in self-confidence and, it appeared, he had never heard of a word called 'modesty'. He smoked ten-inch cigars, loved flamboyant bow-ties, resided in a Bel-Air mansion, and Audrey adored him.

For the first time since her marriage to Mel Ferrer nearly twenty-six years earlier, Audrey was not only alone, but lonely. Along the way, her self-confidence had been shattered. Andrea had essentially deserted her for a life of philandering. Gazzara had spurned her romantic ardour. Now there was Bogdanovich; but from the moment of their rumoured romance, friends of the director were not optimistic about a happy outcome. Their relationship, indeed, was brief – despite reports in some Rome newspapers that Audrey jetted regularly to America to see him.

But Bogdanovich's affection for Audrey, and Audrey's even deeper affection for Bogdanovich, was profoundly overshadowed by the director's incredible passion for twenty-year-old *Playboy* centrefold Dorothy Stratten. This ravishing Canadian beauty, a Playmate of the Year, had only a small part in *They All Laughed*, though she played a very big role in Bogdanovich's life. He loved her, wanted to marry her and make her a star. Bogdanovich had met her at a party given by Playboy chief Hugh Hefner, but she was already married to a small-time pimp named Paul Snider, although they had separated after barely a year of marriage. When she left for location shooting in New York, where Bogdanovich's affair with Stratten began, Snider was enraged and several times threatened to kill her. He bought a shotgun and vowed to friends, 'I'm going to kill Bogdanovich'.

Just a month after completing work on *They All Laughed*, and by that time installed in Bogdanovich's Bel-Air mansion, Stratten went unaccompanied to her old marital home in Los Angeles to ask her husband for a divorce. But instead the insanely jealous Snider blasted her in the face with the shotgun and then shot himself. Their naked bodies were found by the police, who believed Stratten may have been forced to make love at gunpoint in a last bizarre bid by Snider to win her back. Friends said that Bogdanovich should have shielded her, and one bitter insider remarked: 'Personally, I think the husband shot the wrong person.'

They All Laughed was critically acclaimed at the Venice Film Festival, and the American showbiz newspaper *Variety* applauded it as 'probably Bogdanovich's best film to date: rarely does a film come along featuring such an extensive array of attractive characters with whom it is simply a pleasure to spend two hours.' That was good news for the director, and even better news for Audrey who, having been associated with two massive flops in a row, desperately needed a success to restore her professional integrity. Fortunately, it was third time lucky. That alone brought considerable brightness to her life.

Besides, it had marked her elder son's movie-acting début – alongside Mamma – albeit as a bit-part Latin lover named Jose. But, like father Mel Ferrer, Sean insisted that he felt much more comfortable *behind* the camera than in front of it.

Audrey's triumph in the film convinced her that, to regain cinematic credibility, her future lay within the domain of romantic comedy. It would be a case of her career going full circle. After a brace of lead balloons, and a lifetime in films, it was only now that she had realised that her forte was really where it had always been, from that magical epoch when she teamed up with Gregory Peck for *Roman Holiday*: romantic comedy suited her style better than any other.

Peck himself came to the same conclusion at about the same time. 'She had a delicious sense of humour,' he said, 'always making faces like a clown, yet the producers saw her mostly as a "classy lady" and seldom gave her zaniness full expression.' During the writing of this book another of her co-stars, Peter O'Toole, wrote to say that he saw Audrey at her best in 'sophisticated, romantic comedy – though who knows where an actress will go?'

Well, Audrey was now certain. 'As the years go on,' she told an old confidant, 'you see changes in yourself, but you've got to face that – everyone goes through it. I can't be a leading lady all my life. That's why I'd be thrilled if people offered me character parts in the future. I won't resent it. Either you have to face up to it and tell yourself you're not going to be eighteen all your life, or be prepared for a terrible shock when you see the wrinkles and white hair.'

Audrey, indeed, did not tint her hair, and so now there was the occasional grey strand among the rich dark brown. When she was in Rome, Italian hairdresser Sergio trimmed or re-styled it; and she herself washed her hair every five days with a special shampoo, provided by London trichologist Philip Kingsley. She would also permit only one man in the world to create the illusion of youth around the eyes: Alberto de Rossi. And for her day make-up, she would use only the skin-nourishing and skin-protective products of Dr Ernest Laszlo in New York and Dr Elmi in Rome.

Soon after Audrey reached her fiftieth birthday, TV chat-show host Johnny Carson spoke for many at that year's

Academy Awards. 'I'm in love with Audrey Hepburn, like millions of other guys,' he gushed. But guests at another Hollywood party, a year or so later, were stunned to see how incredibly thin the sylph-like beauty had become. She had always been too skinny to throw a shadow, of course, but now people were beginning to worry over signs of emaciation. What those same people failed to take into account was the lady's own philosophy: 'If a woman of fifty is very thin, she can pass for years younger.' But some gossips were saying that, in Audrey's case, just the opposite was true.

Jealousies prevailed. For Audrey continued to make most women green with envy – Italian women particularly. In Rome, she virtually lived on pasta dishes, especially spaghetti. Plus brown bread and potatoes. 'Actually, if I'm not careful I *lose* weight,' she lamented. 'If I didn't eat pasta, I'd get even thinner. . . .' Years of wartime malnutrition had taken their toll. Audrey would never experience the martyrdom of a weight-reducing diet.

Being a sylph was sometimes unavoidable. Sometimes it was in the lap of the gods.

32

'I heard a definition once: Happiness is health and a short memory! I wish I'd invented it, because it's very true.'

O NE SATURDAY MORNING in late September, 1980, Audrey and Andrea met to discuss 'certain matters' in the fuchsia-scented garden of the two-bedroomed villa she was now renting in Rome. With them was a lawyer bearing a brief-case. The meeting was solemn and businesslike. A week later, Vero Roberti – Andrea's stepfather – disclosed that the marriage was finally over and that Audrey had filed for divorce. He blamed the rift on his stepson's 'private life'.

The previous year, in an interview with New York's *Us* magazine, Audrey made a poignant statement. 'The end of any marriage is a tragic thing,' she said. 'I'm determined that my marriage to Andrea will work for a very long time.' Determination, alas, had failed. Now, twelve years after the romantic Mediterranean cruise that had first brought them together, it was *finito* . . . finished.

It surprised few people. It shocked even fewer.

'My husband and I had what you could call an open arrangement,' she admitted after their separation. 'It's inevitable, when the man is younger. I wanted the relationship to last. Not just for our own sake, but for that of Luca, the son we had together. Nowadays, couples seem to think of themselves; I still believe the child has to come first.'

There was a good reason behind Audrey's eagerness to end the marriage, apart from her incompatibility with Andrea. The reason's name was Robert Wolders – the new love in her life. The handsome Dutchman, a former actor and producer, who had been in the *Laredo* series on TV, met Audrey a short while after the death of his celebrated actress wife, Merle Oberon, in 1979. Audrey, an old friend of the Tasmanian-born star who won fame opposite Laurence Olivier in *Wuthering Heights*, came to New York to film *They All Laughed* and, when Ben Gazzara and Peter Bogdanovich departed from her life, so her affections for Rob Wolders deepened.

Whereas Andrea was Audrey's junior by nine years, Rob was a mere seven years younger than his new fair lady. In his marriage to Merle Oberon, after all, there had been an age differential of some twenty-five years. Rob was her fourth husband, after starmaker Sir Alexander Korda, cinematographer Lucien Ballard, and multi-millionaire industrialist Bruno Paglial. She was one of the richest and most elegant hostesses in the world, with palaces in Mexico City, Cuernavaca and Acapulco. The film that brought them together was a Mexican soap opera called *Interval*, about a widow who, recovering from a nervous breakdown after running her husband down with a car, falls in love with a struggling artist in the Mayan ruins of ancient Yucatan. No prizes for guessing who played the two protagonists.

After their marriage in 1975, having lived together for two years, they became familiar members of the international jet-set. Friends close to the couple told stories of Rob's utter devotion to his wife. He worshipped her. He abandoned a promising career for her. He devoted all his energies to pleasing her. And then, on 23 November 1979, at the age of sixty-eight, the glamorous star died after a stroke at their Malibu home. Robert Wolders was grief-stricken. He learned later that, in her will, Merle Oberon had left him two million dollars, a house, cash, and most of her jewellery. It was some small consolation for his failed film career.

Rob, the son of an airline executive, had studied acting at the American Academy of Dramatic Art in New York and, prior to *Laredo*, had won a few minor roles in films like *Tobruk* and *Beau Geste*. He had been a protégé of Noël Coward, who subsequently introduced Rob – then appearing in a number of Italian films – to Merle Oberon. For a while after the actress's death Rob lived a solitary life, rarely venturing from his luxury apartment in Beverly Hills; and then the wealthy society hostess, Connie Wald, invited Rob to a dinner party at her opulent Bel-Air mansion just off Sunset Boulevard.

'She insisted I go,' recalled Rob. 'She told me there would be only a few people there, which was true. Billy Wilder and his wife were among her guests. There was also Audrey Hepburn, who was alone in Hollywood at the time.'

Later, Rob discovered that Connie Wald had also rung Audrey that day. She implored her, 'Do come over. We'll invite somebody you might enjoy meeting. He's Dutch like you.'

That evening the two Netherlanders sat together and talked into the early hours. 'We liked each other immediately,' said Rob. 'It was a normal, friendly kind of contact we had, nothing more. I liked her a lot, and she really did try to put me at ease. Audrey had known Merle and admired her. She understood her death was a great loss to me, and encouraged me to talk about myself.'

Audrey: 'It was certainly friendship at first sight between us. Neither of us was in the frame of mind to fall in love. We had both been through a very difficult and rather sad period. But instantly there was a great friendship and a great deal of understanding.'

Rob: 'To me, a truly extraordinary woman had extended herself to offer solace to the grieving widower of another extraordinary woman.'

Six months went by. Rob then flew to New York on a business trip, whereupon the ever-helpful Connie Wald informed him: 'You may not know it, but Audrey is in New York right now. Why don't you call her?'

They met briefly, after a day's filming on *They All Laughed* was over. Two weeks later Rob returned to New York – this time with the express purpose of meeting up again with Audrey. Two sad, lonely people deepened their friendship in the following weeks – although, explained Rob, it never occurred to Audrey to think of romance: 'She was married and she has always been a faithful wife.' He then added, 'She felt I needed another woman in my life. She even thought she had found someone for me – there's proof that there was no romance between us at the time!'

But their meetings and long-distance calls became more intimate and tender, and a deep friendship was transformed into inevitable love. 'Yes, it's true love,' Audrey admitted eventually. 'I feel as if we were married. Rob is my man. . . .'

Audrey then confided to one close friend that she would marry Rob 'just as soon as I can get free from my present husband – and it can't be too soon for me'. Another intimate talked of Rob as her salvation, adding that 'In her heart Audrey feels he's her last chance for happiness – a sincere, devoted, faithful man who won't leave her.'

Coming after a decade of 'torment', of making light of Andrea's wandering eye, when even her friends could find little in the relationship to commend it, Audrey became a new woman. Her personality bristled with reborn enthusiasms. There were things to do, places to go. Invitations which would once have been tactfully declined were now cheerfully accepted. Galas and parties were attended. Of *course* photographer-royal Patrick Lichfield could take snaps of her for his coffee-table book, *The Most Beautiful Women*. She flew halfway round the world to help honour her co-workers at tributes such as the American Film Institute's Life Achievement award for Fred Astaire (though Ginger Rogers did not turn up). At the AFI banquets and at the Academy Awards she was the youngest movie personality to draw forth prolonged standing ovations, which always seemed to embarrass and genuinely surprise her.

When Billy Wilder was honoured at Rome's Campidoglio, where he was given a gold medallion for his artistic career by deputy mayor Pierluigi Severi on behalf of the municipal government, Audrey was there as the surprise guest. When New York's Fashion Institute of Technology held a gala to honour Hubert de Givenchy, Audrey flew over to say 'thank you' to one of her oldest friends. When, in 1983, the Ballet Rambert held a memorial gala at Sadler's Wells in honour of the company's late founder – Dame Marie Rambert had died the previous year – Audrey graced the proceedings with her presence and gave a gently reflective speech from the stage of the London theatre.

Suddenly, the woman who had always preferred the tranquillity of home-life in Rome and Tolochenaz, was now to-ing and fro-ing across the Atlantic as if she owned shares in the airlines. And always by her side, so obviously in love, was Rob Wolders. 'I'm more self-confident,' she told everybody. 'I'm having a ball, falling in love again and enjoying life.' It was no empty phrase. She glowed like an expectant mother – though she certainly was not pregnant. Even her face and body looked healthier, more filled out.

Love, Rob Wolders – both – agreed with her.

Only one episode at this time intruded on the tranquillity of her new-found buoyancy: the death, in the late summer of

1983, of her old chum, David Niven. At the burial service in the Swiss village of Château d'Oex, where Niven had lived for twenty-five years, Audrey stole unobtrusively into the church half an hour before the service began and sat quietly in a side pew against the rough white wall. She was visibly distraught. She slipped her dark glasses on and off with repeated nervousness and wiped the occasional tear that trickled from her eyes – a sense of grief shared with Prince Rainier of Monaco and other close family friends. It finally became all too much for her when the red-bearded Scottish minister, Pastor Arnot Morrison, recalled the 'happy philosophy of David Niven – his capacity for laughter and his love for his friends'. Audrey buried her head in her hands and wept.

Audrey was now anxious to free herself from the man who made her life miserable with his wild antics and womanising. So anxious, indeed, that as divorces in Italy could take anything up to five years to finalise, she had taken the precaution to also file for divorce in Switzerland. Andrea, however, according to one American newspaper, was dragging his feet; and he only agreed to the divorce in the first place with the stipulation that Luca remained in his custody while he continued his schooling in Rome.One source described Andrea as 'the old-fashioned type of husband', the sort of partner who firmly believes that it is a man's prerogative to have a wife *and* a mistress. He was therefore doing everything within his power to make the divorce both difficult and prolonged.

If ever two men resided at opposite ends of the pole in matters concerning loyalty and devotion in affairs of the heart, then those two men were Rob and Andrea. Where Rob could exist only by directing his love exclusively to one woman, Andrea could exist only by diversification, by directing his attention towards a variety of women. But it required a Dutchman to show the Roman how to really love a woman.

The divorce came through in 1982, but neither Audrey nor Rob were in any hurry to tie the wedding knot. They were now indeed husband and wife in all but the small matter of signing a piece of paper. There was no urgency. Audrey, in any case, wanted to be absolutely certain before committing herself legally the third time around. They had their whole lives ahead of them: that could never change. But would their love withstand the future?

'Audrey has rarely been happy in marital love,' argued her

publicist friend Henry Rogers. 'I hope that one day the right man will come along who will give her the happiness that a woman with her ability to love truly deserves.'

Rob Wolders appears to be such a man. The man who will bring Audrey Hepburn an enduring joy and inner serenity.

Audrey Hepburn is . . .

'Perfection' – David Niven
'Sexy' – Ben Gazzara
'Fragile' – Sean Connery
'Steely' – Cary Grant
'Yar' – Christopher Reeve
'Elfin' – Humphrey Bogart
'Ethereal' – Barbara Rush
'Gutsy' – George Cukor
'Audrey' – Peter O'Toole
'Bones' – John Huston
'Radiance' – Robert Stack
'Chic' – Van Johnson
'Energy' – Gary Cooper
'Gigi' – Colette
'Dream-girl' – Clifton Webb
'*Soignée* – Cecil Beaton
'Princess' – William Wyler, Frank Sinatra
'Classy' – William Holden, Billy Wilder, everybody else

Audrey today is all things to all people; but always, woven into the fabric of any judgement, are the words 'style', 'dignity' and 'breeding'. 'She's a *lady*,' avows Van Johnson. 'When she participates in the Academy Awards, she makes all those starlets look like tramps. Thank you for your class, Audrey – you're quite a lady! I'm devoted to her. If anyone said anything derogatory about her, I'd push them in the river. . . .' David Niven concurs: 'A great lady. It's quite an achievement to spend that long in Hollywood and not become a Hollywood product. She always manoeuvred around that – and that takes intelligence. She was always her own person.'

When Audrey became an eight-pounds-a-week dancing girl in *High Button Shoes*, back in 1948, she really never expected anything special from life. Yet she accomplished more than she ever hoped for, and most of the time it happened without her seeking it. The fast push of events turned out to be quicksilver rather than quicksand. The increasing maturity of her acting affirmed that she had progressed successfully past the limitations of the *ingénue* roles that initiated her success. She picked scripts with a shrewd eye, studied feverishly and worked for only top-grade directors. She ignored her lack of training and worked to prove that the original success was no flash in the pan. Maybe that is why she remains so serenely beautiful today: for beneath all that outward fragility there is a lot of strength and common sense.

Her life has been much more than a fairy tale, although it has been that as well. She has endured her fair share of difficult moments, of the heart and of her art, but it was as if there was always a light at the end of the tunnel. Whatever difficulties she has lived through, she has invariably received a prize at the end. She has been fulfilled as a person. 'One thing I would have dreaded', she says quietly, 'would be to look back on my life and only have movies.'

If she has been fortunate, then that is because she was not content to be merely a fair lady. Nor was she ever a sex symbol. She chose instead to become an actress, and, as an actress, she has been able to age gracefully. She maintains that age has never worried her, yet few actresses over fifty can afford to dismiss it. When she laughs, however, she appears to be about fifteen years old. Her philosophy in the 1980s is simply to accept life as it comes, to respect life even when it deals blows; the blows are a part of life. More and more, Audrey lives by the day and does not expect too much. She does not do too much of anything – eat, drink, overwork or worry; but whatever she does, she does the best she possibly can. She is intelligent and alert, wistful but enthusiastic, frank yet tactful, assured without conceit and tender without sentimentality. The great essential, she believes, is a sense of humour.

The sleek body, the lilting voice, that extraordinary head pedestalled on that elegant neck – they are all still part of Audrey's stunning attractiveness. But her image as the eternal *gamine* is one which makes her laugh today. Whatever she became was not consciously decided on. Her *look* was just something that evolved over the years, partly to hide what she considered were her faults and partly to emphasise her good points. The glamour business was something of which she never really felt a part. It was almost as if it was happening to someone else. She knew the woman she was underneath, but most people did not. The woman they talked about was really the image, the woman she projected.

Looking back on a life that has encompassed childhood opulence and horror, adolescent frustration tinged with hope, two failed marriages, two adored sons, a Dutchman named Rob, and a career where the name 'Audrey Hepburn' is uttered in the same breath as the screen immortals, Greta Garbo, Marlene Dietrich, Joan Crawford, Bette Davis and Katharine Hepburn . . . looking back on all that, Audrey has only a vague, oblique nostalgia for the past. 'You know, one would love to be younger, to have more time,' she says. 'Yet there's a big advantage in being older. Since you've done a lot of things you feel you have to do, there's a luxury in being able to retire before it's time to retire. . . .'

And then, looking forward, she envisions herself growing tomatoes in her garden at Tolochenaz and hoping that all her grandchildren will have the time to visit her and Rob once in a while. She sees her old age as going back to the country, to her roots. She also sees herself emulating Mae West, still making movies occasionally in her eighties: 'I hope I can always play somebody's grandmother. Maybe I should put myself on ice. If I stayed very still, maybe I wouldn't crack.'

Audrey's life is now complete. The screen goddess with the personal, but not the common, touch. She is surrounded by a universal love. She has her man, her sons, her legions of fans all over the world. She is the eternal phoenix, the perennially twinkling star of the movie firmament.

Audrey Hepburn's radiance and spirit are contagious fevers for which there are no known or desirable cures. If they ever discover an antidote, God help us and the movies.

APPENDIX

FILMOGRAPHY
(*with thanks to Gene Ringgold*)

Abbreviations:

AA – Academy Award
AAN – Academy Award
  nomination
ad – art director
AH – Audrey Hepburn
bw – black and white
ch – choreography
d – director

m – composer of background
  music
min. – minutes
m/ly – music and lyrics
p – producer
pd – production designer
ph – director of photography
sp – screenplay writer

1. *Nederlands in 7 Lessen (Dutch in 7 Lessons)*. Dutch independent. 1948. *p* H. M. Josephson. *d* Charles Huguenot van der Linden. Not, as title suggests, an instructional documentary, but a feature film. AH played small role of air stewardess. Filmed in the Netherlands. *bw*, 79 min.

2. *One Wild Oat*. Eros-Coronet, GB. 1951. *sp* Vernon Sylvaine and Lawrence Huntington from Vernon Sylvaine's play. *d* Charles Saunders. Robertson Hare, Stanley Holloway, Constance Lorne, Vera Pearce, June Sylvaine, Andrew Crawford, Gwen Cherrill, Irene Handl, Sam Costa, Robert Moreton, Charles Groves, Joan Rice. A barrister (Hare) attempts to discourage his daughter's infatuation for a philanderer by revealing his past. The plan backfires when the daughter's would-be father-in-law (Holloway) threatens to reveal the barrister's shady background. AH was an unbilled extra. Filmed in England. *bw*, 78 min.

3. *Young Wives' Tale*. Associated British/Allied Artists, GB. 1951. *sp* Anne Burnaby, from Ronald Jeans' stage comedy. *d* Henry Cass. Joan Greenwood, Nigel Patrick, Derek Farr, Guy Middleton, Athene Seyler, Helen Cherry, Audrey Hepburn, Fabia Drake, Anthony Deaner, Carol James, Irene Handl, Joan Sanderson, Selma Vaz Dias, Jack McNaughton, Brian Oulton. AH, a man-shy lodger in a house shared by two couples, is temporarily smitten with one of the husbands (Patrick). It had

only limited release in the US in 1951 but was re-issued there in 1954 after *Roman Holiday* had catapulted AH to overnight stardom. Filmed in England. *bw*, 78 min.

4. *Laughter in Paradise*. Associated British/Pathé, GB. 1951. *p/d* Mario Zampi. *sp* Michael Pertwee and Jack Davies. *ph* William McLeod. *m* Stanley Black. Alastair Sim, Fay Compton, Guy Middleton, George Cole, Hugh Griffith, Ernest Thesiger, Beatrice Campbell, Mackenzie Ward, A. E. Matthews, Joyce Grenfell, Eleanor Summerfield, John Laurie, Veronica Hurst, Anthony Steel, Charlotte Mitchell, Leslie Dwyer, Colin Gordon, Audrey Hepburn. A delightful will-with-strings comedy about an eccentric millionaire (Griffith) who divides his fortune among four relatives whose eligibility to inherit depends on their fulfilling the zany stipulations he decrees. AH is a cigarette girl in a night-club sequence. Filmed in England. *bw*, 95 min. (Remade in 1972 as *Some Will, Some Won't*.)

5. *The Lavender Hill Mob*. Ealing/Rank/Universal, GB. 1951. *p* Michael Truman. *sp* T. E. B. Clarke. *d* Charles Crichton. *ph* Douglas Slocombe. *m* Georges Auric. Alec Guinness, Stanley Holloway, Sidney James, Alfie Bass, Marjorie Fielding, Edie Martin, John Salew, Ronald Adam, Arthur Hambling, Gibb McLaughlin, John Gregson, Clive Morton, Sidney Tafler, Frederick Piper, Peter Bull, Patrick Barr, Patric Doonan, Marie Burke, William Fox, Michael Trubshawe, Audrey Hepburn. After working for the bank of England for twenty years, a mild-mannered shipping clerk (Guinness), with the help of a boarding-house crony (Holloway) and two professional crooks (James and Bass), devises and executes a foolproof scheme for stealing a million pounds in gold from his employers. AH's bit is in a South American sequence. Filmed in England. AA: T. E. B. Clarke. AAN: Alec Guinness. *bw*, 80 min.

6. *The Secret People*. Ealing/Lippert, GB. 1952. *p* Sidney Cole. *sp* Thorold Dickinson and Wolfgang Wilhelm, from an original story by Dickinson and Joyce Carey (uncredited). *d* Thorold Dickinson. *ph* Gordon Dines. *m* Roberto Gerhard. Valentina Cortesa, Serge Reggiani, Audrey Hepburn, Charles Goldner, Megs Jenkins, Irene Worth, Angela Fouldes, Reginald Tate, Norman Williams, Michael Shepley, Athene Seyler, Sidney Tafler, Geoffrey Hibbert, Hugo Schuster. A refugee (Cortesa)

involved in an abortive assassination plot helps the police apprehend the conspirators after an innocent bystander is killed. AH, her younger sister, is a ballerina with a Dublin dance troupe. AH is given her first above-the-title credit. Filmed in England. *bw*, 91 min.

7. *Monte Carlo Baby/Nous Irons à Monte Carlo*. Ventura/Filmakers, GB. 1952. *p* Ray Ventura. *sp* Jean Jerrold, Alex Jaffe and Jean Boyer. *d* Jean Boyer and Jean Jerrold. Cara Williams, Philippe LeMaire, Russell Collins, Audrey Hepburn, John Van Dreelan, George Lannes, Marcel Dalio, Lionel Murton, Andre Lugret, Ray Ventura and his orchestra. When an epidemic of measles temporarily closes a child centre the infant son of a film star (AH) and her estranged husband, a concert pianist (Van Dreelan), is mistakenly given into the custody of a touring musician (Collins). Filmed in France, this British production was also made, with AH, in a French-language version. US producers Collier Young and Ida Lupino acquired the US distribution rights to it after the completion of *Roman Holiday. bw*, 70 min.

8. *Roman Holiday*. Paramount, US. 1953. *p/d* William Wyler. *sp* Ian McLellan Hunter and John Dighton, from an original (uncredited) script by Dalton Trumbo. *ph* Franz Planer and Henri Alekan. *m* Georges Auric. Gregory Peck, Audrey Hepburn, Eddie Albert, Hartley Power, Harcourt Williams, Margaret Rawlings, Tullio Carminati, Paolo Carlini, Claudio Ermelli, Paolo Borbon, Alberto Rizzo, Laura Solari, Gorella Gori. The runaway princess of a mythological kingdom (AH) spends a night and a carefree day touring Rome and falling in love with an American newsman who is unaware of her true identity (Peck). After spending four years attempting to finance and film *Roman Holiday*, Frank Capra sold this property to Wyler. Filmed in Italy. AA: Audrey Hepburn, Ian McLellan Hunter. AAN: best picture, script, William Wyler, photography, Eddie Albert. *bw*, 118 min.

9. *Sabrina* (GB title: *Sabrina Fair*). Paramount, US. 1954. *p/d* Billy Wilder. *sp* Billy Wilder, Samuel Taylor and Ernest Lehman, from Samuel Taylor's play. *ph* Charles Lang Jnr. *m* Frederick Hollander. Humphrey Bogart, William Holden, Audrey Hepburn, Walter Hampden, John Williams, Martha Hyer, Joan

Vohs, Marcel Dalio, Marcel Hillaire, Nella Walker, Francis X. Bushman, Ellen Corby, Marjorie Bennett, Emory Parnell, Nancy Kulp, Emmett Vogan, Colin Campbell, Kay Riehl, Kay Kuter, Paul Harvey, Harvey Dunn, Marion Ross, Charles Harvey, Grey Stafford, Bill Neff, Otto Forrest, David Ahdar. Returning to the Long Island estate of her father's employers after flunking a cookery course at a Paris school, a chauffeur's daughter (AH), long infatuated with the family's playboy son (Holden), discovers she really loves his older, hard-working brother (Bogart). Filmed in US. AAN: Audrey Hepburn, Billy Wilder, Charles Lang Jnr. *bw*, 112 min.

10. *War and Peace*. Carlo Ponti/Dino de Laurentiis/Paramount, US/Italy. 1956. *p* Carlo Ponti and Dino de Laurentiis. *sp* Bridget Boland, Robert Westerby, King Vidor, Mario Camerini, Ennio DeConcini and Ivo Perelli, from Leo Tolstoy's novel. *d* King Vidor (battle scenes by Mario Soldati). *ph* Jack Cardiff (battle scenes by Aldo Tonti). *m* Nino Rota. *ad* Mario Chiari. Audrey Hepburn, Henry Fonda, Mel Ferrer, Herbert Lom, Oscar Homolka, Vittorio Gassman, Anita Ekberg, Helmut Dantine, Barry Jones, Lea Seidl, Wilfrid Lawson, Jeremy Brett, Sean Barrett, Tullio Carminati, Milly Vitale, Anna Maria Ferrero, May Britt, Patrick Crean, Gertrude Flynn, John Mills. AH plays Natasha in this flawed but fascinating cinemation of Tolstoy's novel. Filmed in Italy and Yugoslavia. AAN: King Vidor, Jack Cardiff. Technicolor, VistaVision, 208 min.

11 *Funny Face*. Paramount, US. 1957. *p* Roger Edens. *sp* Leonard Gersche. *d* Stanley Donen. *ph* Ray June. *m/ly* George and Ira Gershwin, with additional songs by Roger Edens and Leonard Gersche; title and songs derived from the 1927 Broadway musical. Fred Astaire, Audrey Hepburn, Kay Thompson, Michel Auclair, Robert Flemyng, Dovima, Virginia Gibson, Suzy Parker, Sue England, Sunny Harnett, Ruta Lee, Jean Del Val, Alex Gerry, Iphigenie Castliglioni, Albert D'Arno, Nina Borget, Marilyn White, Louise Glenn, Heather Hopper, Cecile Rogers, Nancy Kilgas, Emilie Stevens, Don Powell, Bruce Hay, Dorothy Colbert, Carole Eastman, Paul Smith, Diane Du-Bois, Karen Scott, Gabriel Curtiz. A May–December romance involving the transformation of a Greenwich Village introvert (AH) into a dazzling *haute-couture* mannequin by a fashion-magazine photographer (Astaire). Originally an

MGM property called *Wedding Day*, Paramount acquired it for AH whom it had under contract and would not lend out. Filmed in Hollywood and France. AAN: Leonard Gersche, Ray June. Technicolor, VistaVision, 103 min.

12. *Love in the Afternoon*. Allied Artists, US. 1957. *p/d* Billy Wilder. *sp* Billy Wilder and I. A. L. Diamond, from Claude Anet's novel, *Ariane*. *ph* William Mellor. *m* Franz Waxman. *ad* Alexander Trauner. Gary Cooper, Audrey Hepburn, Maurice Chevalier, John McGiver, Van Doude, Lise Bourdin, Olga Valery, Gyula Kokas, Michael Kokas, George Cicos, Victor Gazzoli. A Lubitsch-like comedy about a middle-aged playboy (Cooper) fascinated by the daughter (AH) of a private detective (Chevalier) who has been hired to entrap him with the wife of a client. It had been made in France as a silent in 1926 and as *Ariane* with Elizabeth Bergner in 1931. Filmed in France. *bw*, 125 min.

13. *Green Mansions*. MGM/Avon, US. 1959. *p* Edmund Grainger. *sp* Dorothy Kingsley, from W. H. Hudson's novel. *d* Mel Ferrer. *ph* Joseph Ruttenberg. *m* Bronislau Kaper and Hector Villa-Lobos. Anthony Perkins, Audrey Hepburn, Lee J. Cobb, Henry Silva, Sessue Hayakawa, Nehemiah Persoff, Michael Pate, Estelle Hemsly, Bill Saito, Yonco Iguchi. Abel, a political refugee (Perkins), searching for gold in the Venezuelan jungle to finance a rebellion against his father's assassins, encounters Rima, a wistful, mysterious child-of-nature (AH), who is feared by the natives as a possessor of evil spirits. Filmed in Hollywood (location footage shot in British Guiana, Colombia and Venezuela). Metrocolor, Panavision, 104 min.

14. *The Nun's Story*. Warner Bros, US. 1959. *p* Henry Blanke. *sp* Robert Anderson, from Kathryn C. Hulme's book. *d* Fred Zinnemann. *ph* Franz Planer. *m* Franz Waxman. Audrey Hepburn, Peter Finch, Edith Evans, Peggy Ashcroft, Dean Jagger, Mildred Dunnock, Patricia Collinge, Beatrice Straight, Rosalie Crutchley, Ruth White, Barbara O'Neil, Margaret Phillips, Patricia Bosworth, Colleen Dewhurst, Stephen Murray, Lionel Jeffries, Niall MacGinnis, Eva Kotthaus, Molly Urquhart, Dorothy Alison, Jeanette Sterke, Errol John, Diana Lambert, Orlando Martins, Giovanna Galletti, Marina Wolkonsky. A nun felled by tuberculosis while nursing in the Belgian Congo (AH) realizes she can never give complete obedience to her order, repu-

diates her vows and joins a Second World War underground movement to help fight the Nazi invaders of her homeland. AH's favourite role. Filmed in Africa, Belgium and Italy. AAN: best picture, Robert Anderson, Fred Zinnemann, Franz Planer, Franz Waxman, Audrey Hepburn. Technicolor, 150 min.

15. *The Unforgiven*. United Artists/James Productions/Hecht-Hill-Lancaster, US. 1960. *p* James Hill. *sp* Ben Maddow, from Alan LeMay's novel. *d* John Huston. *ph* Franz Planer. *m* Dmitri Tiomkin. Burt Lancaster, Audrey Hepburn, Audie Murphy, Lillian Gish, Charles Bickford, Doug McClure, John Saxon, Joseph Wiseman, Albert Salmi, June Walker, Kipp Hamilton, Arnold Merritt, Carlos Rivas. Prejudiced neighbours rebel against a panhandle ranch family whose adopted daughter (AH), an Indian orphan, becomes a pawn in a savage Kiowa uprising. Filmed in Mexico. Technicolor, Panavision, 125 min.

16. *Breakfast at Tiffany's*. Paramount/Jurow-Shepherd, US. 1961. *p* Martin Jurow and Richard Shepherd. *sp* George Axelrod, from Truman Capote's novella. *d* Blake Edwards. *ph* Franz Planer. *m* Henry Mancini. Audrey Hepburn, George Peppard, Patricia Neal, Buddy Ebsen, Martin Balsam, John McGiver, Mickey Rooney, José-Luis de Villalonga, Alam Reed, Dorothy Whitney, Beverly Hills, Stanley Adams, Claude Stroud, Elvia Allman, Joseph Lanphier, Robert Patten, Gil Lamb, Nicky Blair, Fay McKenzie, Glen Vernon, Joyce Meadows, Joan Staley. Holly Golightly, a Texas innocent working as a fifty-dollar-a-trick call-girl (AH), seeks security, via a rich husband, among Manhattan's most offbeat Bohemians. Filmed in US. AA: Henry Mancini, song 'Moon River' (*m* Henry Mancini, *ly* Johnny Mercer). AAN: Audrey Hepburn, George Axelrod. Technicolor, 115 min.

17. *The Children's Hour* (GB title: *The Loudest Whisper*). United Artists/Mirisch, US. 1961. *p/d* William Wyler. *sp* John Michael Hayes, from Lillian Hellman's adaptation of her play. *ph* Franz Planer. *m* Alex North. Audrey Hepburn, Shirley MacLaine, James Garner, Miriam Hopkins, Fay Bainter, Karen Balkin, Veronica Cartwright, Mimi Gibson, Debbie Moldow, Diana Mountford, William Mims, Florence MacMichael, Sallie Brophy, Hope Summers, Jered Barclay. The founders of a girls' school (AH and MacLaine) lose a libel suit against the grand-

mother (Bainter) of a malicious student (Balkin) who accused them of lesbianism. Originally filmed, *sans* perversion, by Wyler and Samuel Goldwyn in 1936 as *These Three*, with Miriam Hopkins, Merle Oberon and Joel McCrea in the MacLaine-AH-Garner roles. Filmed in US. AAN: Franz Planer, Fay Bainter. *bw*, 108 min.

18. *Charade*. Universal, US. 1963. *p/d* Stanley Donen. *sp* Peter Stone, from a story ('The Unsuspecting Wife') by Stone and Marc Behm. *ph* Charles Lang Jnr. *m* Henry Mancini. Cary Grant, Audrey Hepburn, Walter Matthau, James Coburn, George Kennedy, Ned Glass, Jacques Marin, Paul Bonifas, Dominique Minot, Thomas Chelimsky. An American widow (AH), threatened by her late husband's associates into revealing where a quarter of a million dollars in stolen gold is hidden, seeks protection from the US Embassy in Paris and receives help from a mysterious stranger (Grant), whom she thinks may be a master criminal. Filmed in Paris. AAN: song 'Charade' (*m* Henry Mancini, *ly* Johnny Mercer). Technicolor, 113 min.

19. *Paris When It Sizzles*. Paramount, US. 1964. *p* Richard Quine and George Axlerod. *sp* George Axelrod, from a story and screenplay by Julien Duvivier and Henri Jeanson. *d* Richard Quine. *ph* Charles Lang Jnr. *m* Nelson Riddle. William Holden, Audrey Hepburn, Grégoire Aslan, Raymond Bussières, Christian Duvellex, Thomas Michel; voices of Fred Astaire and Frank Sinatra. Guest stars: Marlene Dietrich, Tony Curtis, Mel Ferrer, Noël Coward. An American living in Paris (Holden) attempts to write a complete film script in forty-eight hours with the help of an imaginative typist (AH). A re-make of Duvivier's French movie, *Holiday for Henrietta* (1954), with Michel Auclair and Hildegarde Neff in the Holden–Hepburn roles. Originally called *The Girl Who Stole the Eiffel Tower*, it was completed before *Charade* and shelved for two years. Filmed in Paris. Technicolor, 110 min.

20. *My Fair Lady*. Warners/CBS, US. 1964. *p* Jack L. Warner. *sp* Alan Jay Lerner, from his adaptation of George Bernard Shaw's screenplay for the 1938 film version of his play *Pygmalion*. *d* George Cukor. *ph* Harry Stradling. *m* Frederick Loewe. *ch* Hermes Pan. *ad* Gene Allen. *costumes* Cecil Beaton. Audrey Hepburn, Rex Harrison, Stanley Holloway, Wilfred Hyde

White, Gladys Cooper, Jeremy Brett, Theodore Bikel, Isobel Elsom, Mona Washbourne, Walter Burke, John Holland, Henry Daniell, Grady Sutton, Moyna Macgill, Alan Napier, Betty Blythe, Lillian Kemple-Cooper, Marjorie Bennett, Queenie Leonard, John Alderson, John McLiam, Veronica Rothschild, Owen McGivney, Barbara Pepper. AH is Eliza Doolittle (singing dubbed by Marni Nixon). Filmed in US. AA: best picture, George Cukor, Rex Harrison, Harry Stradling, Gene Allen, Cecil Beaton, best sound (Francis J. Scheid and Murray Spivack) and best adaptation of a musical score (André Previn). AAN: Alan Jay Lerner, Stanley Holloway, Gladys Cooper. The film won all the major Oscars save that for best actress. Technicolor, Super Panavision 70, 175 min.

21. *How to Steal a Million*. 20th Century-Fox/World Wide, US. 1966. *p* Fred Kohlmar. *sp* Harry Kurnitz, from George Bradshaw's story. *d* William Wyler. *ph* Charles Lang. *m* Johnny Williams. Audrey Hepburn, Peter O'Toole, Charles Boyer, Hugh Griffith, Eli Wallach, Fernand Gravet, Marcel Dalio, Jacques Marin, Moustache, Roger Treville, Eddie Malin, Bert Bertram. The daughter of an art forger (AH) enlists the aid of a private detective she believes to be a crook (O'Toole) to help her steal a Cellini sculpture from a museum before insurance appraisers discover her father's generous donation is really one of his clever forgeries. Filmed in Paris. De Luxe, Panavision, 127 min.

22. *Two for the Road*. 20th Century-Fox. 1967. *p/d* Stanley Donen. *sp* Frederic Raphael. *ph* Christopher Challis. *m* Henry Mancini. Audrey Hepburn, Albert Finney, Eleanor Bron, William Daniels, Claude Dauphin, Nadia Grey, Georges Descrieres, Gabrielle Middleton, Cathy Jones, Carol Van Dyke, Karyn Balm, Mario Verdon, Roger Dann, Irene Hilda, Jacqueline Bisset, Judy Cornwell, Dominique Joos, Libby Morris, Joanna Jones, Helene Tossy. *En route* to the Côte d'Azur, a successful architect (Finney) and his wife (AH) review, in their minds, the events in their twelve-year marriage, shown in non-chronological flashbacks, that have led to their boredom and infidelity. Filmed in France. AAN: Frederic Raphael. De Luxe, Panavision, 112 min.

23. *Wait Until Dark*. Warner Bros, US. 1967. *p* Mel Ferrer.

sp Robert and Jane Howard-Carrington, from Frederick Knott's play. *d* Terence Young. *ph* Charles Lang. *m* Henry Mancini. *ad* George Jenkins. Audrey Hepburn, Alan Arkin, Richard Crenna, Efrem Zimbalist Jr, Jack Weston, Samantha Jones, Julie Herrod, Frank O'Brien, Gary Morgan, Francis DeSales, Jim Raymond, Lucy Ann Cook, Alan Paige. AH, as the recently blinded wife of a photographer (Zimbalist), is terrorised by a gang of narcotic smugglers (Arkin, Crenna, Weston) during her husband's absence. Filmed in US. AAN: Audrey Hepburn. Technicolor, 108 min.

24. *Robin and Marian*. Columbia/Rastar, US. 1976. *p* Denis O'Dell. *sp* James Goldman. *d* Richard Lester. *ph* David Watkin. *m* John Barry. *pd* Michael Stringer. Sean Connery, Audrey Hepburn, Robert Shaw, Nicol Williamson, Richard Harris, Denholm Elliott, Ronnie Barker, Kenneth Haigh, Ian Holm, Bill Maynard, Esmond Knight, Veronica Quilligan, Peter Butterworth. Robin Hood (Connery) returns to Sherwood Forest after fighting for King Richard (Harris) in the Crusades and in France for twenty years, and finds that the Sheriff of Nottingham (Shaw) is still grinding the faces of the poor and that Maid Marian (AH) is now an abbess. Filmed in Spain. Technicolor, 107 min.

25. *Bloodline*. Paramount/Geria, US. 1979. *p* David V. Picker and Sidney Beckerman. *sp* Laird Koenig, from the novel by Sidney Sheldon. *d* Terence Young. *ph* Freddie Young. *m* Ennio Morricone. *ad* Ted Haworth. Audrey Hepburn, Ben Gazzara, James Mason, Claudia Mori, Irene Papas, Michelle Phillips, Maurice Ronet, Romy Schneider, Omar Sharif, Beatrice Straight, Gert Fröbe, Wolfgang Preiss. A pharmaceutical tycoon is murdered and his daughter-heir (AH) begins to receive death threats. Filmed in New York, Copenhagen, Rome, Munich, London, Paris, Sardinia and Zürich. Movielab, 117 min.

26. *They All Laughed*. PSO/Moon Pictures/Time-Life, US. 1981. *p* George Morfogen and Blaine Novak. *sp-d* Peter Bogdanovich. *ph* Robby Müller. *m* Colleen Camp's songs arranged and conducted by Earl Poole Ball; 'Kentucky Nights', words and music by Eric Kaz; 'One Day Since Yesterday', words and music by Earl Poole Ball and Peter Bogdanovich. *ad* Kert Lundell.

Audrey Hepburn, Ben Gazzara, John Ritter, Colleen Camp, Dorothy Stratten, Patti Hansen, George Morfogen, Blaine Novak, Sean Ferrer, Linda MacEwen. A European tycoon's lonely wife (AH) visits New York for a short interlude of romance and escape, and her husband assigns a private detective (Gazzara) to keep an eye on her. Comedy with plot similarity to *Roman Holiday*, though with a number of differences the second time around. Filmed in US. De Luxe, 121 min.

FILM DOCUMENTARY

A World of Love. UNICEF. 1971. *p* Alexander Cohen. *d* Clark Jones. UNICEF documentary film, starring Audrey Hepburn, Richard Burton, Barbra Streisand, Harry Belafonte, and others. Filmed in Europe and US.

TELEVISION

Mayerling. NBC Television. 1957. Presented as one of the US network's 'Producer's Showcase' specials. *d* Anatole Litvak. Audrey Hepburn, Mel Ferrer, Raymond Massey, Diana Wynyard, Basil Sydney and cast of 120. In 1881 the heir to the Habsburg Empire (Ferrer) is forced into a suicide pact with his mistress (AH). It was Litvak who directed the original film version in French in 1936, which made stars of Charles Boyer and Danielle Darrieux. Made in New York. Colour, 90 min.

TELEVISION COMMERCIALS

In 1971, Audrey Hepburn made four one-minute television commercials for a Tokyo wig manufacturer for showing on Japanese television. All-Japanese crew. Filmed in Italy.

THEATRE

1. *Gigi*. A comedy by Anita Loos, adapted from Colette's novel. Following previews at the Walnut Theatre, Philadelphia, opened on Broadway at the Fulton Theatre, New York, 24 November 1951. *p* Gilbert Miller. *d* Raymond Rouleau. Settings by Raymond Sovey. Audrey Hepburn (Gigi), Josephine Brown (Mme. Alvarez, her grandmother), Cathleen Nesbitt (Alicia de St. Ephlam, her aunt), Doris Patston (her mother), Michael Evans (Gaston Lachaille), Francis Compton (Victor), Bertha Belmore (Sidonie). Two acts and six scenes. Not to be confused with the 1958 film *musical* starring Leslie Caron. Setting: Paris, 1900. A young wide-eyed rebel is trained by her aunt to be a *cocotte*, but when married off to a playboy she reforms him. When the show closed, AH flew to Rome to make *Roman Holiday* and then returned to the US for an extensive road tour of *Gigi*.

2. *Ondine*. A romance by Jean Giraudoux, adapted by Maurice Valency. Following previews in Boston, opened on Broadway at the 46th Street Theatre, New York, on 18 February 1954; closed 26 June same year. Staged by the Playwrights' Company (Maxwell Anderson, Robert Anderson, Elmer Rice, Robert E. Sherwood, Roger L. Stevens, John F. Wharton). *d* Alfred Lunt. *m* Virgil Thomson. Settings by Peter Larkin. Costumes by Richard Whorf. Lighting by Jean Rosenthal. Three acts and three scenes. Setting: the Middle Ages. Audrey Hepburn (Ondine), Mel Ferrer (Ritter Hans), John Alexander (Auguste), Edith King (Eugenie), Alan Hewitt (the Lord Chamberlain), Marian Seldes (Bertha), Robert Middleton (the Old One). Other parts played by Dran Seitz, Tani Seitz, Sonia Torgeson, Lloyd Gough, James Lanphier, Peter Brandon, Faith Burwell, Gaye Jordan, Jan Sherwood, Barry O'Hara, Lily Paget, William le Massena, Stacy Graham, William Podmore, Robert Crawley. A water nymph (AH) magically ascends from the sea and falls in love with a handsome knight (Ferrer). The role brought her a Tony award for best stage actress; she won an Oscar the same year for *Roman Holiday*.

ACKNOWLEDGEMENTS

'If I blow my nose it gets written about all over the world,' Audrey Hepburn once said. 'But the whole image people see of me is on the outside. Only we ourselves know what really goes on; the rest is all in people's minds.' Much of what follows is by way of saying thank you to all those who, over the years, in one form or another, have watched Audrey Hepburn blow her nose – watched her forge a career and a life – and either recorded the fact on the printed page or committed it to memory for and until that moment when, duly prompted, a biographer opted to reconstruct the sequestered whispers of the past into something resembling a portrait. Many individuals – actor colleagues, producers, directors, make-up, wardrobe and design people, cameramen, business associates, publicists, friends, an enemy or two – have contributed recollections. To these, and to the many other people who gave me their time and co-operation – far too many to acknowledge individually – I extend my gratitude.

In particular, however, I must thank: Fred Astaire, Ronnie Barker, Douglas Byng, Helen Cherry, T. E. B. Clarke, George Cole, Sidney Cole, Judy Cornwell, Diana Coupland, Richard Crenna, Roald Dahl, Thorold Dickinson, Denholm Elliott, Derek Farr, Robert Flemyng, Logan Gourlay, Alec Guinness, Kenneth Haigh, Radie Harris, William Holden, Stanley Holloway, John Huston, Lionel Jeffries, Van Johnson, Richard Lester, John McCallum, James Mason, Anthony Mendleson, Bob Monkhouse, Lionel Murton, Patricia Neal, David Niven, Peter O'Toole, Michael Pertwee, Marie Rambert, Frederic Raphael, Christopher Reeve, Henry C. Rogers, Barbara Rush, Ann Skinner, Eleanor Summerfield, Mona Washbourne, Irene Worth, and Fred Zinnemann. Many other people offered much valuable information on the understanding that their identity would remain anonymous and, of course, their wishes have been respected.

In Britain, the Reference Division of the British Library, London, provided so many essential facilities that it would be impossible to adequately express my gratitude and indebtedness. The *Daily Express* Library, the Library Services department of the British Film Institute, and the BBC Script Library, all in London, and the BBC Written Archives at Caversham Park, Reading, also kindly placed their extensive files at my disposal.

In the Netherlands, I have been greatly aided by the expertise of Chr. van Etten of the Communication Techniques Department of the Netherlands Information Service (Rijksvoorlichtingsdienst), in The Hague, who led me down many intriguing avenues of research. I am also indebted to P. J. Yperlaan, director of Huis-Doorn; Gemeente Doorn, Doorn; and the Iconographisch Bureau, Gravenhage, for enlightening me on Audrey Hepburn's ancestry. In addition, K. Schaap, the official archivist at Arnhem, through extensive correspondence, helped to throw much light on the Dutch underground movement, particularly as it applied to Audrey Hepburn's Arnhem.

In the United States, I would like to thank Val Almendarez, Co-ordinator of the National Film Information Service of the Academy of Motion Picture Arts and Sciences, Hollywood, for putting me in touch with a substantial amount of the American literature (newspapers, magazines, books, studio biographies and press material) as it relates to Audrey Hepburn. A similar vote of thanks must go to David A. Weiss and Packaged Facts, New York, for giving admirable attention to detail to the onerous task of researching and photocopying most of the important feature articles on Audrey Hepburn in America. Kathy Davis of the American Film Institute, Washington, was also extremely kind.

In Australia, Michelle Deer undertook extensive research among the continent's major newspaper and magazine files, work which was as methodically executed as it was invaluable. She was a godsend.

In South Africa, the Republican Press (Pty) Ltd, Durban, and B. Murray, the Librarian of S. A. Associated Newspapers, Johannesburg, contributed greatly to my knowledge of Audrey Hepburn material in South Africa.

For granting permission to quote from newspapers and magazines, I am grateful to the authors (listed in parentheses), editors and publishers mentioned as follows: Adelaide *News* (Ian Rae), *American Film* (Stanley Kauffmann), *Australian Women's Weekly* (Camilla Beach, George Haddad-Garcia), *Daily Express* (Anne de Courcy, John Ellison, Peter Evans, David Lewin, Cecil Wilson), *Daily Mail* (Edward Goring, Hugh Kuranda, Ronald Singleton, Paul Tanfield), *Daily Mirror* (John Sampson, Donald Zec), *Daily Telegraph* (George W. Bishop), *Family Circle* (USA) (Myrna Blyth: reprinted from the 26 June 1979 issue of *Family Circle* © 1979 The Family Circle, Inc.),

Family Weekly (USA) (Peer J. Oppenheimer), *Film Dope* (David Badder, Bob Baker), *Films and Filming* (Clayton Cole, Gordon Gow, John Francis Lane, Sergio Viotti), *Films in Review* (USA) (Gene Ringgold, Ken Doeckel), *Guardian* (Bart Mills), *Harper's Bazaar* (USA: © 1981 The Hearst Corporation. Courtesy of *Harper's Bazaar*), *International Herald Tribune* (Mary Blume), Johannesburg *Star*, Johannesburg *Sunday Express* (Henry Gris, John Newnham, Maxie Pienaar), Johannesburg *Sunday Times*, *Ladies' Home Journal* (USA) (Judith Krantz, D. Audrey Judge: © 1976 and © 1981 by Family Media, Inc. Reprinted with permission of *Ladies' Home Journal* and Judith Krantz), *Life* (USA), London *Evening Standard* (Alexander Walker, Thomas Wiseman), *McCall's* (USA) (Curtis Bill Pepper: reprinted with permission of the author and his agent, The Julian Bach Literary Agency, 747 Third Avenue, New York, NY 10017), Melbourne *Herald* (Robert MacDonald), *New York Post* (Gene Grove: 26 February 1965 issue; Sidney Skolsky: 20 July 1958 issue; and 24 February 1981 issue), *New York Sunday News* (16 June 1968 issue; Liz Smith: 7 September 1975 issue; Rex Reed: 21 March 1976 issue. © 1968, 1975 & 1976 New York News, Inc. Reprinted by permission), *New York Times* (Brooks Atkinson, Gloria Emerson, Michiko Kakutani, Murray Schumach), *New Zealand Herald* (David Stone), *People* (USA) (Jim Watters), *Photoplay* (UK) (Mike Connolly, Gary Cooper, Rupert Croft, Colin Dangaard, Pip Evans, George Haddad-Garcia, Radie Harris, Rose Jamieson, Mary Worthington Jones, Eric Random, Bert Reisfeld, Dick Reves, Dave Smith, Pauline Swanson, Peter Tipthorp), *Photoplay* (USA) (Anita Allen, Carl Clement, Mary W. Jones, John Maynard, Ruth Waterbury), Reuters, *Sunday Express* (Logan Gourlay, Roderick Mann, Milton Shulman), *Sunday Mirror* (Peter Stephens), *Sunday People* (Frederic Mullally), Sydney *Daily Mirror*, Sydney *Daily Telegraph* and Consolidated Press (Betty Best), Sydney *Morning Herald*, Sydney *Sun-Herald*, Sydney *Sunday Mirror*, Sydney *Sunday Telegraph*, *Telegraph Sunday Magazine* (Nicholas Freeling), *Time* (USA) (Jay Cocks: © 1970 and 1976 Time, Inc. All rights reserved. Reprinted by permission from *Time*), *Times*, *Us* (USA) (M. George Haddad), *Variety* (USA), *Vogue* (USA) (Curtis Bill Pepper), Wellington *Evening Post* (New Zealand) (Guy Austin, Beth Saunders), *Woman* (William Hall: 13 December 1975 issue), *Woman's Day* (Australia) (Nikkie Barrowclough, Rebecca Morehouše), *Woman's Own* (Diana Day, Henry Gris, William

Hall: 17 March 1979 issue), *Woman's Realm* (George Haddad-Garcia).

The following discontinued publications were also consulted and in many instances quoted: *American Weekly* (magazine of the *New York Journal-American*) (Charles van Heusen), *Argus Weekly* (Australia) (Louis Berg), *Daily Graphic* (Paul Holt), *Daily Herald* (Paul Holt), *Daily Sketch* (Herbert Kretzmer, Arthur Pottersman), *Empire News* (Ralph Cooper), London *Evening News*, *Look* (USA), *Movie* (N. V. Perkins, Mark Shivas), *Movieland* (USA) (Margaret Gardner), *Movie News* (Singapore), *Newark Evening News* (USA) (Sheilah Graham, Edward Sothern Hipp), *New York Herald Tribune* (and its magazine, *This Week*) (Joe Hyams, Walter Kerr, Eric Lasher), *New York Journal-American* (Philip K. Scheuer), *New York World-Telegram & Sun* (William Hawkins, William Peper), *Sound Stage* (USA), *Sunday Dipatch* (Perry Miller), *Sunday Graphic* (Ken Passingham, Peter Chambers), *Sunday Pictorial* (Bernard McElwaine), *Weekend Magazine* (courtesy of Torstar Corporation, Today Magazine, Inc., Toronto, Canada) (Marci McDonald).

And for granting permission to quote from their books, I wish to thank the following authors, their executors, and publishers (all published in London, except where stated): George Allen & Unwin Ltd for *Bravo Maurice!* by Maurice Chevalier (edited and translated by Mary Fitton); W. H. Allen & Co Ltd for *Bogie* by Joe Hyams (reprinted by permission of the author and his agents, Scott Meredith Literary Agency, Inc., 845 Third Avenue, New York, NY 10022), *Gregory Peck* by Michael Freedland, and *Sophia* by Donald Zec (courtesy of the author and The Jon Thurley Literary Agency); Angus & Robertson (UK) Ltd for *Peter Finch: A Biography* by Trader Faulkner; Arrow Books Ltd for *Finch: My Life with Peter Finch* by Yolande Finch; Arthur Barker Ltd for *Maurice Chevalier* by Michael Freedland; B. C. W. Publishing Ltd (Isle of Wight) for *Journey Down Sunset Boulevard: The Films of Billy Wilder* by Neil Sinyard and Adrian Turner; Bodley Head Ltd for *Six Men* by Alistair Cooke; Jonathan Cape Ltd for *By Myself* by Lauren Bacall; Elm Tree Books Ltd for *Big Bad Wolves: Masculinity in the American Film* by Joan Mellen; Leslie Frewin Ltd for *Wiv a Little Bit o' Luck* by Stanley Holloway; Granada Publishing Ltd for *Halliwell's Film Guide* by Leslie Halliwell, and *Sparks Fly High* by Stewart Granger; Hamish Hamilton Ltd for *Before I Forget* by James Mason; Harper and Row Publishers, Inc. (New York) for *Eddie:*

My Life, My Loves by Eddie Fisher; Hart-Davis MacGibbon Ltd for *Who's Afraid of Elizabeth Taylor?* by Brenda Maddox; William Heinemann Ltd for *Life with Googie* by John McCallum; Hutchinson Publishing Group for *Michael Balcon presents . . . A Lifetime of Films* by Michael Balcon; Michael Joseph Ltd for *This is Where I Came In* by T. E. B. Clarke; Macmillan Publishers Ltd for *An Open Book* by John Huston; William Morrow & Co., Inc. (New York) for *Walking the Tightrope: The Private Confessions of a Public Relations Man* by Henry C. Rogers; Peter Owen Ltd for *Both Ends of the Candle* by Alfred Shaughnessy; Robson Books for *The Last Hero: A Biography of Gary Cooper* by Larry Swindell; Martin Secker & Warburg Ltd for *Unholy Fools* by Penelope Gilliatt; George Weidenfeld & Nicolson Ltd for *Cecil Beaton's Fair Lady* by Cecil Beaton, *Golden Boy: The Untold Story of William Holden* by Bob Thomas, *Keep on Dancing* by Sarah Churchill, *Self Portrait with Friends: The Selected Diaries of Cecil Beaton, 1926–1974*, edited by Richard Buckle, and *Unity Mitford: A Quest* by David Pryce-Jones.

Every effort has been made to trace the ownership of copyright material quoted in this book. If I have inadvertently omitted to acknowledge any publication, publisher or individual I would be grateful if this could be brought to my attention, care of W.H. Allen & Co. Ltd, for correction at the first opportunity.

Grateful thanks, finally, must go to my wife, Zenka, for typing the book and for having to live with me during its gestation.

'The world has always been cynical, and I think I'm a romantic at heart,' Audrey Hepburn confessed. 'I hope for better things, and I thank God the world is also full of people who want to be genuine and kind.' Most of the aforementioned would seem to share that noble conviction.

INDEX

302

305

307